CW01395655

HERITAGE MATTERS

PRESENTING THE ROMANS

INTERPRETING THE FRONTIERS OF
THE ROMAN EMPIRE WORLD HERITAGE SITE

Hadrian's Wall
Trust

Heritage Matters

ISSN 1756–4832

Series Editors
Peter G. Stone
Peter Davis
Chris Whitehead

Heritage Matters is a series of edited and single-authored volumes which addresses the whole range of issues that confront the cultural heritage sector as we face the global challenges of the twenty-first century. The series follows the ethos of the International Centre for Cultural and Heritage Studies (ICCHS) at Newcastle University, where these issues are seen as part of an integrated whole, including both cultural and natural agendas, and thus encompasses challenges faced by all types of museums, art galleries, heritage sites and the organisations and individuals that work with, and are affected by them.

Previously published titles are listed at the back of this book

Presenting the Romans

Interpreting the Frontiers of the Roman Empire World Heritage Site

Edited by

NIGEL MILLS

THE BOYDELL PRESS

© Contributors 2013

All rights reserved. Except as permitted under current legislation
no part of this work may be photocopied, stored in a retrieval system,
published, performed in public, adapted, broadcast,
transmitted, recorded or reproduced in any form or by any means,
without the prior permission of the copyright owner

First published 2013
The Boydell Press, Woodbridge

ISBN 978–1–84383–847–0

The Boydell Press is an imprint of Boydell & Brewer Ltd
PO Box 9, Woodbridge, Suffolk IP12 3DF, UK
and of Boydell & Brewer Inc.
668 Mt Hope Avenue, Rochester, NY 14620–2731, USA
website: www.boydellandbrewer.com

The publisher has no responsibility for the continued existence or accuracy
of URLs for external or third-party internet websites referred to in this book,
and does not guarantee that any content on such websites is,
or will remain, accurate or appropriate.

A CIP record for this book is available
from the British Library

Papers used by Boydell & Brewer Ltd are natural, recyclable products
made from wood grown in sustainable forests

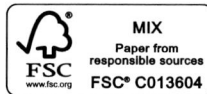

MIX
Paper from
responsible sources
FSC
www.fsc.org   FSC® C013604

Printed and bound in Great Britain by
CPI Group (UK) Ltd, Croydon, CR0 4YY

Contents

Illustrations

TABLES

The editor, contributors and publisher are grateful to all the institutions and persons listed for
permission to reproduce the materials in which they hold copyright. Every effort has been made
to trace the copyright holders; apologies are offered for any omission, and the publishers will be
pleased to add any necessary acknowledgment in subsequent editions.

Acknowledgments

Without David Brough's generous contribution of time, his diligence in the editing process and his insightful contributions, it is unlikely that this volume would ever have been completed. I would like to thank Professor Peter Stone for his interest in publishing the book and for nearly a lifetime's intellectual stimulation, and Catherine Dauncey for steering it through the final stages. Finally I would like to thank all those who contributed to the session at the 2009 Limes Congress and their interest and commitment to bringing the many stories of Rome to life for modern audiences.

Nigel Mills

Abbreviations

CAD	Computer Aided Design
CEO	Chief Executive Officer
CGI	Computer-generated imagery
CNC	Computer Numerical Control
EPSRC	Engineering and Physical Sciences Research Council
ERA	Economics Research Associates
EU	European Union
GIS	Geographic information system
GPR	Ground Penetrating Radar
GPS	Global Positioning System
ha	hectare
HCI	Human–Computer Interaction
HWHL	Hadrian's Wall Heritage Ltd
ICCROM	International Centre for the Study of the Preservation and Restoration of Cultural Property
ICIP	ICOMOS International Committee on Interpretation and Presentation of Cultural Heritage Sites
ICOMOS	International Council on Monuments and Sites
IFA	Institute of Field Archaeologists
ILN	*Illustrated London News*
SHP	Schools History Project
SICSA	Scottish Informatics and Computer Science Alliance
TWAM	Tyne & Wear Archives & Museums
UNESCO	United Nations Educational, Scientific and Cultural Organization
WHS	World Heritage Site

Preface

Peter Stone

'But Dad, history is boring and the Romans are the most boring bit of it all.' I may have paraphrased my son's attempted justification for not doing homework but the essence of his argument is, and was, very plain. A similar argument was deployed always when discussing going to visit one of the site museums on Hadrian's Wall; and yet a walk along the Wall where 'British war parties' (children), waiting in ambush for Roman supply columns (parents), were routinely 'flushed-out' by Roman scouts (the dog) but rallied to win the ensuing battle, were, for a time, one of the most attractive of weekend activities.

Where have we, as teachers, academics and interpreters gone so badly wrong? How have we managed to make the Romans such a hated topic? Readers may think I overreact but on a very brief and totally unsystematic survey (conducted in the last few minutes with two of my children and eight of their friends, home for lunch from school), the result was almost unanimous: the Romans *are* the most boring part of history – with one dissenter identifying 'Medicine Through Time' (although, when pressed by his peers, he acknowledged that the worst bit of this was 'The Romans and the beginning of public health' as there was no gruesome dissection or surgery to talk of …).

This book goes some way to try to address this issue. The Romans *shouldn't* be boring: we know so much about them, and yet there is still so much to learn. We have names, places, events and stories that make, or should make, the Romans real, tangible, *touchable*. We have numerous opportunities to link the past to the present, to get us thinking not necessarily about the highfaluting discourse of academic and museum specialists but rather to draw parallels, to prompt debate, to provoke thought. One such piece of interpretation is the new gallery at Tullie House Museum in Carlisle where the 'living wall' display prompts the reader to think not only about the Romans and Hadrian's Wall but also about walls and frontiers – and why we build them in the first place. Here Hadrian's Wall sits alongside walls and frontiers old and new across the world: the 'Peace Wall' in Belfast, the Great Wall of China, and many, far too many, more. This is a brilliant piece of provocative interpretation and prompted one visitor to write: 'I've been coming to Hadrian's Wall for 30 years; I had never <u>thought</u> about it before'. What an accolade!

Read on and enjoy some more of the attempts to do just that; to move away from death by 1000 objects in yet another museum dedicated to the Roman Army/Empire/Frontier to an interpretation that provokes the visitor to *think* … 'Tis a consummation devoutly to be wished.

Introduction: Presenting the Romans – Issues and Approaches to Interpretation

Nigel Mills

Nigel Mills

Purpose and Discussion

The aim of this book is to explore and address a number of perceived issues in the public presentation of the archaeology of Hadrian's Wall and of the Frontiers of the Roman Empire. It is relevant also to wider issues of public presentation of the Roman world in Britain and elsewhere and to the application of principles of good interpretation to periods of the past in which archaeology is a major source of evidence. The issues can be summarised as follows:

1. Public presentation is generally very academic, focusing on the imparting of knowledge from academics and professionals to visitors rather than responding to the interests and questions of the visitors (and potential visitors) themselves.

2. Public presentation has tended to focus on the display of objects for their own sake, avoiding and excluding approaches which seek to use objects to illustrate themes and narratives.

3. Academic and professional archaeologists are often very conservative in their understanding of how archaeological evidence might be used for public presentation.

4. There is generally a poor understanding of the basic principles of good interpretation in the academic and museums world, with a perception that anything beyond straightforward presentation of objects and well-authenticated reconstruction implies 'Disneyfication', 'dumbing down' or 'marketing'. Use of the word *storytelling* by interpreters tends to equate with the word *fairytales* in the minds of many academic and professional archaeologists and curators.

5. Public presentation of the Roman Frontiers has a tendency to focus on the Roman army and its military infrastructure and to avoid broader political, economic and social issues.

6. Public presentation usually focuses on the detailed archaeology of particular sites rather than their broader context. In Britain as a whole this has led to a situation where there is no museum that specifically explores the nature of the Roman occupation of Britain. Where many sites are essentially similar, as is the case with Roman forts, public presentation tends to be repetitive.

7. Popular understanding of the Romans amongst British people is constrained by the education system in which children come across the Romans in primary school through simple facts and stereotypes. This encourages a perception as adults that the Romans are essentially boring and that most of the important things are known about them.

In addition to these specific issues there are some broader contextual elements which provide a setting for the book and for the interest and value of reviewing and reappraising how we present the Roman Frontiers and the Roman world to the public.

First, popular understanding of the Romans is constrained and influenced by preconceptions and stereotypes in the way the Romans are perceived and presented by academics, in educational and popular literature, in film, television and other media. That we tend to reinterpret the past in the light of the present is nothing new. It takes time, though, for new approaches to filter through into the public domain. A theme of this book is that new academic approaches of the last ten years combined with the opportunities offered by new technology provide a particular opportunity for engaging public presentation and reaching new audiences. Together they have the power to transcend how we present the past, making it accessible, stimulating, valuable and relevant to a far wider range of people.

Mattingly's (2007) book deliberately sets out a post-colonial history of the Roman occupation of Britain that produces an entirely different perspective from those of the colonial histories produced in the 19th and earlier 20th centuries (Corbishley, this volume, Chapter 14). In the same way, AD 410 is seen as a mythical date in British history, alongside 1066: the moment when Roman power collapsed, chaos and the dark ages began and nothing was the same. New approaches and new evidence allow a more nuanced and complex picture to emerge, of people endeavouring to maintain and adapt existing structures and lifestyles and of significant elements of continuity (Dark 2001; Wickham 2010), notwithstanding the fact that for many the experience of imperial decline was indeed dramatic and catastrophic (Ward-Perkins 2006). The idea that the frontier garrisons did not leave Britain (they had nowhere to go!) but helped to form the power bases of local warlords (probably high-ranking Romano-Britons) opens up fascinating areas of study to question existing stereotypes concerning the birth of English nationhood and the Brythonic/Anglo-Saxon/Roman interface.[1] These new approaches and ideas inform a broader narrative relevant to public presentation concerning the nature, origins and future of Britain as a political, cultural and economic entity (Great Britain, the UK, the British Isles?) which is explored by writers such as Norman Davies (2000) in his book *The Isles*, and by David Miles (2006) in *The Tribes of Britain*.

As Wickham (2010) illustrates, the legacy of the Romans is far more, and far more subtle, than roads, drains and legal systems. These ideas are relevant to a wider European public, for which the Roman Empire has had a multi-faceted and lasting legacy which still finds expression in many issues currently facing the European Union. For Hadrian's Wall, Hingley (this volume, Chapter 16) shows that the concept of the Roman Wall and its physical presence in the landscape has a lasting legacy.

Second, public understanding and engagement is of particular significance for World Heritage Sites for which education and learning is a key UNESCO objective, aspiring to promote UNESCO's core objectives of encouraging respect, toleration and cooperation amongst the peoples of the world. As a focus for conflict and separation in the past, the Frontiers of the Roman Empire WHS provides an excellent opportunity to promote these core UNESCO values but, to achieve this, public presentation needs to move beyond a narrow archaeological and militaristic focus to explore wider issues and contemporary resonances.

Presentation of World Heritage Sites tends to focus on the limited concept of their Outstanding

---

1   See, for example, Laycock (2009) for an interesting insight into Anglo-Saxon/British relationships.

Universal Value. In the case of Hadrian's Wall, this could easily limit public presentation to the physical monument itself. To understand Hadrian's Wall, as with any frontier, an understanding of the political, economic and social context in which it was created is needed. To limit presentation to the physical monument would fail to enable the public to understand the monument as a frontier, limit opportunities to engage visitors with the site and limit opportunities to engage with the wider context of UNESCO's core values.

Third, exploration of these broader narratives in presenting the Romans to the public is constrained both by many of the specific issues summarised above and by the process through which many major presentation projects are undertaken. This process tends to marginalise the role of interpreters in the design of new museum galleries, giving the lead roles to exhibition designers and curators. Interpreters tend to be brought in once the basic design concept has been developed and the curators have decided which objects they wish to display. The interpreters' role is then limited to providing text to explain the objects. The result is often a beautifully designed space filled with lots of objects that lacks conceptual or narrative coherence. Hazenberg (this volume, Chapter 10) notes that in developing the interpretive approach to displaying the Roman archaeology of Woerden, initial attempts to work with professional designers failed repeatedly due to a clash between the desire of the archaeologists to bring the narratives of Roman Woerden to life, and the focus of the designers on form.

An alternative approach (Mills *et al*, this volume, Chapter 19) is to bring forward involvement of the interpreter to an initial phase during which the narrative concept for the gallery is developed through dialogue between interpreter, curator and education specialists. Objects for display are selected on the basis of their potential to illustrate the narrative, which is in turn informed by the nature and range of objects in the collection. This narrative concept is used to inform the brief for the exhibition designers who then work as part of an interdisciplinary team. Several authors emphasise and illustrate the value of interdisciplinary, team-based approaches to public presentation (Kronberger, Hazenberg, Devine, Mills *et al*).

Another aspect of this approach is the opportunity to explore with existing and potential audiences how best to engage them with the past. The chapters by Kronberger, Hazenberg, Devine, Spearman, Adkins *et al*, Mills and Adkins, and Mills *et al* illustrate the vital contribution of audience research in informing development of interpretive displays, helping to frame the narratives, themes and questions used to structure the design and layout including selection of objects and interpretive media. People are interested in people, and it is through people past and present that the best opportunities for engaging modern audiences with the past exist. The Roman world is full of opportunities through the many individuals known by name from inscriptions across the Empire. For some of these, like Marcus Maenius Agrippa from Maryport (this volume, Chapter 19) or Flavius Cerialis and his wife Lepidina at Vindolanda (this volume, Chapter 13), we know a surprising and intriguing amount. The Roman world has left many legacies and has many resonances with the present whilst remaining fundamentally different. The Roman people and the resonances provide doors through which to invite audiences to enter and engage with the Roman world at the same time as increasing understanding and engagement with the present.

Fourth, public presentation needs to be seen in a much broader context than simply providing visitors with information or educating them about the past. Heritage is an increasingly important driver of economic benefit through sustainable tourism development. The better the visitor experience, the more the public can engage with the past, the easier it is to attract visitors and to encourage them to stay longer, a point emphasised in the chapters by Golubović and Korać

(Chapter 7), by Kronberger (Chapter 9), by Hazenberg (Chapter 10) and Mills and Adkins (Chapter 18). Heritage is also an important contributor to local distinctiveness and the sense of pride and identity amongst local communities. In an increasingly globalised world it has the potential to make people and places stand out and be themselves. Enabling local people to engage with their heritage and to be champions and advocates in presenting their heritage to visitors is fundamental to this, a point well made by Hazenberg.

Perhaps most importantly though, engagement of local people and visitors is essential to ensure better protection of the archaeology itself through enhanced public understanding and appreciation. Devine concludes that the Voices from the Past project's

> … focus on using museum artefacts to draw on real people from the past, and place them in their archaeological and historical contexts, provided learning opportunities that were highly engaging for the pupils, and which raised their awareness of the importance of the archaeological sites and heritage collections on their doorsteps to a level from which they felt a personal sense of ownership and pride.   (Devine, this volume, Chapter 12)

This point is made by several authors in this volume including Golubović and Korać, Hazenberg and Spearman.

Fifth, the use of different media and technology is not an end in itself and needs to be adapted and used in response to the messages to be conveyed and the spaces available. The Roman museum in Vienna (this volume, Chapter 9), the multi-storey car park in Woerden (Chapter 10) and the Frontier Gallery at Tullie House (Chapter 19) are examples where seemingly difficult spaces have been turned into opportunities for imaginative and dramatic display. Multimedia technology was deliberately avoided by Hazenberg and his team at Woerden (this volume, Chapter 10) in the interests of economy, but also of empowering local people to deliver and animate interpretation through guided walks and events. At Viminacium the emphasis is on putting the archaeology itself on display as a means of demonstrating the scale and significance of what is in the ground and engaging local people in valuing and protecting it, as well as encouraging visitors. Devine (this volume, Chapter 12) and Spearman (this volume, Chapter 13) emphasise the opportunities that new technology presents for people-focused interpretation as part of a mix of different media adapted to message and to site.

Sixth, an interesting dimension which is hinted at but not explored in this volume is that of the cultural aspect of interpretation and public presentation. Anglo-Saxon approaches to interpretation have been much influenced by the work of Tilden (1977) in the 1950s for the United States National Parks Service. Tilden's six principles emphasise a people-focused approach which has been widely applied in the UK in countryside interpretation, but less so in the heritage and museums sector. Are the issues identified above more relevant to the museums and heritage sectors in Anglo-Saxon countries than elsewhere? There is an apparent tendency, for instance, for public presentation in the Germanic world to focus on detailed modelling and reconstruction, as illustrated by approaches to presentation adopted at Aalen (this volume, Chapter 5). There are far more popular publications focusing on archaeology and history available for sale in French newsagents than in equivalent shops in the UK. Does this reflect differences in education systems, in cultural attitudes, in social class?

Structure and Outline

This book has its origins in a two-day session entitled 'Presenting the Romans' at the 2009 Limes Congress of Roman Frontier Studies held in Newcastle upon Tyne. In recent years the conference has broadened its essentially militaristic focus to encompass broader issues including supply and communications, civilian settlements and the role and contribution of women and families to life in the Roman army. 'Presenting the Romans' broke more new ground for the conference by focusing on the way that information about the Roman Frontiers is presented to the public. The idea behind the session came, in turn, from the involvement of the editor in the development of an Interpretation Framework for Hadrian's Wall, for which the 'Presenting the Romans' session provided an opportunity to explore and test emerging ideas within an academic Roman archaeology context.

The structure of this book is based on the structure of the session at the 2009 Limes conference and reflects the preoccupation of professional and academic archaeologists with evidence and authenticity when faced with the need and the opportunity for public presentation. The early chapters focus on archaeological evidence and the use of that evidence to visualise what buildings and people looked like in the past, through various approaches to reconstruction.

In Chapter 1, Breeze outlines his approach to editing the new *Handbook to the Roman Wall*, a detailed guidebook to Hadrian's Wall which has the ambition to be '*the* statement of current knowledge of the archaeology of the Wall' and of interpretations of the evidence which command the respect of Wall archaeologists. He suggests 'it would not be pitching its claims too high to say that it is the bible for Hadrian's Wall, the place where all readers seeking knowledge about the frontier would turn first'.

Yet even here as Breeze points out, different archaeologists have different viewpoints on fundamental aspects of our understanding of the Wall, its defensive nature for instance. Breeze recognises that the *Handbook* could have highlighted these differences more clearly. Differences of opinion provide opportunities to engage readers and visitors in debate and to contribute their own ideas, thereby stimulating further interest and understanding.

Moving beyond basic presentation of evidence as represented by the *Handbook*, reconstruction (including re-enactment, physical architectural reconstruction, graphical illustration and virtual and physical modelling) is a highly effective means of presenting the past to visitors and is discussed by Bishop (Chapter 2: re-enactment), Greaney (Chapter 3: reconstruction drawings), Flügel and Obmann (Chapter 4: architectural reconstruction), Kemkes (Chapter 5: architectural reconstruction, virtual and physical modelling), Trumm and Flück (Chapter 6: architectural reconstruction, virtual and physical modelling) and Young (Chapter 8: UNESCO perspectives on architectural reconstruction).

The authenticity of reconstruction is a constant concern to ensure that visitors are not misled and that they receive as accurate an impression as possible of the Roman world. Authenticity is constantly under review in the light of new evidence and can itself be informed by the process of reconstruction. Bishop explores these issues and notes the contribution enactors can make to academic knowledge through practical testing of military equipment; there is a three-way relationship between enactors, academics and audiences. As Bishop points out though, the only people who really knew what it was like to wear and use the kit were the Romans themselves!

Greaney explores the dialogue between illustrator and archaeologist in the creation of graphic representations of buildings and activities and the potential dangers of reinforcing stereotypes.

Greaney emphasises, too, the value of the process in contributing to archaeological debate and understanding, and in challenging preconceptions.

One of the problems with visualising the appearance of Roman buildings is that archaeological evidence is usually restricted to foundation plans and rarely provides firm evidence of upper storeys and roofing. Flügel and Obmann use the evidence of fibulae decorated with architectural designs to reappraise the scale of Roman fort gates as represented by many existing reconstructions. They conclude that the gateways were higher and grander in scale than previously thought, a conclusion which has important implications for our understanding of the role of gateways as monumental architecture expressing the power of the Roman Empire and for public presentation. Many existing reconstructions are too low and convey a misleading impression to visitors.

Kemkes describes the use of a range of different reconstruction techniques in the refurbishment of the Limes Museum at Aalen, including virtual reconstruction, a model and a partial reconstruction of a Roman cavalry barracks at 1:1 scale. Much of the archaeology of the Upper German-Raetian Limes lies hidden in the ground and it is difficult for visitors to visualise the extent and scale of Roman buildings. A key objective of using the different techniques is that each should provide a complementary experience and that collectively they should help to establish the Limes in the public consciousness, in turn helping to ensure long-term protection of the archaeology. A schematised model enables visitors to grasp the overall layout of the fort and garrison settlement in relation to the modern town; the 1:1 reconstruction enables visitors to experience the physical scale of the original buildings; the virtual reconstruction brings to life the fort and civil settlement at the same time as providing a source of graphic illustration that can be used across the site to reinforce visual impressions. Finally an animated film places the Roman site at Aalen in the context both of the Limes as a whole, and of provincial Roman rule.

Trumm and Flück describe a similar approach to tackling similar problems at the site of Vindonissa in Switzerland, although here abstract, schematised frames are used to convey the scale of the original buildings, thereby avoiding a potential problem of a full reconstruction giving visitors the impression that what they see is entirely accurate and factual. A highly detailed scale model of the fort and its surroundings was also created, using new technologies, that enable detailed representation of the functioning of the fort, of spatial relationships and of services such as waste management and the operation of craft workshops. Young highlights issues surrounding 1:1 reconstruction of UNESCO World Heritage Sites, since this approach to public presentation appears to be explicitly rejected by UNESCO for the Frontiers of the Roman Empire WHS in the interests of protecting the Outstanding Universal Value.

Chapters 8–10 focus on sites where the nature of the archaeology and the development pressures on it have prompted a range of interpretive responses to the particular local opportunities and constraints. Common themes are the desire to engage local people in appreciating their local heritage and participating in its protection, discovery and presentation, and the use of multidisciplinary teams in this process.

The archaeological remains of the Roman city and fortress of Viminacium cover a vast area of over 650 hectares. Golubović and Korać (Chapter 8) describe how archaeologists have responded to development pressures by creating a multidisciplinary research team in a project designed to link research, cultural tourism, engagement of local people and regeneration. Public presentation has focused on the uncovering and display of key archaeological features and has, in some cases, involved the total removal and redisplay of well-preserved remains in advance of opencast mining. An archaeological park has been created in the area of the necropolis of the Roman city to display these translocated and other *in situ* remains together with an archaeological research centre. Particular care has been taken in the design of structures to protect the remains whilst enabling the best experience for visitors. The research centre provides a focus for active research, finds storage, community engagement and tourism, and the Viminacium project as a whole is seen as a showcase for the use of heritage as a basis for economic and cultural development whilst promoting its understanding and protection amongst local people.

In Chapter 9, Kronberger describes how a multidisciplinary team in Vienna set about bringing to life the Roman city hidden beneath the modern streetscape. The narrow vertical planes dictated by the building prompted an imaginative approach to the use of space, moving the stairs to create a dramatic vertical area for graphic display across three floors. Audience research led to a thematic approach to display, with objects selected to illustrate key narratives and themes and to answer specific questions, linking the objects to the people who made and used them. The new display spaces were designed around the responses to the audience research, the interdisciplinary team working together to create an exhibition that would make often complex scientific content accessible to a wide range of audiences. A specific decision was made to display and interpret the objects in context rather than leaving them to 'speak for themselves'. The displays involved a mix of presentation techniques including cases, handling collections, interactive computer stations, graphic illustrations and multimedia.

Hazenberg (Chapter 10) describes how at Woerden in Holland local authorities, developers, local people and archaeologists worked together to bring to life the invisible Roman past of the city in response to the development of a major new shopping complex. The general public was asked to participate in developing ideas about how to present archaeological information resulting from excavations on the site of the shopping centre car park. The result has led to an integrated approach to presenting a number of Roman sites across the city in which local people acting as guides are the principal animators. The project has created an interpretive infrastructure which local people can use to bring the Roman past to life using simple, tried and tested presentation techniques, an interpretive focus for, by and about people and an approach which integrates the Roman past into modern city life rather than isolating it in a museum.

Chapters 11, 12 and 13 focus on the use of multimedia techniques and the opportunities they offer for innovative presentation that can transcend the limitations of the archaeology. Dobat, Walkshofer and Flügel (Chapter 11) explore the use of mobile phone technology in bringing to life archaeological sites in the landscape that would otherwise be invisible and difficult for visitors to visualise, at the same time linking the sites to objects discovered on them that are housed in distant museums. Their contribution emphasises the importance of taking a holistic view in which the development of an audio-visual resource for museum use can supply visual material for mobile applications, thereby cutting costs and enabling effective linkage between museum and site.

Devine (Chapter 12) also emphasises the importance of teamwork, this time between heritage professionals, academics, interpreters, the commercial sector and potential audiences, to maximise effective use of limited financial resources in realising the potential of digital technologies to provide access to cultural resources in new and innovative ways. Devine worked with children aged 8 to 16 to bring to life the story of Verecunda, a female known from a gravestone found on the Antonine Wall in Scotland, and to enable Verecunda herself to be a guide to the Bar Hill Roman fort for present-day visitors. Further work with schoolchildren enabled a suite of characters drawn from Roman inscribed stones in the Hunterian collection to be brought to life, which helped modern visitors to explore the Roman world through them.

Spearman (Chapter 13) also emphasises the importance of incorporating people into interpretive displays and the opportunities that new technologies provide for doing this, in populating the reconstruction images, in identifying and exploring different points of view, in exploring the lives of real people identified through the archaeology and in framing the questions and themes through which the archaeology is presented:

> For heritage professionals this process (of piecing together the past) and its associated debate is the stuff of history. For exhibition interpreters it is less the debate and more the conclusions that matter. For the majority of the public it is the story. Balancing these sometimes very different levels of interest has never been easy. An acceptable level of accuracy for one group can be a source of obfuscation for another. The successful combination of these different approaches is nevertheless essential if we are to make accessible the processes and results of historical debate to the wider public.   (Spearman, this volume, Chapter 13)

Chapters 14, 15 and 16 explore perceptions of the Roman world from different perspectives. Corbishley (Chapter 14) and Henson (Chapter 15) consider how the Romans have been portrayed in books and in film and how these portrayals may influence the preconceptions visitors have when they visit Roman sites and museums. Corbishley notes how attitudes to presenting the Romans have changed, from the overt imperial comparisons of the 19th and early 20th centuries to more nuanced and investigatory approaches today. Henson observes that the Rome seen in theatre, film and television is a mythical Rome, used to explore contemporary issues. Hingley (Chapter 16) explores perceptions of the Wall historically, and in the minds of artists and popular writers. He argues that this living dimension of the monument and the impact of its continuing presence in the landscape is an aspect of its legacy as deserving of public presentation as its archaeological and historical significance.

The final set of Chapters (17–19) explores the development of an Interpretation Framework for Hadrian's Wall. The 11 managed sites and museums offer particular opportunities and difficulties in presenting the Romans to the public. On the one hand, there is a risk that if not thought through and coordinated, each site and museum will tell an essentially similar story, putting visitors off rather than encouraging them to visit. On the other hand, the range of sites and museums creates opportunities to explore many different narratives and aspects of the Roman world. Extensive audience research was undertaken in developing the Framework (Chapter 17). Importantly, the research included qualitative analysis through focus groups which enabled different approaches to be explored and tested with potential and existing audiences. The Framework advocates a people-focused approach to presenting the Romans, selecting objects to illustrate narratives and exploring modern resonances. It suggests a range of themes which could be used to broaden interpretation at the different sites to create differentiated but complementary visitor offers that explore many different aspects of the Roman world and the Frontiers of the Roman Empire World Heritage Site (Chapter 18). The application of these approaches is illustrated in Chapter 19 with reference to the Roman Frontier Gallery at Tullie House Museum and Art Gallery in Carlisle, and to proposals for a new museum and visitor attraction at Roman Maryport on the Cumbrian coast.

Bibliography and References

Dark, K, 2001 *Britain and the End of the Roman Empire*, Tempus, Stroud

Davies, N, 2000 *The Isles: A History*, Pan Macmillan, London

Laycock, S, 2009 *Warlords – The Struggle for Power in Post-Roman Britain*, The History Press, Stroud

Mattingly, D, 2007 *An Imperial Possession: Britain in the Roman Empire*, Penguin, London

Miles, D, 2006 *The Tribes of Britain*, Phoenix, London

Tilden, F, 1977 *Interpreting our Heritage*, 3 edn, University of North Carolina Press, Chapel Hill

Ward-Perkins, B, 2006 *The Fall of Rome and the End of Civilisation*, Oxford University Press, Oxford

Wickham, C, 2010 *The Inheritance of Rome, a history of Europe from 400 to 1000*, Penguin, London

1

Tradition and Innovation:
Creating a New *Handbook to the Roman Wall*

David J Breeze

The *Handbook to the Roman Wall* is an unusual publication. On one level it is a guidebook, albeit a detailed guidebook, to a single monument – Hadrian's Wall – but as that monument is massive in its size and complex in the range of its elements, the *Handbook* is perforce a considerably larger guidebook than normal. Further, the *Handbook* is generally regarded as *the* statement of current knowledge and of those interpretations which command the support of the archaeologists working on the Wall. Hence, it is directed at a wide readership of visitors, archaeologists, cultural resource managers and the mythical general reader. It would not be pitching its claims too high to say that it is the bible for Hadrian's Wall, the place to which all readers seeking knowledge about the frontier would turn first.

The task of preparing a new edition of the oldest archaeological guide in Britain, as I was invited to do in 1998 by the Society of Antiquaries of Newcastle upon Tyne, was therefore a daunting prospect. How was I to deal with the weight of tradition and the authority of one's predecessors? How far was change possible? Was any innovation possible? How was I to ensure that all available evidence was taken into account in preparing the new edition? Was it possible to produce a corporate view?

The Oldest Archaeological Guidebook

The claim that the *Handbook to the Roman Wall* is the oldest archaeological guidebook requires some justification. In 1848, the Newcastle schoolteacher and Nonconformist minister John Collingwood Bruce (Fig 1.1) went on a tour of Hadrian's Wall. Over the following winter, he gave lectures to the Literary and Philosophical Society in Newcastle, to an audience that was somewhat sceptical about his descriptions of the Wall. In order to demonstrate that the Wall did indeed survive as well as Bruce averred, he offered to lead a tour along the frontier. This took place in 1849 and became known as the first Pilgrimage of Hadrian's Wall (the Pilgrimage continues as an event held every ten years: Edwards and Breeze 2000). In 1851, Bruce took a further step forward in his new career as interpreter of Hadrian's Wall when he published a new detailed account, *The Roman Wall*. A second edition followed two years later, with the third and most authoritative edition in 1867. In the meantime, Bruce had produced a synoptic version, *The Wallet-* (later *Hand-*) *Book to the Roman Wall* in 1863. This was billed as 'A Guide to Pilgrims journeying along the Barrier of the Lower Isthmus', amended to 'A Guide to Tourists traversing the Barrier of the Lower Isthmus' in his later editions of 1884 and 1885, wording which was retained until 1947. After Bruce's death in 1892, Robert Blair edited the next five editions (1895,

Fig 1.1. John Collingwood Bruce in his prime.

1907, 1909, 1914 and 1921), R G Collingwood one in 1933, Sir Ian Richmond three (1947, 1956 and 1966) and Charles Daniels one (1978): a list of the editions of *The Roman Wall* and the *Handbook* is provided at the end of this chapter.

A Review of Previous *Handbooks*

Bruce's own *Handbooks* were a good starting point for consideration of the style and contents of a new edition. Bruce himself had kept his own publications on Hadrian's Wall books up-to-date, in particular revising the accounts of the Wall running through his native Tyneside. This gave encouragement to a new editor to consider change (Breeze 2007).

A review of all previous editions demonstrated considerable change over the last 140 years. Blair retained the Bruce format. Collingwood, however, undertook a root-and-branch review for his edition of 1933. He dropped ancillary chapters on 'Supporting Stations' and 'Antiquities from Hadrian's Wall' but added a short section on the 'Cumberland Coast', which he had started to explore, and a bibliography. Both have been retained by subsequent editors, the latter now forming the most detailed published bibliography for the Wall.

The crucial lesson of the review was that change was possible, and indeed essential for the *Handbook* to remain as the principal in-depth guidebook to Hadrian's Wall. The review, however, taught me something altogether different. It became clear that over 13 editions, interpretation had been heaped upon interpretation with editors often not going back to the original sources and examining the basic facts. This led me to realise that a full review of all the available literature was required – and also a visit to every section of the Wall described in the *Handbook*. The visitation, I soon realised, was important in another way. It would appear that several editors had not inspected some parts of the Wall at all, or certainly not when it came to revising their editions, but relied too much upon memory (as we all do). The problem became more acute the further west along Hadrian's Wall I walked. This is not surprising considering that four of the five previous editors had been based in Newcastle; Collingwood lived in Oxford though he had been brought up in Cumbria.

The Preparation of the *Handbook*

The inspection of the Wall and its ancillary works took five years to complete. Walking, examining and recording were slow in the areas where much survived, but, over and above that, the Wall is a complex monument. There is the linear barrier itself, that is the wall, together with the ditch, upcast mound, Vallum, Military Way and Stanegate, forming a series of features which run along all or most of the length of the Wall. Then there are the forts, civil settlements, milecastles, turrets and bridges as well as the forts, milefortlets and towers on the Cumbrian Coast, and the forts, fortlets and towers on the Stanegate. Beyond these elements themselves, there is their relationship to each other and their position in the landscape. There were also other people's theories to consider in the field. The exercise was compounded by new publications which appeared while I was working on the *Handbook*, resulting in repeat visits to some sectors. It is not surprising, therefore, that progress was slow. Nor was it entirely complete. Each linear element should have been walked separately and considered as a feature in its own right, possibly even where it is not visible. I sought to do this. Separate visits were devoted solely to the Vallum and to the Stanegate but, in the end, some stretches of each were observed from the car rather than walked.

FIG 1.2. THIS WOODCUT OF AN INSCRIPTION FROM BIRDOSWALD HAS APPEARED
IN EVERY EDITION OF THE *HANDBOOK*.

In parallel to the walking was the reading. There is a considerable literature on Hadrian's Wall. This includes reports on excavations undertaken over the last hundred years and more. None of these reports were written in a vacuum. The conclusions of the excavators, and indeed their observations of the archaeological deposits, were intimately related to the prevailing theories of the day. The most important of these is the concept of Wall periods. Earlier excavators acknowledged the existence of levels within military structures, but it was the excavators of milecastle 48 (Poltross Burn) in 1909–10, J P Gibson and F G Simpson, who first formulated a coherent theory (Breeze 2003a, 10; Bruce 2006; Dobson 2008). Gibson and Simpson divided the occupation of the milecastle into periods, offering dates for each. Excavations at Birdoswald in 1929 led to the dates assigned to the beginning and end of each period being changed. Thereafter, archaeologists adapted the history of each site to the Wall period theory: earlier work was reinterpreted to fit the new dates and the results of every newly excavated site were presented within the framework of the 1929 orthodoxy. In 1967 M G Jarrett first argued that the history of each site should be taken on its own merits (Jarrett 1967). During the 1960s and 1970s the Wall-periods theory was reviewed and largely discarded. Now, care is taken not to squeeze events into a straitjacket. In considering each excavation report, therefore, I sought to bypass the interpretation of the day and go back to the raw data while bearing in mind the beliefs at the time the report was written. The basic information about each site was then presented in the *Handbook* with the minimum of interpretation.

The necessity to go back to the basic information in the field or in the excavation report was not confined to the archaeological evidence. To take an epigraphic example, a range of inscriptions at Maryport on the Cumbrian coast provides a fascinating insight into an activity of the Roman army: the taking of the annual oath of allegiance to the emperor and the Roman state (Breeze 1997). Fifteen altars date to the reign of Hadrian and provide a near-complete record of the dedications of his reign. The average length of service of each commander was three years and that is the figure widely quoted in publications on the Roman army.

The order in which the commanding officers held their appointments at Maryport is, however, not known. There are two different pieces of evidence that may be called into play. One commanding officer, Maenius Agrippa, is recorded on an inscription erected in Italy as a host of the Emperor Hadrian. It has often been assumed that this indicates that he was in post at Maryport during the visit of Hadrian to the Wall – what one might term the romantic interpretation – though there is no evidence for this; it is perhaps more likely that the event occurred in Italy. The assumption, however, has led to Agrippa being placed first in the list of commanders (Jarrett 1976, 21; Breeze 1997, 72, 77). Secondly, the title of the commanding officers at Maryport changed during the reign of Hadrian. Two, including Agrippa, are given the title 'tribune' and the others the title 'prefect'. The former title is normally used for the officer commanding a unit of 1000 men and the latter for the commander of 500 men. Thus, it would appear that the unit was either doubled in size while at Maryport or lost part of its strength to service elsewhere. Agrippa's friendship with Hadrian, combined with the large size of the fort, appropriate for a thousand-strong unit, has led to the proposal that the unit was reduced in size, perhaps losing troops to fight in the Bar Kokba Rebellion of the early 130s (Breeze 1997, 73–4). Frere has offered a different interpretation of the use of the title of tribune, pointing out that the unit is nowhere recorded as being 1000 strong (Frere 2000, 26–7). He suggested that the two commanders with the rank of tribune were accorded special status because they were carrying out additional duties. Frere suggested that these might relate to the use of the fort as a supply base, which in turn would account for its size, or because the commanders were undertaking a task of limited duration such as the construction of a harbour. This is possible, though it is worth noting that there is no independent evidence for either suggestion.

There is, however, yet another dimension. Maenius Agrippa was sent to Britain to participate in a military campaign, only later taking up the post of tribune at Maryport. The campaign is not dated, though the career of another officer who took part in what we presume was the same campaign, T Pontius Sabinus, suggests that the event did not take place before 125 (Breeze 2003b). This dating of the event is of direct relevance to the order of service of the commanding officers at Maryport and therefore to the history of the site. But the argument also relates to wider Hadrian's Wall issues and is therefore considered in the general discussion in chapter 1 of the *Handbook* rather than in the account of Maryport (Bruce 2006, 26–7).

The issues raised by these 15 altars are complex and there was insufficient space in the *Handbook* to do more than briefly set out the evidence and indicate the existence of the different interpretations and wider complications. This was unfortunate in view of the international importance of the altars, though the Bibliography points to further reading on the site and its problems. In addition, the debate about the Maryport altars and their interpretation continues but it is not possible to state in every such instance that the solution offered is merely an interim statement.

This leads on to a consideration of the amount of detail to include in the *Handbook*. The first chapter was simply updated, but the second chapter, A General Account of the Works, was more problematic. This grew to be larger than planned but, once finished, it was difficult to cut because the amount of detail seemed necessary to aid an understanding of the Wall for the reader and the visitor. A new section in this chapter was a consideration of the purpose and operation of Hadrian's Wall. The main part of the book is a description of the remains within a geographical framework. Here again, I provided more detail than previous editors and here again this was deemed necessary in order to provide a wider view of the sites. It seemed to me that the results of recent work required appropriate description and discussion. And once such detail was

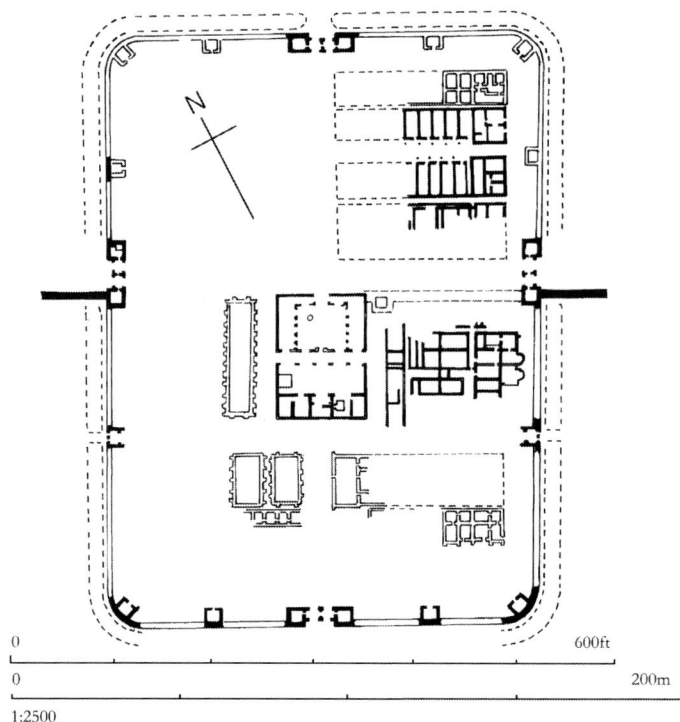

FIG 1.3. THE PLAN OF THE
FORT AT CHESTERS PREPARED
BY SANDRA ROWNTREE.

provided, for example on the turrets excavated by Charmian Woodfield in the 1960s, then more details were required for other sites to maintain a balance of treatment (Woodfield 1965). That said, there is an imbalance. The smaller sites are generally discussed in greater detail than the forts; this, as any writer of a guidebook will acknowledge, is an inherent problem of the genre.

With regard to the structure of the book, I took an early decision to separate out the entries on the Stanegate sites and place them in their own chapter. This, it seemed to me, helped the user of the *Handbook*, and is approved by Collins and Symonds in their review (2010, 652). I also decided to exclude the outpost forts from detailed discussion as it is only through our interpretation that they are regarded as part of the Wall complex. If these forts were to have been included, then so too should have been the hinterland forts, and that would have made the *Handbook* too wide in its scope. Otherwise, the editorial committee and myself were determined to retain the basic structure of the *Handbook* and the somewhat old-fashioned look; there are plenty of glossy, full-colour guidebooks for visitors who want to buy that style of publication; a similar point is made by Wilmott in his review (2010, 479).

Earlier editions had contained some background information on the area. Some passages were useful and were retained, but several relayed the local myths and hardly reached above the level of anecdote. These were expunged, not least because anyone interested in such aspects could either consult earlier editions or turn to more authoritative and up-to-date treatments of such material (accepted by Collins and Symonds (2010, 652), though Bidwell is nostalgic about these 'colourful snippets' in his review (2007, 369)).

Fig 1.4. The plan of the geophysical survey at Maryport.

Illustrations were carefully considered. Some woodcuts were retained from earlier editions, though re-photographed from the best available publication. Full use was made of new material, such as the geophysical plans of forts and civil settlements by TimeScape. All plans were drawn by Sandra Rowntree to basic scales for comparison. New detailed maps prefaced each section. These were a re-introduction as maps had been dropped by Ian Richmond in the 12th edition published in 1966.[1] When all was gathered together, a start was made on designing the new *Handbook*. This took Linda Kay a year to complete, but her careful endeavours led to an integrated and, I believe, user-friendly production.

---

1   Alan Biggins and David Taylor of TimeScape generously allowed many of the geophysical surveys of forts and civil settlements to be included.

PUBLICATION AND AFTER

The publication of the new edition of the *Handbook* in November 2006 led to various press interviews. Amongst the questions I was asked was: what is the importance of the *Handbook*? I replied, perhaps rather lamely, that all future guidebooks to Hadrian's Wall would be based upon the information within it. This is indeed largely true. It is for that reason that I laboured so hard to bring all colleagues on board with the final text. It is my firm belief that the *Handbook* ought to be – and largely is – the considered statement of Hadrian's Wall for its generation. Where it is not, it is my fault. I foolishly tried to tinker with Humphrey Welfare's considered position on the date of the removal of milecastle causeways (2000) and argued too strongly against a wall-walk. Although I reviewed the evidence for a wall-walk, my interpretation of it was coloured by my own belief that a wall-walk did not exist. That belief was based upon my own view of the purpose and operation of Roman frontiers, a view which is shared by several other archaeologists and historians but not by Paul Bidwell and Nick Hodgson, for example (see the review by Bidwell 2007, 370). A text produced by either archaeologist, I suspect, would have more reference to defence and to the Wall sitting in a defensive location in the landscape, whereas I would assume that it simply follows the shape of the land, as discussed by Poulter (2010, 121–32).

This point has a wider resonance. Collingwood published a paper in 1921 in which he argued that the wall-walk – the existence of which he assumed, as had his predecessors – was not a fighting platform but an elevated sentry walk (Collingwood 1921). Yet, when he came to prepare a new edition of the *Handbook* he left within the text all the references to the Wall here and there adopting a line for better defence (Breeze 2003a, 6).

The publication of the 14th edition of the *Handbook to the Roman Wall* in November 2006 coincided with the annual conference of the Arbeia Society in South Shields. Paul Bidwell and his colleagues had agreed to hold the conference on Hadrian's Wall and kindly allowed me a free hand in inviting the lecturers. I was – and am – conscious as co-author of the basic text book on Hadrian's Wall, Breeze and Dobson's *Hadrian's Wall*, which was first published in 1976, that such books can sometimes depress research in the (mistaken) belief that the last word has been said on the subject (Breeze and Dobson 1976). Accordingly, I invited several colleagues to speak whose views differed from my own as well as archaeologists who had offered new views of the Wall over recent years and two foreign contributors which would help us place Hadrian's Wall in a wider context. In the end, there was perhaps not such a level of disagreement as I had expected, but the papers, published as *Understanding Hadrian's Wall*, form a significant contribution to Wall studies and, on a personal note, encouraged me to change my own views, in particular on the existence of a wall-walk (Bidwell 2008, 129–43; Breeze 2009, 97). I would now accept that the evidence will support the existence of a wall-walk. I have, however, offered a different reason for the possible/probable existence of a wall-walk to that offered by Bidwell (namely that it was necessary for the proper function of the Wall as a defensive barrier), which is that Hadrian's Wall was designed by the Emperor Hadrian himself, this accounting for other unique elements recognisable on the frontier (Breeze 2009).

How far do I believe that I have succeeded in the aims set out at the beginning of this chapter? Firstly, although the text of the *Handbook* has received general approval from those archaeologists working on the Wall, this is not to say that we are all right! What has been offered are the interpretations for our generation. Obviously, so far as possible they are based upon agreed and recorded facts, but it should also be remembered that the very act of excavating is an interpretation, and so some elements of the *Handbook* are an interpretation based upon an interpretation. Both are subject to revision as knowledge and experience grows.

With hindsight, one aspect I believe I should have acknowledged more strongly is the fundamental differences between archaeologists studying the Wall in terms of its function. Indeed, these significant differences render the attempt to produce a corporate statement, itself a new concept, impossible to achieve fully.

Five years on, would I change the *Handbook*? Apart from eradicating the errors I have noted, and taking into account new research and their implications and my own improving knowledge, the answer is negative. Reviewers have approved of the general approach, the stripping out of unnecessary anecdotes, and the ability to use the *Handbook* as a guidebook (Beale 2007, 26; Summerly 2007). The main area of discussion has been the size of the 14th edition. By size, I do not mean the dimensions, which are the same as before, but its thickness. It has increased from 355 to 512 pages and is noticeably thicker than the 13th edition. This incurred criticism from Andrew Selkirk, but acceptance of the necessity by Ian Caruana (Selkirk 2007; Caruana 2007).

The 14th edition took eight years to produce from taking the first steps at Chesters in July 1999 to publication in November 2006. I was fortunate in terms of the publisher: the Society of Antiquaries of Newcastle. The sole aim of the Society was to achieve the publication of the best possible *Handbook*; money was not its primary concern, so I was allowed to take as long as was necessary. It is not given to every author to work for such an enlightened body. I was further fortunate in the advisers appointed by the Society who brought to the task a range of experience and knowledge. This was supplemented by Sandra Rowntree taking on the enormous task of producing new maps and plans and Linda Kay's patience in designing 512 pages. Finally, I was fortunate in the generosity of my colleagues in reading and re-reading the text, advising on the best form of the bibliography, of the maps, plans – indeed every aspect. The *Handbook* was certainly a communal effort and is the better for that.

Bibliography and References

Beale, A, 2007 Review, *The Journal of Classics Teaching* 11 (3), Summer, 25–6

Bidwell, P, 2007 Review, *Archaeologia Aeliana* 36 (5), 369–70

Bidwell, P (ed), 2008 *Understanding Hadrian's Wall*, The Arbeia Society, South Shields

Breeze, D J, 1997 The regiments stated at Maryport and their commanders, in *Roman Maryport and its setting* (ed R J A Wilson), Cumberland and Westmorland Antiquarian and Archaeological Society, extra series 28, Maryport, 67–89

— 2003a John Collingwood Bruce and the study of Hadrian's Wall, *Britannia* 34, 1–18

— 2003b Warfare in Britain and the Building of Hadrian's Wall, *Archaeologia Aeliana* 33 (5), 13–16

— 2007 The Making of the Handbook to the Roman Wall, *Archaeologia Aeliana* 36 (5), 1–10

— 2009 Did Hadrian design Hadrian's Wall?, *Archaeologia Aeliana* 38 (5), 87–103

Breeze, D J, and Dobson, B, 1976 (1978, 2nd edn; 1987, 3rd edn; 2000, 4th edn), *Hadrian's Wall*, Penguin Books Ltd, London and Harmondsworth

Bruce, J C, 1851 *The Roman Wall*, John Russell Smith, London, William Sang and G Bourchier Richardson, Newcastle upon Tyne

— 1853 *The Roman Wall*, 2nd edn, John Russell Smith, London

— 1863 *The Wallet-book of the Roman Wall*, Longman, Green, Longman, Roberts and Green, London, D H Wilson, Newcastle upon Tyne

— 1867 *The Roman Wall*, 3rd edn, Longmans, Green, Reader and Dyer, London, Andrew Reid, Newcastle upon Tyne

— 1884 *The Hand-book to the Roman Wall*, 2nd edn, Alfred Smith, London, Andrew Reid, Newcastle upon Tyne

— 1885 *The Hand-book to the Roman Wall*, 3rd edn, Longmans, Green & Co, London, Andrew Reid, Newcastle upon Tyne

— 1895 *The Hand-book to the Roman Wall*, 4th edn (ed R Blair), Longmans, Green & Co, London, Andrew Reid, Newcastle upon Tyne

— 1907 *The Hand-book to the Roman Wall*, 5th edn (ed R Blair), Longmans, Green & Co, London, Andrew Reid, Newcastle upon Tyne

— 1909 *The Hand-book to the Roman Wall*, 6th edn (ed R Blair), Longmans, Green & Co, London, Andrew Reid, Newcastle upon Tyne

— 1914 *The Hand-book to the Roman Wall*, 7th edn (ed R Blair), Longmans, Green & Co, London, Andrew Reid, Newcastle upon Tyne

— 1921 *The Hand-book to the Roman Wall*, 8th edn (ed R Blair) (reprinted 1925 and 1927), Longmans, Green & Co, London, Andrew Reid, Newcastle upon Tyne

— 1933 *The Handbook to the Roman Wall*, 9th edn (ed R G Collingwood) (reprinted 1937), Longmans, Green & Co, London, Andrew Reid, Newcastle upon Tyne

— 1947 *Handbook to the Roman Wall*, 10th edn (ed I A Richmond) (reprinted 1951), Harold Hill & Son Ltd and Andrew Reid & Co, Newcastle upon Tyne

— 1956 *Handbook to the Roman Wall*, 11th edn (ed I A Richmond), Newcastle upon Tyne

— 1966 *Handbook to the Roman Wall*, 12th edn (ed Sir I Richmond) (reprinted 1970), Harold Hill & Son Ltd and Andrew Reid & Co, Newcastle upon Tyne

— 1978 *Handbook to the Roman Wall*, 13th edn (ed C M Daniels), Harold Hill & Son Ltd, Newcastle upon Tyne

— 2006 *Handbook to the Roman Wall*, 14th edn (ed D J Breeze), Society of Antiquaries of Newcastle upon Tyne, Newcastle upon Tyne

Caruana, I, 2007 Review, *Newsletter of the Cumberland and Westmorland Antiquarian and Archaeological Society* 55, Summer, 12

Collingwood, R G, 1921 The Purpose of the Roman Wall, *Vasculum* 8 (1), 4–9

Collins, R, and Symonds, M, 2010 Forts and frontiers: recent Limesforschung from Britannia, *Journal of Roman Archaeology* 23, 651–6

Dobson, B, 2008 Moving the Goalposts, in *Understanding Hadrian's Wall* (ed P Bidwell), The Arbeia Society, South Shields, 5–9

Edwards, B J N, and Breeze, D J, 2000 *The 1999 Pilgrimage of Hadrian's Wall*, Cumberland and Westmorland Antiquarian and Archaeological Society and Society of Antiquaries of Newcastle upon Tyne, Kendal

Frere, S S, 2000 M Maenius Agrippa, the *Expeditio Britannica* and Maryport, *Britannia* 31, 23–8

Jarrett, M G, 1967 Actuelle Probleme der Hadriansmauer, *Germania* 45, 96–108

— 1976 *Maryport, Cumbria: A Roman Fort and its Garrison*, Cumberland and Westmorland Antiquarian and Archaeological Society, extra series 22, Kendal

Poulter, J, 2010 *The Planning of Roman Roads and Walls in Northern Britain*, Amberley, Stroud

Selkirk, A, 2007 The Roman Wall, *Current Archaeology* 207, Jan/Feb, 50

Summerly, J, 2007 Review, *Archaeological Journal* 164, 279

Welfare, H, 2000 Causeways, at Milecastles, across the Ditch of Hadrian's Wall, *Archaeologia Aeliana* 28 (5), 13–25

Wilmott, T, 2010 Review, *Britannia* 41, 479–80

Woodfield, C C, 1965 Six Turrets on Hadrian's Wall, *Archaeologia Aeliana* 43 (4), 87–200

2

Re-enactment and Living History – Issues about Authenticity

M C Bishop

Introduction

No re-enactor can ever come anywhere near to the experience of being a Roman soldier, in much the same way as neither Laurence Olivier nor Kenneth Branagh could ever *be* Henry V. Each could and can think themselves into the part, assuming the mantle of the persona, but it will always (and can only) be *mimesis*, an impression of the desired model, perhaps coloured by the experiences and imagination of the individual playing the part and informed by research into the subject, but it is never the thing itself. Re-enactors (despite some extreme examples) cannot really eat, think, walk, drink, talk or live like a Roman. Thus, we must acknowledge from the very beginning that the only truly authentic Roman soldiers were those in the service of Rome many years ago.

Performance

It is no accident that a re-enactor will talk of their impression of a particular character from the past, for they too are acknowledging the gap between what they can achieve and the reality of life in the Roman period. They adopt a Roman name and this helps give them a focus for their character. The character is a fabrication based on many different sources, as is the appearance of the re-enactor, since a similarly disparate range of information will have helped shape the clothing they wear (Sumner 2009) and equipment they carry (Bishop and Coulston 2006). For the early imperial period, this will usually be as heavily influenced by the fine series of tombstones from Britain, the Rhineland and the Danube as it is by the equipment recovered from the archaeological record; later periods are more dependent upon the artefactual evidence.

Moreover, this distance, as it were, between the re-enactor and the re-enacted is tacitly acknowledged by both the players and their audience, to revisit the earlier metaphor – and perhaps Shakespeare's preferred term *spectators* (Shapiro 2006, 368–9) is more appropriate here. There is a sort of embarrassed acceptance that all is not what it seems, but nevertheless it is what it is. Strict rules are usually enforced, banishing anachronistic details such as the wearing of watches or modern jewellery, or even being glimpsed participating in an out-of-character activity such as having a cup of tea, in order not to hinder the suspension of disbelief on the part of the spectators by committing what, in modern cinematic terms, would be an *edge violation*. Nevertheless, the fact that the re-enactor is not a native speaker of Latin (and many, one suspects, leave much to be desired in the realms of pronunciation) and is, ultimately, an inhabitant of the

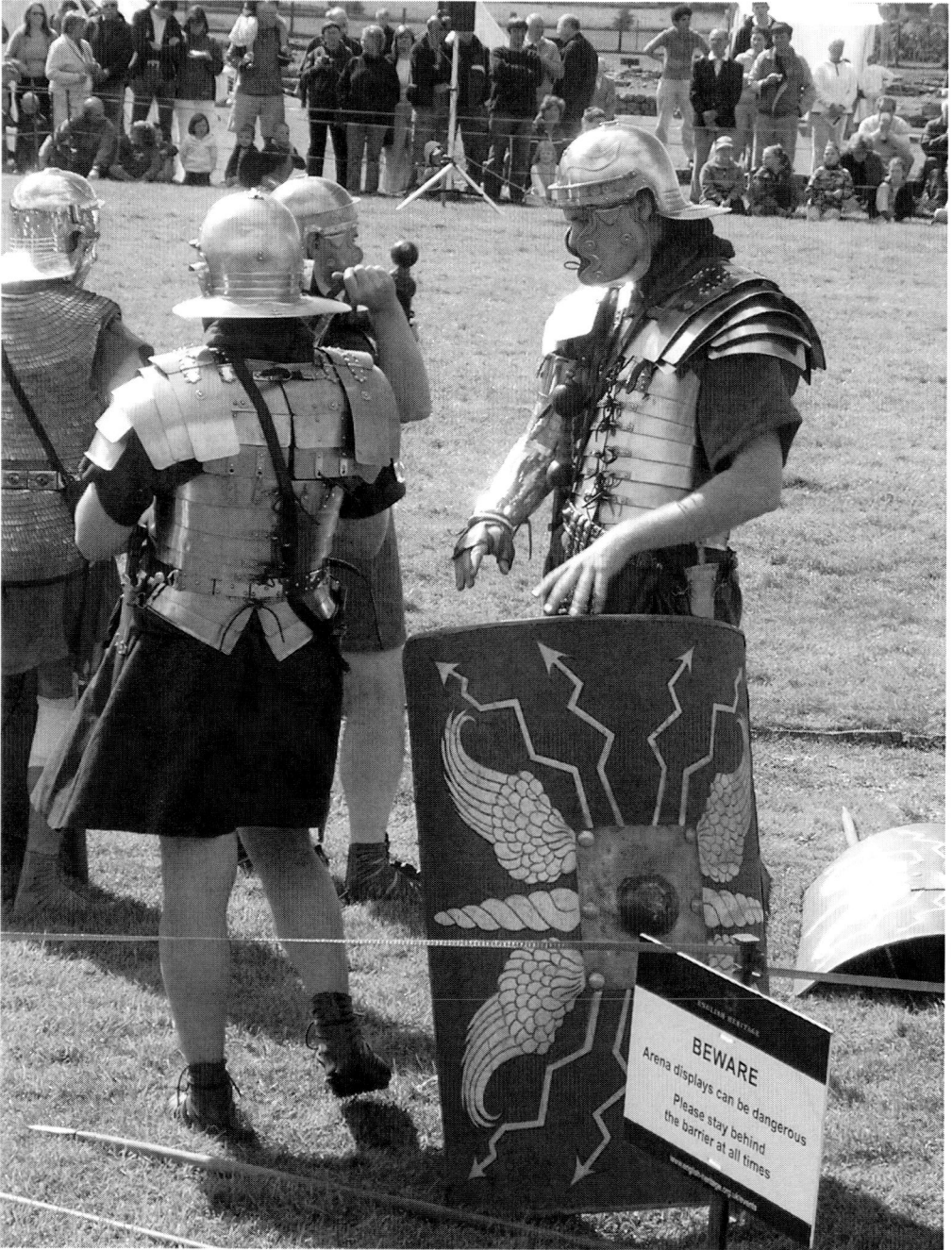

Fig 2.1. Roman re-enactors (complete with safety barrier and PA system) discuss their impressions of 1st-century legionaries.

21st century will inevitably communicate itself in some way. Moreover, prevailing conditions at events, most noticeably the pervasive modern obsession with health and safety, scarcely help matters. Safety fencing and public address systems are likewise obstacles to the perception of the past as the re-enactor might want it (Fig 2.1), but they are not insurmountable. Thus re-enactment is a performance that inevitably incorporates and must work with a distance between the performer and the spectators, but that does not mean it cannot strive to be as accurate, useful and interesting as possible and one must be careful to assess it on its own terms, rather than against absolutes which are unachievable without the aid of a time machine and a snatch squad.

So how did this curious state of affairs originate? Historical re-enactment has what can punningly be described as a long history, being founded in pageants of past ages, like those mounted in Colchester in 1909 (Wallace 1988) and Chester in 1910 (Lloyd-Morgan 1987, 96–7) or those associated with Kaiser Wilhelm II and the Saalburg (Obmann and Wirtz 1997), but it began to be taken seriously – by its participants at least – in the early 1960s with American Civil War centennial events (Hadden 1999, 4). In Britain, the late 1960s saw the rise of the Sealed Knot recreating the English Civil War period and it was not long after that, during the early 1970s, that the first serious Roman re-enactment society, the Ermine Street Guard, was born out of a village historical pageant (Haines 2007, 133). Roman re-enactment remained a largely British affliction until the 1980s when it began to be found in the USA, in continental Europe and ultimately it has spread right around the world.

Roman re-enactment is now everywhere. From full centuries of heavily equipped legionaries through to a handful of civilians and even a bloodthirsty solo *medicus* (a *tour de force* which is a favourite with children), all Roman provincial life is there. A small industry exists to supply the needs of re-enactors, be it with lovingly crafted small fittings closely based on archaeological originals, or mass-produced sets of *lorica segmentata* shipped in from India and available for around £160.

Interestingly, whilst re-enactment (or, as it is slightly euphemistically called these days, 'living history') had its origins in the re-creation (as distinct from recreation!) of past battles by American or English Civil War societies, the Roman branch has remained surprisingly pacific, concentrating on everyday life and crafts or, in the case of military units, demonstrating drills and the occasional tactical formation. For a long time, the most alarming thing about the Ermine Street Guard, apart from their knees, was a charge towards those spectators not wise enough to have worked out where not to sit or stand beforehand (Fig 2.2); nowadays, sadly, health and safety requirements impose a polite distance between chargers and charged. War, after all, can be a messy business. When it is available, shooting torsion artillery (not firing, of course, for that requires gunpowder) is always a prominent feature of such displays, but shooting *at* anyone tends to be discouraged, even in the case of less enlightened or troublesome elements amongst the spectators. Similarly, the opportunity to display cavalry is always enthusiastically greeted, particularly by little girls of a certain age, who tend to be more concerned with the horse than issues of authenticity (Fig 2.3). Staged combats are rare, which is probably a good thing, since, unless they are played for laughs (itself an ethically rocky path), they seldom look anything except staged (but at least re-enactors, unlike Hollywood fight arrangers, know enough to parry with the shield and not the sword). Many groups prefer to show some sort of active training sequence, reminiscent of Josephus' oft-quoted aphorism about the similarities between training and combat for the Roman army (Josephus, *Bellum Iudiacum*, 3.76 tr. Williamson 1969). In that respect, both then and now, simulated combat more closely resembles the playground battles of childhood,

FIG 2.2. THE ERMINE STREET GUARD MOUNTING A SPIRITED CHARGE IN THE DAYS BEFORE SAFETY BARRIERS.

FIG 2.3. A CAVALRYMAN SURROUNDED BY AN ADMIRING CROWD. ARGUABLY THE EPITOME OF CAREFUL RESEARCH INTO EQUIPMENT AND DRESS, IT IS NEVERTHELESS THE HORSE THAT ATTRACTS THE ATTENTION.

where participants get up at the end and live to fight another day – in so doing distancing the re-enactment from the full horrors of ancient warfare, where death, maiming, looting, rape and enslavement were regular and uncontentious features of proceedings for the perpetrators, if not all of the participants.

VALUE

As for the equipment that is used, this is where re-enactment arguably has its greatest value (Haines *et al* 2000). Beyond replicas for museum display, there is little impetus in academic spheres to reconstruct and use ancient military equipment. The work of David Sim (1995; 1997; Sim and Kaminski 2011) in recreating Roman weaponry and armour, both in terms of studying the likely construction processes, as well as examining usage and attrition in a scientific fashion, is one notable exception. Another is to be found in the carefully researched reconstructions of Peter Connolly (1990; Connolly and van Driel-Murray 1991), undertaken to inform his illus-trated books (Connolly 1988), but it largely falls to re-enactors to experiment with the long-term effects of everyday use upon reconstructed Roman arms and armour (Haines *et al* 2000, 123–4).

Taking the use of articulated plate armour as an example, Henry Russell Robinson's collabora-tion with Charles Daniels on reconstructing the armour from the Corbridge Hoard, found in 1964 (1988, 97–100), allowed him to exhibit his reconstructions at the 1969 Roman Frontiers Congress in Cardiff (Robinson 1969). This work, published in his popular *The Armour of Impe-rial Rome* (1975), and also outlined in the earlier Congress proceedings (1974), became the basis for re-enactors to produce their own versions, often in collaboration with Robinson (Haines 2007, 133). Whilst replicas in museum cases look attractive, the sheer familiarity of repeated use of such equipment can be invaluable. For example, one section of the armour from the Hoard clearly showed how a flawed design (in this case the overlap of backplates) could manifest itself archaeologically, and this is confirmed by observation of unwitting re-enactors (Bishop 2002, 43 with Fig 5.13).

A second illustration that can be usefully introduced is that of the Roman military horse harness and especially the Celto-Roman saddle. Thanks to a series of important discoveries of fragments of leather from saddles, Peter Connolly and Carol van Driel-Murray were able to reconstruct the likely original form of the Celto-Roman saddle and have it tested initially by Anne Hyland (Connolly and van Driel Murray 1991; Hyland 1990, 130–4). However, once Roman military horse harness began to be reconstructed by re-enactors, a much wider body of experience was brought to bear on the use, strengths and weaknesses of the system, not least since many of the new Roman horse riders had experience riding a range of modern and recon-structed pre-modern systems of harness and could compare their capabilities. Quite apart from such practical considerations, re-creation of Roman horse harness allows simple things like the sound of a trotting Roman cavalry horse to be heard and, when research-body-funded schemes to pursue such reconstructions are few and far between, it is in such intangibles that the value of re-enactment can be truly appreciated.

ASSUMPTIONS

Much has to be assumed, of course, and it is here that the pitfalls lie. Re-enactment is not like reconstruction illustrations, where plumes of smoke or squalls of rain can be used to obscure uncertainties. The patchy nature of the source material has to be padded out to make a plausible whole. Everybody knows soldiers march, and most nowadays assume they have always marched in step (they have not), so the sight of a body of legionaries traipsing past muttering 'sin, sin, sin dex sin' has become familiar to an event-going public when there is no fact to back up the assumptions that have been made, and every chance that the meme that Roman soldiers marched in step and muttered to keep pace will flourish. Cadenced marching, as it is known, was a fairly late introduction, probably being adopted around 1730 by the Prussians under Friedrich II or, alternatively, by Marshal Saxe (Furse 1901, 191), but armies have always shambled along and the world record for a forced march, popularised in Stephen Ambrose's book and the subsequent TV series *Band of Brothers* (Ambrose 2001, 28–9), was not performed in step (Moore 2007). Vegetius, often quoted on the subject, talks only of soldiers being required to harmonise their speed, not cadencing (Vegetius, *Epitoma Rei Militaris,* 1.9 tr Stelton 1990). Nevertheless, marching in step is certainly a possibility for the Roman army, perhaps more so than the dubiously abbreviated chant, but it is an assumption that has become a factoid.

Tunic colour is another area of contention that can verge on a religious war amongst the cognoscenti. Some prefer red, others blue, whilst others opt for white, off-white, or some non-committal shade of brown, and our sources are appropriately oblique on the matter, although much has been accomplished in print recently by Graham Sumner (2009, 119–59) to rectify the uncertainties in this area and lay out the evidence for consideration. Nevertheless, such turf wars (shield size and colour, tunic colour, shininess of armour, who has got the biggest piece of artillery) punctuate the otherwise sedate and comfortable lives of re-enactors and help provide no little interest in the whole process for the otherwise baffled academic onlooker, whose conflicts tend to be of a wholly different kind.

Whilst Hollywood has, with the odd exception, floundered around with depictions of Roman soldiers that have ranged from the not bad to the execrable, television has increasingly taken to using re-enactors to add a little bit of dramatic colour in documentaries, so the practice – if that is what it may be called – has reached an even larger public than that of just event-going spectators. With it has gone all the research and attention to detail, as well as the odd dubious assumption and creative instinct on the part of directors, to provide a cultural construct, *the Roman Soldier*, which may, or may not, resemble the original more or less closely.

Re-enactors are an extension of the mannequins favoured by museums and first used in the 19th century by Lindenschmit in the Römisch-Germanisches Zentralmuseum, Mainz, where he reconstructed a Roman legionary based on the depiction on the tombstone of G Valerius Crispus from Wiesbaden (Frey 2009, 50). Re-enactors have the advantage that they are, on the whole, more animated than museum dummies. They have the disadvantage of possessing an element of free will that can make them slightly unpredictable and occasionally positively mischievous. Either way, three-dimensional realisations of practical and academic research clearly have both a value and an attraction for the general public.

CONCLUSIONS

Ultimately, the test is to gauge the success of the quest for authenticity amongst re-enactors against two very different yardsticks: on the one hand will be the engagement of the re-enactors with the academics, and equally of the academics with the re-enactors; but on the other must be the interaction between re-enactors and the public. In the early 1980s, when the first Roman

Military Equipment Research Seminar was held (Bishop 1983), Roman re-enactors were not taken seriously by most academics, but a new generation of military equipment postgraduates, inspired by Russell Robinson's book, saw the value of their work and, most importantly, their potential (Feugère 1982, 82) and they now form a familiar part of the Roman Military Equipment Conferences, presenting both displays and papers, whilst publications by re-enactors abound (Junkelmann 1986; 1996; Haines *et al* 2000). Now the donners of armour *are* given the time of day in wider academic circles, invited to openings of exhibitions (Haines 1995, 46), used to boost visitor numbers at events (Haines 2007, 134), marched round and round at televised archaeological excavations (Anon 1998, 72), even helping defend a PhD thesis (Constable 1987), not just for a little added colour but also because there is a perceived inherent desire for accuracy on the part of all involved. They even have an important educational role, whether it be individual soldiers visiting schools or school groups going to museums. Make no mistake, there are good re-enactors and there are bad, and it can sometimes be hard to distinguish the serious part-time scholars from the cavorting ninnies. There are enthusiastic re-enactors, stupid and stubborn ones, and those who would be better off in some sort of fantasy role-playing organisation, but there are very few who do not want to improve what they do and that has to be a good thing.

BIBLIOGRAPHY AND REFERENCES

Ambrose, S E, 2001 *Band of Brothers. E Company, 506th Regiment, 101st Airbourne from Normandy to Hitler's Eagle's Nest*, Simon and Schuster, London

Anon, 1998 Guard news, *Exercitus* 3:3, 71–5

Bishop, M C (ed), 1983 *Roman Military Equipment. Proceedings of a Seminar Held in the Department of Ancient History and Classical Archaeology at the University of Sheffield, 21st March 1983*, privately published, Sheffield

Bishop, M C, 2002 *Lorica Segmentata Vol I: A Handbook of Articulated Roman Plate Armour, JRMES* Monograph 1, The Armatura Press, Chirnside

Bishop, M C, and Coulston, J C N, 2006 *Roman Military Equipment: From the Punic Wars to the Fall of Rome*, Oxbow Books, Oxford

Connolly, P, 1988 *Tiberius Claudius Maximus: the Cavalryman*, Oxford University Press, Oxford

— 1990 The saddle horns from Newstead, *Journal of Roman Military Equipment Studies* 1, 61–6

Connolly, P, and van Driel-Murray, C, 1991 The Roman cavalry saddle, *Britannia* 22, 33–50

Constable, C, 1987 Going Dutch, *Exercitus* 2:3, 48–9

Daniels, C, 1988 The conservation and reconstruction of the armour, in *Excavations at Roman Corbridge: The Hoard* (eds L Allason-Jones and M C Bishop), English Heritage, London, 97–100

Feugère, M, 1982 L'équipement militaire et l'armement romains: recherches et travaux récents en Grande Bretagne, *Cahiers archéologiques de la Loire* 2, 79–85

Frey, A, 2009 Wissenschaftliche Schausammlung und Museum – die Ausstellungen des RGZM, in *Ludwig Lindenschmit d. Ä. Begleitbuch zur Ausstellung aus Anlass seines 200. Geburtstages im Römisch-Germanischen Zentralmuseum, 10. September 2009 bis 10. Januar 2010* (ed A Frey), RGZM, Mainz, 49–50

Furse, G A, 1901 *The Art of Marching*, W Clowes & Sons, London

Hadden, R L, 1999 *Reliving the Civil War: A Reenactor's Handbook*, Stackpole Books, Mechanicsburg

Haines, C, 1995 Guard news, *Exercitus* 3:2, 43–6

— 2007 A short history of the Ermine Street Guard, *Exercitus* 3:6, 133–6

Haines, T, Sumner, G, and Naylor, J, 2000 Recreating the world of the Roman soldier: the work of the Ermine Street Guard, *Journal of Roman Military Equipment Studies* 11, 119–27

Hyland, A, 1990 *Equus: the Horse in the Roman World*, Batsford, London

Josephus, *The Jewish War* (trans G A Williamson), 1969, Penguin, Harmondsworth

Junkelmann, M, 1986 *Die Legionen des Augustus. Der römische Soldat im archäologischen Experiment*, von Zabern, Mainz

— 1996 *Reiter wie Statuen aus Erz*, von Zabern, Mainz

Lloyd-Morgan, G, 1987 Professor Robert Newstead and finds of Roman military metalwork from Chester, in *Roman Military Equipment: the Accoutrements of War. Proceedings of the Third Roman Military Equipment Research Seminar* (ed M Dawson), BAR International Series 336, Oxford, 85–97

Moore, H B, 2007 *115-Mile March to Atlanta, 2nd Battalion, 506th PIR, December 1–3, 1942* [online], available from: http://www.506infantry.org/his2ndbnwwiiphoto09.html [4 July 2011]

Obmann, J, and Wirtz, D, 1997 'Sie muß den Kaiser auf der Saalburg sehen' – Die Feier zur Grundsteinlegung des wiedererrichteten Römerkastells am 11. Oktober 1900, in *Hundert Jahre Saalburg. Vom römischen Grenzposten zum europäischen Museum* (ed E Schallmayer), von Zabern, Mainz, 33–54

Robinson, H R, 1969 *Roman Armour*, National Museum of Wales, Cardiff

— 1974 Problems in reconstructing Roman armour, in *Roman Frontier Studies 1969* (eds E Birley, B Dobson and M G Jarrett), National Museum of Wales, Cardiff, 24–35

— 1975 *The Armour of Imperial Rome*, Arms and Armour Press, London

Shapiro, J S, 2006 *1599: A Year in the Life of William Shakespeare*, Faber and Faber, London

Sim, D, 1995 Weapons and mass production, *Journal of Roman Military Equipment Studies* 6, 1–3

— 1997 Roman chain-mail: experiments to reproduce the techniques of manufacture, *Britannia* 28, 359–71

Sim, D, and Kaminski, J, 2011 *Roman Imperial Armour: The Production of Early Imperial Military Armour*, Oxbow Books, Oxford

Sumner, G, 2009 *Roman Military Dress*, History Press, Stroud

Vegetius (*Epitoma Rei Militaris*), tr Stelton, F, 1990, Lang, New York

Wallace, C, 1988 The Colchester Pageant of 1909, *Exercitus* 2:4, 66

3

Reconstruction Drawings: Illustrating the Evidence

Susan Greaney

Introduction

This paper was originally put together and presented by the author and Dr Sarah Tatham, Interpretation Officer for the Free Sites Project at English Heritage, at the XXIst International Limes (Roman Frontiers) Congress in Newcastle upon Tyne in August 2009. The following chapter differs somewhat from the presentation given that day, for two reasons. The first is that the original paper was largely visual and by its nature a chapter in a book is more restrictive in terms of graphics. Secondly, the author's thoughts and research on this topic have developed over the intervening two years. What follows is therefore more discursive and covers wider issues of academic accuracy, authenticity and artistic style in more depth.

Why Do We Commission Reconstruction Drawings?

Reconstruction drawings of the past are produced for a variety of purposes and audiences – for museum displays, guidebooks, graphic panels and to illustrate professional archaeological texts. All have the same objective: to put flesh on the bare bones of the past by restoring – on paper, at least – what time has taken away.

English Heritage and its predecessors, beginning with the Ministry of Works in the 1950s, have commissioned and displayed many hundreds of reconstruction artworks, largely produced to help visitors to England's historic sites in guardianship understand and relate to the past. Many of these paintings are archived in the National Monuments Record in Swindon and form a unique record of the development of the discipline (see Davison 1997 for a broad overview). Today, reconstruction drawings are regularly commissioned for guidebooks and for on-site information panels. A graphic panel with a reconstruction drawing forms the bread and butter of many of English Heritage's presentation schemes. In recent years, staff working on the Free Sites Project, to improve our free and unstaffed properties where panels are often the only form of interpretation, have commissioned reconstructions extensively.

In whatever format they are presented, reconstruction drawings are designed to help the public understand how archaeological or historical sites appeared in the past; they are a graphic recreation of a particular time and place (Hodgson 2004, 137). Reconstruction drawings can impart information about an entire landscape or about a specific room; about certain historic events or about the long-term function of a building; about the details of architectural structure or the feeling of a particular place.

The old adage that 'a picture is worth a thousand words' is certainly true. Where space is at a premium, always the case with an interpretation panel, a reconstruction drawing can impart information that would cover several pages or even a chapter of a book. Audience research has shown that people who read graphic panels tend to look first at the pictures and secondly at the captions; only the very interested will persevere with the body text. Images transcend barriers of age, understanding and language.

Despite considerable advances in digital technology, online graphics and computer reconstruction over the last 20 years, the time-honoured creation of a static reconstruction image is still an important skill, whichever method is used to produce the final product.

In the context of chapters within this volume, reconstruction using a paintbrush or a computer never damages or alters a site. Whereas full-scale, physical reconstructions no doubt have considerable impact, the exercise is 'expensive, uncertain and generally unconvincing, if not comic, to the next generation of archaeologists' (Rigold 1965, 7). Unlike these, new painted reconstructions, drawings and also physical models of a site can be commissioned very easily if our ideas about the interpretation of a site shift. If used in imaginative schemes, balanced with text and other graphics, reconstructions can be just as helpful for visitors to understand the past as full-size reconstructions or re-enactment events.

The process of commissioning a reconstruction drawing leads to benefits not only for the visitor, but also for the archaeologist or historian. Producing such an image helps to progress our thinking about a site and develop our ideas about the past. It makes us examine aspects of an archaeological site that would otherwise go unnoticed. What colour were the walls? What did the furniture look like? How was the room heated or lit? What did people wear at that time? These questions lead us to closer interrogation of the existing archaeological evidence and standing fabric of a site. If the evidence is lacking, it forces us to turn to evidence from similar buildings or sites elsewhere, or to contemporary depictions. Each reconstruction is the result of close collaboration and discourse between artist and archaeologist as described by Ambrus and Aston (2001).

RECONSTRUCTING THE ROMANS

There has been a long history of reconstruction drawing depicting Roman life and showing buildings, forts and frontiers. The history and origins of reconstruction paintings in general is too vast a subject to entertain in detail here, but Hodgson (2004) provides an overview of their evolution. The Roman period is a popular subject for reconstruction drawings as it is a visually familiar period to most people. Our archaeological evidence, backed up by contemporary art and material culture, is considerable. There is no lack of parallel sites from which to draw comparison. As Alan Sorrell explained, the period is popular amongst reconstruction artists as 'the Romans sprang no surprises in their planning, and were the most predictable of builders. You can always be reasonably sure of right-angled turns in their structures …' (Sorrell and Sorrell 1981, 25).

The beginnings of Roman reconstruction artwork can be traced from the work of Italian Renaissance artist Andrew Mantegna in the late 15th and early 16th centuries, to 18th-century paintings of historical events, such as Nicholas Blakey's depiction of the landing of Julius Caesar on Britain's shores. Victorian paintings like those of Lawrence Alma-Tadema tended to show upper-class Roman domestic scenes (Hodgson 2004, 79–80). Perhaps one of the first true Roman reconstruction paintings is William Bell Scott's *Building a Roman Wall*, painted between 1855 and 1860, and showing subdued Britons slaving under Roman rule to build Hadrian's Wall (Smiles 1994, 144–5).

Modern reconstruction painting came into its own with the explosion of illustrated papers, magazines and books in the late 19th and early 20th century. The *Illustrated London News* (ILN) made the greatest use of reconstructions to illustrate archaeological discoveries and news, employing Amédée Forestier, whose 1928 book *The Roman Soldier* featured scenes of everyday British Roman life. Reconstruction drawings of the Roman world increased with the growth of illustrated children's books and illustrated historical fiction, and later the demand for guidebooks, museum displays and other printed material led to the emergence of the discipline of reconstruction art that we recognise today. Forestier's successor at the ILN was the prolific and popular artist Alan Sorrell; one of his early commissions included a series of reconstruction drawings of the Roman Forum at Leicester which appeared in 1937, and between 1937 and 1940 he worked on a series of Welsh Roman sites for the National Museum of Wales (Sorrell and Sorrell 1981, 13). Alan Sorrell's dominance and influence on the emerging world of archaeological reconstruction drawing cannot be underestimated (Sorrell and Sorrell 1981; Sorrell 1965). More recently, artists such as Terry Ball, Ivan Lapper and Peter Dunn have all tackled reconstruction images of Roman sites and scenes. Specialist Roman reconstruction artists are rare; perhaps only the late Peter Connolly, a renowned scholar in his own right, and Graham Sumner, with his carefully researched and informed figurative and military costume illustrations, can lay claim to that accolade.

Purpose of the Reconstruction Drawing and Viewpoint

When commissioning a reconstruction drawing, for a Roman or any other type of site, there are several elements that should be carefully thought through. These include the purpose and audience for the image and therefore the viewpoint and style. The choice of artist and the briefing and reference material provided are vitally important.

The intended purpose of the reconstruction drawing will dictate the viewpoint and style of the final image. What are the key messages that you want the viewer to understand? This may relate to the overall layout and impression of a site or area, the function of a particular building or the social or ritual arrangements of a particular space. Several different viewpoints can be used to convey different messages.

A ground- or eye-level view of a scene can be produced from exactly the same position as the modern visitor might see it and is therefore involving and very easy to understand. If done well, it can give a sense of large dramatic spaces and elevations, and also the detail of people and their activities from close quarters. This can be particularly informative when the reconstruction drawing is of a known event or intimate moment. However, sometimes the perspective can be difficult, the viewpoint can be restrictive and the medium often does not suit the cut-away method of showing interiors or architecture.

Aerial views, by contrast, can show the whole plan of sites and this can be useful for large or very complex sites. The viewpoint can include the landscape around a town or fort, placing the site into its contemporary surroundings (see Fig 3.1). However, aerial views can lead to a certain detachment for the viewer and are less easy to relate to the real surroundings of an archaeological site. Where the reconstruction drawing is to be displayed on a fixed panel, this can be mitigated to some extent by keeping the angle of view the same as for the viewer of the image. A viewpoint that is too vertical can lead to an overload of tiled roofs; this has previously proved a problem for reconstructions drawings of Roman sites such as Wroxeter and Richborough.

FIG 3.1. AN AERIAL RECONSTRUCTION OF WALLTOWN CRAGS FROM STEEL RIGG, HADRIAN'S WALL, BY ALAN SORRELL (1959).

FIG 3.2. A CUT-AWAY RECONSTRUCTION OF THE ROMAN BATH HOUSE AT JEWRY WALL, LEICESTER, BY MICHAEL CODA (1998).

A common device is the cut-away, where a portion of wall and/or roof is removed to enable to viewer to see into interior spaces of buildings. Although not an easy technique for the artist to master, it allows the exterior and interior of a building to be seen at the same time, and can therefore impart function and appearance of rooms. It is useful for explaining how complex or unusual structures functioned; particularly details of hypocausts or bath houses (see Fig 3.2), although they can be more difficult for the viewer to understand.

CHOICE OF ARTIST AND STYLE

The choice of artist will dictate the final finish of the painting, but may also affect the dialogue and discourse between archaeologist and artist. For some projects, a particular type of artist may be deemed suitable. A recent interpretive display at Lullingstone Roman Villa in Kent used a children's illustrator to provide scenes of Roman domestic life, as the exhibition was designed particularly with families in mind.

An artist with at least a basic understanding of archaeology or architecture is usually required. Some reconstruction artists have an in-depth understanding of archaeology and history and are willing to do their own research to inform their art. Others may require more detailed information from the commissioning expert. The more informed and interested the artist, the more challenging and enlightening the discourse can be for both sides, and the higher the level of accuracy of the final product. A good artist will come back to the expert with questions that challenge: How was this room lit? Where were the stairs? How were the walls finished?

Over the last 10 or 15 years, reconstructions drawn using computer graphics software have developed in leaps and bounds, and are now commonplace. Whereas in the past artists such as Terry Ball made 3D cardboard models to help produce a painting, today a digital wireframe model will often be created, which can be digitally altered to get the correct viewpoint and perspective before being worked up into a painting, as exemplified by Phil Kenning in his painting of Ashby de la Zouch castle (Sherman and Westlake 2009). Sometimes, however, the entire reconstruction drawing will be created digitally. Used on its own, or in combination with photography, this type of total digital reconstruction can be a very effective way of recreating a viewpoint in the past (Fig 3.3).

Other techniques, such as ghosting-in figures onto a scene, or using simple line-drawing in an otherwise colour graphic for parts of an unexcavated building, can help circumnavigate issues of authenticity and give the sense that not everything about this scene is known for certain. Computers can make this technique easier. Where the image is intended for an online or digital publication, digital graphics have the enormous advantage that the image can be made interactive. This can allow the user to switch between two or three slightly different interpretations of the same scene, rather like creating three different reconstruction drawings of the same building (see James 1997, 30–2).

Nevertheless, the creation of a reconstruction drawing should still be firmly regarded and approached as an art, portraying feelings of mood and emotion. The almost photorealism of a static computer-produced graphic can add a sense of certainty about the past, which may sometimes be unhelpful. The more precise and detailed the drawing, the more convincing it is, but the more guesses it contains (James 1997, 26). The success of artists such as Alan Sorrell or Ivan Lapper rests on the stylistic quality of their work, with a painterly aspect making it clear that the work is one of imagination, albeit based on fact (Hodgson 2004, 467). This artistic approach can

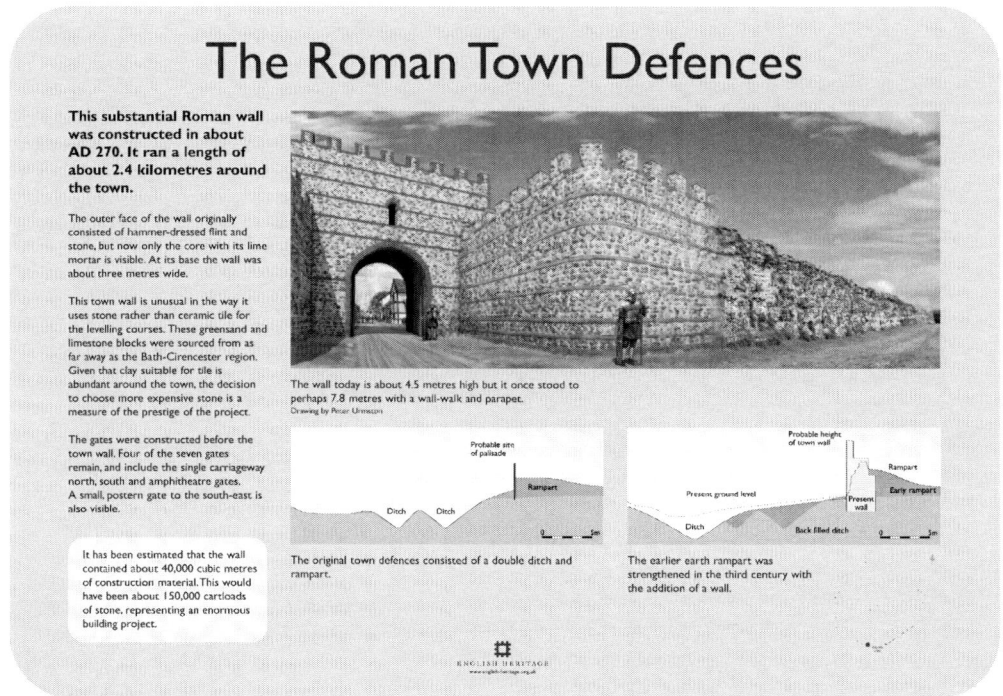

The Roman Town Defences

This substantial Roman wall was constructed in about AD 270. It ran a length of about 2.4 kilometres around the town.

The outer face of the wall originally consisted of hammer-dressed flint and stone, but now only the core with its lime mortar is visible. At its base the wall was about three metres wide.

This town wall is unusual in the way it uses stone rather than ceramic tile for the levelling courses. These greensand and limestone blocks were sourced from as far away as the Bath-Cirencester region. Given that clay suitable for tile is abundant around the town, the decision to choose more expensive stone is a measure of the prestige of the project.

The gates were constructed before the town wall. Four of the seven gates remain, and include the single carriageway north, south and amphitheatre gates. A small, postern gate to the south-east is also visible.

It has been estimated that the wall contained about 40,000 cubic metres of construction material. This would have been about 150,000 cartloads of stone, representing an enormous building project.

The wall today is about 4.5 metres high but it once stood to perhaps 7.8 metres with a wall-walk and parapet.
Drawing by Peter Urmston

The original town defences consisted of a double ditch and rampart.

The earlier earth rampart was strengthened in the third century with the addition of a wall.

ENGLISH HERITAGE
www.english-heritage.org.uk

Fig 3.3. An interpretation panel at Silchester Roman town, installed in 2009. This image, created by Peter Urmston, is a combination of digital reconstruction and modern photography.

sometimes be a useful technique to mask the unknowns, using carefully placed weather, smoke, trees or even clever use of perspective, although this may be an unfavourable technique for the artist (Sorrell and Sorrell 1981, 22). There is something to be said for retaining a distinctive artistic style in archaeological reconstruction drawings.

Using Reconstruction Drawings on Heritage Sites

For whom is the final artwork intended? The final location of the reconstruction drawing is important to consider – is it for the general public on a site graphic panel, or is it for an academic monograph to illustrate an excavation? Illustrations depicting complex architectural forms may be interesting for the artist and archaeologist to work through and produce, but whether they are helpful and understandable to the non-specialist viewer should be considered. It is vitally important to include people in a reconstruction drawing, not only to provide scale but also to give a sense of activity and life to the image.

A common form of reproduction is on an on-site graphic interpretation panel. These perform a very valuable function; archaeological sites are often visually uninteresting to the general public, unless the visitor knows something about what they are viewing. The golden rule is that a reconstruction drawing on a graphic panel should be orientated to the same direction as the viewer, even if that viewpoint is elevated. This way the viewer can more easily relate what they are looking at on the panel to what they can see in front of them (Fig 3.3).

The graphic panel should be designed with the reconstruction drawing in mind. What other graphics will help the viewer's understanding? Clever use of photographs of archaeological finds, maps or plans can further enhance the impact of the reconstruction drawing and understanding of the site.

When commissioning reconstruction drawings it is also important to think beyond the immediate use of the image. If it is to be used subsequently in a guidebook or museum display, what are the needs of these media? The final reconstruction painting should be kept in a suitable secure environment. Ideally, the painting should be made available for future scholars and interested members of the public, and for this reason high-resolution colour-matched digital scans should be taken. It is vitally important that the evidence of the discourse between artist and archaeologist (eg drafts, notes, reference material and comments) is also kept and archived. Recent work by the Alan Sorrell Project (Johnson and Perry 2011) has shown that the creation of a reconstruction drawing is a fascinating process of archaeological thinking, which should be preserved for the future.

AUTHENTICITY: REFERENCE MATERIAL AND PARALLELS

Just how far should we go in trying to reconstruct the past? Indeed, should we do it at all? The creation of a reconstruction drawing involves making the best guess we can, with the available evidence. It does not set out to provide a once-and-for-all authoritative view of the past. It aims to inform, but also to provoke.

No reconstruction drawing of the past can do more than illustrate the state of archaeological knowledge at the time that it was created. Some techniques have been mentioned above that can help to hide or draw attention away from certain sections of the image. However, as archaeologists and historians – the commissioners of these influential images – we have a responsibility to ensure that the very best and latest available evidence feeds into each reconstruction drawing.

As much information as possible should be given to the artist about the site: excavated ground plans, aerial and ground photographs, images of artefacts or mosaics found. Nothing can replace a site visit by the archaeologist and artist in order to view and discuss the site; 'it is desirable for the artist to walk over the site, plan in hand' (Sorrell and Sorrell 1981, 24). Some artists will want to take their own photographs, work up preliminary sketches on site or even, for artists like Victor Ambrus, finish complete artworks by the trench side. Beyond direct evidence from the site itself, explanatory and comparison material should be provided. This might include, for example, a diagram of the workings of a hypocaust; reconstructions of other sections of the same frontier; artefacts and decoration schemes (eg mosaics) from other contemporary sites; information about clothing, jewellery and shoes. The Osprey series of military history books are invaluable for the detailed information they provide in this area (eg Sumner 2002). These are always produced in close collaboration with, or often by, reconstruction artists themselves.

Where sources from parallel sites are used to inform a reconstruction drawing, they should be chosen carefully. Where possible, examples should be drawn from sites that are close both spatially and temporally to the scene being represented. For example, when commissioning a reconstruction drawing of a Roman fort at Hadrian's Wall, it would be best to turn to other contemporary wall forts first, before looking further afield.

There should never be a tension between academic accuracy and producing something for the general public. The process of creating a reconstruction for the public is not dumbing down but actually forces an archaeologist or historian, perhaps for the first time, to grapple with unexplored ideas or to come down on one side or the other of a particular debate. As Barry Cunliffe recalled, 'we were all made to think hard and (certainly in my case) to learn something new of the building we thought we knew' (1981, 7). An excavator can be fully engaged with a site for many years before a simple question, perhaps about windows or interior decoration, can make them reassess their own work.

James has highlighted how reconstruction drawings can unhelpfully reinforce stereotypes, sanitising the past or creating it in our own image (1997, 34). But this is a problem inherent in all archaeological interpretation; it is just more obvious in graphic form. In some ways, an archaeological reconstruction drawing is the perfect way to challenge preconceptions of the viewer: a woman placed in a traditionally male role, or a brightly coloured interior decoration where now only rough rubble foundations survive.

How certain of our facts do we need to be? There are times when it is impossible to reconstruct a particular site or viewpoint with any certainty and the temptation to illustrate this type of site should be resisted. However, it is otherwise difficult to stipulate a tipping point beyond which the evidence can be thought sufficient: if we have only 80% of the information necessary to reconstruct a place or an event, should we leave it there or make a guess at the other 20% in order to round off the scene and make it work? It is important to understand that archaeological evidence will always be, to some extent, incomplete.

CONCLUSION

This chapter has outlined the complex archaeological discourse and artistic thinking that goes into the creation of a reconstruction painting. In the past, some have advised that we should not refer to these images as *reconstructions* as this is a misleading term implying elusive certainty, but that we should instead call them *artist's impressions*. Not only does the term imply 'something fuzzy and completely undependable' (Sorrell and Sorrell 1981, 26), but reconstruction drawings are rarely the creation of an artist working alone. They are the end-product of a lengthy and detailed discourse between an informed archaeologist and an informed artist. Their purpose is to educate and to excite, and to encourage people to take an interest in their past. Nothing does this in the same direct way as a reconstruction painting.

ACKNOWLEDGMENTS

With thanks to Dr Sarah Tatham for co-presenting the original version of this paper and to Nigel Mills for inviting us to speak at the conference. I am also indebted to Paul Pattison, Richard Lea and John Goodall who have taught me much about both Romans and reconstructions during my time at English Heritage.

BIBLIOGRAPHY AND REFERENCES

Ambrus, V, and Aston, M, 2001 *Recreating the Past*, History Press, Stroud

Cunliffe, B, 1981 Foreword, in *Reconstructing the Past* (eds A Sorrell and M Sorrell), Batsford, London

Davison, B, 1997 *Picturing the Past: through the eyes of reconstruction artists*, English Heritage, London

Forestier, A, 1928 *The Roman Soldier: some illustrations representative of Roman military life, with special reference to Britain*, A & C Black, London

Hodgson, J, 2004 Archaeological Reconstruction Illustrations: an analysis of the history, development, motivations and current practice of reconstruction illustration, with recommendation for its future development, unpublished PhD thesis, Bournemouth University [online], available from: http://eprints.bournemouth.ac.uk/11960/ [18 June 2011]

James, S, 1997 Drawing inferences: visual reconstructions in theory and practice, in *The Cultural Life of Images: visual representation in archaeology* (ed B L Molyneaux), Routledge, London and New York, 22–48

Johnson, M, and Perry, S, 2011 *The Alan Sorrell Project* [online], available from: http://alansorrellproject.org/ [18 June 2011]

Rigold, S E, 1965 Foreword, in *Living History* (ed A Sorrell), Batsford, London

Sherman, L, and Westlake, S, 2009 Seeing is believing, *Journal of the Association for Heritage Interpretation* 14 (1), 7–10

Smiles, S, 1994 *The Image of Antiquity: Ancient Britain and the Romantic Imagination*, Yale University Press, New Haven and London

Sorrell, A, 1965 *Living History*, Batsford, London

Sorrell, A, and Sorrell, M (eds), 1981 *Reconstructing the Past*, Batsford, London

Sumner, G, 2002 *Roman Military Clothing (1): 100 BC - AD 200*, Osprey Publishing, Oxford

4

Images from the Past: Fibulae as Evidence for the Architectural Appearance of Roman Fort Gates

Christof Flügel and Jürgen Obmann

Introduction

This chapter explores the use of designs found on fibulae as evidence of the architectural appearance (design, features, scale, dimensions, proportions) of Roman fort gates. The evidence suggests that the gateways were higher and grander in scale than previously thought. This conclusion has important implications both for our understanding of the role of gateways as monumental architecture expressing the power of the Roman Empire and for reconstructions of these gateways for public presentation. Many existing reconstructions are too low and convey a misleading impression to visitors.

The Evidence

In 1990 a fibula (Fig 4.1) showing a three-storey gateway building with arched windows was discovered (Flügel 2007; Flügel and Obmann 2009) during the excavation of a *villa rustica* at Chieming in the district of Traunstein in Bavaria. In Roman times this area was part of the province of *Noricum*. The different storeys over the rounded gateway are separated by clearly marked quarter-round dividing cornices, as is often the case in Roman architecture (eg Trier, Porta Nigra). The fact that this real-world feature was depicted as a key visual element on a small-scale reproduction leads to the conclusion that the producer of our fibula had a clear picture in mind of how a Roman gateway looked. Using this symbolic citation (Zanker 1987), the fibula's designer wanted to convey this idea to the potential user of his product.

The Chieming fibula yields no clear indications as to whether a military or civilian gateway is depicted. This is not the case for a second fibula (Fig 4.2) from Vukomericke Gorice, south of Zagreb in Croatia (Flügel and Obmann 2009, 149) which clearly depicts a military gateway. This unfinished specimen reveals two gateways with an inscription as well as dividing cornices and merlons. The realistic depiction of the gate pillars, which can be compared to Roman military architecture (Bidwell forthcoming) as at Birdoswald, the stylised reproduction of the inscription, the arched windows and the quarter-round cornices separating the storeys are comparable to the famous architectural clay model from the legionary fortress of Intercisa in Hungary. We therefore have a clear indication of what the Vukomericke fibula, which uses the same visual key elements as the clay model by the Pannonian potter Ilarius, depicts: the central gateway of a Roman military *porta cum turribus*, as it is often named in Roman inscriptions. The conclusion, that the architectural fibulae can be interpreted as evidence for Roman military reality, is

FIG 4.1. CHIEMING (BAVARIA). ARCHITECTURAL FIBULA.

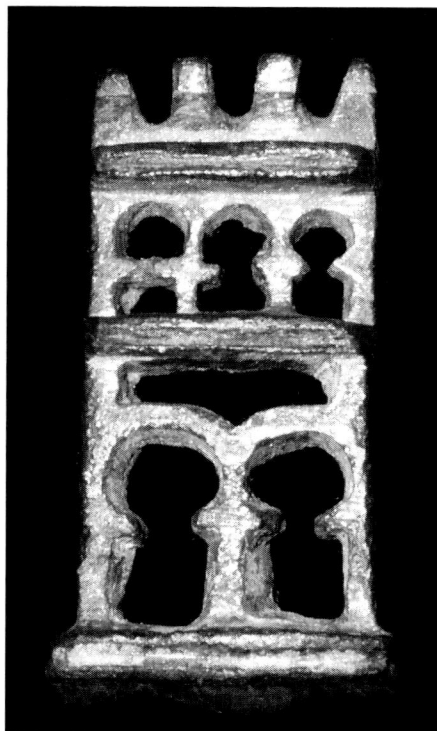

FIG 4.2. VUKOMERICKE GORICE (CROATIA). ARCHITECTURAL FIBULA.

supported by a large number of Roman brooches showing items of everyday military life used by the individual bearers of the fibula like *cornua, spathae* with peltiform scabbard-chapes and helmets (Flügel 2007, pl 4, 5–7, 10–12). Similarly, the strongly symbolic picture language of Roman military propaganda is used as motifs for fibulae, as evidenced by a silver brooch in *opus interrasile* from Töging in Bavaria. This shows Victoria crowning a legionary eagle with a laurel wreath (Flügel 2007, pl 4, 9). Another example is the hitherto unpublished fibula depicting an attacking Roman cavalryman with a fallen barbarian beneath his horse, which recalls the triumphant rider on Romano-British tombstones (Bull 2007).

A gate fibula (Fig 4.3) from an unknown findspot, seen in a London auction (Christie's sale 2058/2009, lot 292), indicates that singular elements could be combined in an unrealistic manner without losing their function as key stimuli for transmitting messages with military content. In this example the head of Sol, which is probably a displaced augmented depiction of the keystone of the entrance arch, seems to indicate that the motif should be interpreted as the front elevation of a Roman gate. The three-storey roofed towers with a central window and a *tympanon* show painted *opus rusticum* as well as plain stucco. Both treatments of the surface are evident in Roman military architecture (cf a reconstructed section of Hadrian's Wall with various possibilities of Wall design at Wallsend). It cannot be ruled out however, that the detailed depiction of the dressed blocks is merely an artistic visual feature to communicate the message

FIG 4.3. UNKNOWN FINDSPOT. GILDED ARCHITECTURAL FIBULA. (CHRISTIE'S LONDON SALE 2057, LOT 292)

of a fortified and solid wall, as is common on Roman mosaics (eg in Orbe, Switzerland). The most intriguing feature on the London fibula is the archway into the two towers which clearly does not make sense if we assume that what we see is the front elevation of a fort gate. However, if we interpret the London fibula as representing a gate seen from the reverse side, this would contradict the impression of the front elevation given by all other architectural fibulae and the head of Sol on the London specimen.

Whilst we can accept the idea that fibulae may be used as contemporary evidence for the appearance of Roman military architecture, we must also bear in mind that due to the small size of the objects, their designers had to confine their depiction to certain key visual elements in order to make their final product understandable to the military public. The representations cannot therefore be interpreted simply as if they were photographs from the past; we also have to consider that key visual elements served purely as ornamental decoration. For example, two belt-plates in *opus interasile* from a second/third century grave of a *beneficiarius consularis* (as evidenced by the beneficiary lance on the larger belt-plate) from Abritus (on display in the Museum of Rasgrad, north-eastern Bulgaria) show two- and three-vaulted gateways with clearly marked imposts, two storeys with arched windows and an ornamentally stylised row of merlons above. The hinges are used for the depiction of the four-level roofed towers, reaching approximately the same height as the central gateway block. The Abritus belt-plates indicate that the

FIG 4.4. PFÖRRING (BAVARIA). SIMULATION OF SIDE GATE OF AUXILIARY FORTRESS (2012).

beneficiarius consularis using this equipment simply wanted to convey the idea of being respon-sible for a fortified location, using the same ornamental elements for a two- and a three-vaulted gateway. The possibility that he intended to illustrate a specific gate can therefore be ruled out.

However, the selective use of key architectural elements in the motifs can give us an indica-tion of what was important to the contemporary users of these brooches in their perception of architecture. Naturally, a reconstruction of the appearance of fort gates has first of all to be based on the local archaeological evidence and should also take account of the different geographic regions; fort gates in the Libyan desert (Mackensen 2010; 2011) may differ from those along the Northern frontier of the Roman Empire. Another point of uncertainty is that we do not know for sure if auxiliary or legionary architecture is shown.

CONCLUSION

Through assessment of the key architectural elements represented in the ornamental motifs we can try to draw the following picture of an ideal Roman fort gate: a central gateway with vaulted arches and an inscription (Vukomericke Gorice) or *tympanon* (London fibula) above is followed by two storeys, completed by a pitched roof (Intercisa model) or merlons, indicating a parapet walk between the two towers. The different storeys are divided by double quarter-round profiles. The three- or four-storey towers themselves are roofed (London fibula; Abritus belt plates) and show a central window below the *tympanon* (London fibula).

If we compare this ideal Roman gate to known architectural elements we can roughly calculate the approximate original height of the central block:

Crown height of entrance arch	3.70m
Height of inscription or *tympanon*	1.00–1.50m
(Minimum three) double quarter-round profiles @ 0.30m	0.90m
Height of two storeys @ 4.20m (according to Regensburg legionary fortress, *porta praetoria*)	8.40m
Merlons (according to Wörth auxiliary fortress; Steidl 2008) (or, alternatively, a pitched roof)	1.60m
TOTAL HEIGHT (for the version with merlons)	16.10m

It immediately becomes clear that existing 1:1 reconstructions of Roman fort gates, mainly from the 1980s and especially along the German Limes (eg Weißenburg or Pfünz), can generally be considered as too low. Roman architecture clearly has a tendency to enormous heights, in civilian contexts also: a total height of 12m can be reconstructed for an annex building in the *villa rustica* of Oberndorf-Bochingen (south-west Germany), which collapsed during an earthquake (Sommer 2005).

To convey this new perspective on Roman monumental military architecture in the north-western provinces to the general public, the erection is planned of an iron and steel simulation of a side gate of the Roman auxiliary fortress of Pförring in Bavaria on the original site of the gate. The construction is reversible and stands above the concrete-sealed original Roman foundations in accordance with UNESCO standards (Fig 4.4). The complete documentation of the excavation results and the considerations leading to this simulation will be published in the periodic publication series of the Bavarian State Conservation Office (Schriftenreihe Bayerisches Landesamt für Denkmalpflege; Flügel and Obmann forthcoming).

BIBLIOGRAPHY AND REFERENCES

Bidwell, P, forthcoming 'The Height of Gate-Pillars (Imposts) at Forts on Hadrian's Wall and Elsewhere', in *Excelsae turres quater divisae – Rekonstruktion römischer Lagertore und Wehrbauten*, proceedings of conference held in Munich on 5 July 2010 (eds C Flügel and J Obmann), to be published in the series Schriftenreihe Bayerisches Landesamt für Denkmalpflege, Munich

Bull, S, 2007 *Triumphant Rider: The Lancaster Roman Cavalry Tombstone*, Lancashire Museums, Lancaster

Flügel, C, 2007 'Eine Scheibenfibel mit Architekturdarstellung aus Chieming, Lkr. Traunstein. Zu mittelkaiserzeitlichen Fibeln mit militärischen Motiven', *Bayerische Vorgeschichtsblätter* 72, 327–40

Flügel, C, and Obmann, J, 2009 'Römische Architekturfibeln – Ein Beitrag zur römischen Militärarchitektur', in *Nuove ricerche sulle fibule romane / Neue Forschungen zu römischen Fibeln* (ed M Buora), Atti Convegno, Udine, 21–22 April 2008, Quaderni Friulani di Archeologia 18, 145–53

— forthcoming 'Visualisierung römischer Kastelltore: Das Beispiel der porta principalis dextra des Alenkastlles Celeusum/Pförring', in *Excelsae turres quater divisae – Rekonstruktion römischer Lagertore und Wehrbauten*, proceedings of conference held in Munich on 5 July 2010 (eds C Flügel and J Obmann), to be published in the series Schriftenreihe Bayerisches Landesamt für Denkmalpflege, Munich

Mackensen, M, 2010 'Das severische Vexillationskastell Gheriat el-Garbia am limes Tripolitanus (Libyen), Vorbericht über die erste Kampagne 2009', *Römische Mitteilungen* 116, 363–458

— 2011 'Das severische Vexillationskastell Myd (---) und die spätantike Besiedlung in Gheriat el-Garbia (Libyen), Bericht über die Kampagne im Frühjahr 2010', *Römische Mitteilungen* 117, 247–375

Sommer, C S, 2005 '12 m bis zum First. Die villa rustica von Oberndorf-Bochingen', in *Imperium Romanum. Roms Provinzen an Neckar, Rhein und Donau*, Exhibition Catalogue Stuttgart 2005, 282–5

Steidl, B, 2008 *Welterbe Limes, Roms Grenze am Main*, Exhibition Catalogue Munich 2008, Logo Verlag, Obernburg am Main

Zanker, P, 1987 *Augustus und die Macht der Bilder*, Beck Verlag, Munich

5

Multimedia Interpretation Techniques for Reconstructing the Roman Past at the Limes Museum in Aalen and at the Limes in Baden-Württemberg

Martin Kemkes

Introduction

In 2005, the Limes Museum in Aalen was provided with new media equipment, including a virtual reconstruction of Roman Aalen. At the same time a partial reconstruction of a Roman cavalry barracks was constructed at 1:1 scale in the adjacent archaeological park. These new installations jointly convey to visitors an impressive and easily understandable picture of the Roman past. These reconstructions play a vital educational role in establishing the Limes in the public consciousness, thereby helping to ensure better protection of the archaeology.

The fact that large parts of the Upper German-Raetian Limes lie hidden in the ground, invisible to the observer, distinguishes the Limes from many other World Heritage Sites. An understanding of the sensitive archaeological monument is significantly impeded for many visitors by its invisibility. Interpretation of the Limes for visitors both within the landscape and in museums brings special challenges that cannot be addressed without the use of reconstructions. Existing interpretation points for the Limes can be grouped into four types, each with specific strengths and weaknesses (Kemkes 2008).

The Limes Archaeological Monument in the Landscape

The majority of the Limes frontier system, including the course of the earth banks and ditches and of the Limes wall where it existed, as well as the majority of military installations from watchtower to fort, are either invisible or barely visible on the surface of the ground. Since there are no easily visible traces in the landscape, a considerable intellectual effort is required from the visitor, which has to be stimulated by appropriate signs or mobile information systems.

However, this apparent drawback of invisible world heritage is compensated for by the fact that the visitor has before them a fragment of undamaged world heritage retaining authentic evidence of the site's history intact, sealed in a soil archive for future generations. In the modern world the idea of people protecting their environment in various ways is common. In theory, it should therefore be possible for people to be made aware of the need to protect the invisible monument in these locations.

PRESERVED AND RESTORED FOUNDATION WALLS

The majority of visible elements of the Limes that can be visited today comprise restored or preserved foundation walls. A major disadvantage of this means of presenting the monument is that it reveals only the ground plan of the building. Unless explanatory panels are available, the visitor has to imagine the three-dimensional form of the original.

In most cases these visible elements are situated in public parks and are associated with a basic visitor infrastructure that includes seating areas. However, as places for learning, these sites offer no more than a locational reference for the monument. Depending on the way the remains are presented, they may appear artificial, divorced from their historical and functional context. In these situations it might be helpful to provide complementary information, to give the visitor a context for the remains and to avoid false impressions.

FULL-SIZE RECONSTRUCTIONS

In the past, at some locations along the Limes, parts of the monument were rebuilt to what was thought to be their original size and appearance. These reconstructions range from rebuilding the Roman fort at Saalburg and some fort gates as at Welzheim, to sections of the Limes with palisades, earth banks and ditches and numerous watchtowers.

The reconstructed watchtowers – there are about 20 of them along the Limes – illustrate the problems of such rebuilding. The various parties involved built the watchtowers in good faith as accurate representations of the originals, but had no archaeological evidence for their design above the foundations. As a result all the reconstructed watchtowers differ quite significantly from each other, while featuring common elements that contribute to a persistent image for the visitor of building types that are not proven for Roman times, such as blockhouse architecture.

Despite their deficiencies, these reconstructions have the key advantage that they present the visitor with a comprehensible and memorable image of the Limes, even if he or she has only a casual interest or happens upon them by chance. Enhanced by the reconstruction, the other features of the monument in the vicinity become sufficiently remarkable to remain with the visitor for a long time. Due to their conspicuous presence in public spaces, these reconstructions also offer strong potential for local people to identify with *their* world heritage. As locations for interpretation they have the advantage of providing easy access to the historical context of the site. This effect can be enhanced through provision of additional interpretation services such as tours by guides in Roman clothing and/or appropriate events. Finally, these reconstructions are tourist attractions and represent essential elements of the regional tourism package, providing opportunities ranging from promotional material to site visits and tours.

MUSEUMS AND INFORMATION CENTRES

The interpretation points identified above usually focus on a specific section or element of the monument. Museums offer the unique opportunity to provide visitors with supplementary information about the Limes. For effective interpretation it is particularly advantageous that museum and monument be located close to each other so that the authenticity of the historical site is evident to visitors (Fig 5.1), as is the case with the Limes Museum in Aalen.

A museum can also be a focus and venue for major promotional events such as Roman festi-

FIG 5.1. AERIAL PHOTOGRAPH OF THE LIMES MUSEUM AALEN AND ARCHAEOLOGICAL PARK; THE FOUNDATION WALLS OF THE *PRINCIPIA* CAN BE SEEN IN THE CENTRE.

vals, which are increasingly popular. For example, the bi-annual Roman Days in Aalen attract 10,000–15,000 visitors with an interest in the Romans and the Limes. These events often attract audiences that are different from traditional museum visitors. However, we should not forget a key role of the museum: while the visitor may come primarily to see the preserved or reconstructed monument, it is only in a museum that he or she can engage with the original archaeological finds from the site. These finds are an intrinsic part of the protected Limes monument and illustrate the cultural heritage lost where the monument has been destroyed.

Large museums especially present the subject of the Limes in many different ways, including through multimedia applications. These applications usually include reconstructions, as these enable the visitor to visualise the past in three dimensions. The use of a range of complementary media contributes to the provision of variety for visitors, creating a lasting impression of their visit. The multimedia interpretation used at the Limes Museum in Aalen is described in detail below as an example of such an approach to presentation.

MULTIMEDIA INTERPRETATION AT THE LIMES MUSEUM IN AALEN

The Limes Museum in Aalen is located on the site of the largest fort on the Limes, extending over six hectares (Kemkes *et al* 2006, 189–205). Around 1900, at the time of the Reichslimeskommission (Imperial Commission of the Limes), the fort site was undeveloped except for a cemetery in the area of the *praetentura*. Up until construction of the museum in 1964, the central area of the fort was still clear of any buildings – a pristine archaeological monument from a modern

FIG 5.2. VIRTUAL RECONSTRUCTION OF ROMAN AALEN WITH CAVALRY FORT AND SURROUNDING *VICUS*.

perspective. When the museum was constructed, the *porta principalis sinistra* which lay in front of the present museum entrance was excavated and subsequently conserved. Three-dimensional representation of the Limes by means of watchtower models and a diorama of tin figures was an important element of the displays in the Limes Museum from the start. Images illustrating part of the diorama with a watchtower and an access point where Germanic people are inspected by Roman soldiers are to be found in numerous textbooks over the decades since the 1960s. These illustrations have shaped the image of the Limes for several generations of students – an early and important example of the impact of reconstructions on the public.

In the 1970s it was proposed to cover the open, central area of the fort with buildings (Fig 5.1). The city of Aalen cooperated with the Baden-Württemberg state government to prevent construction of the buildings and destruction of the underlying monument. Instead, the site was purchased by the state and the Limes Museum generously extended. The *principia* was completely excavated in the period up to 1986 and its foundations conserved in a park behind the museum. In 1999 the museum was expanded again and the permanent exhibition revised.

Despite all these measures, the presentation of Roman Aalen remained unsatisfactory in the context of a modern urban museum facility. Two-dimensional plans are difficult or impossible for visitors to understand. This was the case for the foundations of the *principia* behind the museum, which served as a key reference for the historical authenticity of the site. Many visitors did not realise that the remains are the foundations for the walls of the *principia,* originally 18m high. Some thought the foundations are the actual walls of the fort. Proposals to represent the dimensions and layout of the *principia* through a steel structure failed to progress due to financial costs. To remedy this situation prior to the awarding of World Heritage status by UNESCO, the museum's multimedia services were significantly improved in 2004–5. The different display techniques now complement each other to produce an integrated and varied approach to presentation.

Fig 5.3. Partial reconstruction of cavalry barracks at 1:1 scale. Information boards about the virtual reconstruction can be seen in the foreground.

The Virtual Reconstruction of Roman Aalen

One of the two main projects was the virtual reconstruction of the fort at Aalen and the surrounding civil settlement. A film of approximately 12 minutes duration (Cebulla *et al* 2008) allows the viewer to look at the fort and *vicus* from different angles. The focus is on the excavated and preserved *principia* directly behind the museum (Kemkes *et al* 2006, 188–205) and photo-like imagery was used to enable visitors to understand the appearance of the Roman town (Fig 5.2). Many of the details are based on archaeological research at Aalen over the last 120 years, while others are based on evidence from civil settlements associated with other forts.

A crucial point is that the virtual reconstruction serves not only as a film, bringing the fort and civil settlement to life, but also helps to orientate the visitor within the archaeological park (Fig 5.3). Panels in the archaeological park inform visitors of their location and the associated reconstruction image displays the original building in front of them as it appeared in the film. During a two-hour tour through museum and archaeological park, visitors encounter reconstruction images at several locations, anchoring the images in their consciousness.

Model of Roman Aalen

A new table model was designed for the permanent exhibition alongside the very naturalistic virtual reconstruction. The 1:700 scale model covers an area of approximately 3 × 2.5m and is located in the centre of the Roman Aalen exhibition. The model shows the buildings of the fort and the *vicus* in abstract form on a modern map. The method of presentation is completely different from that used in the virtual reconstruction. The objective is to encourage the viewer to see the same object from a different perspective, stimulating different senses and thereby reinforcing the experience in the memory.

RECONSTRUCTION OF THE CAVALRY BARRACKS

The second major reconstruction project was the partial physical reconstruction of a cavalry barracks on a scale of 1:1 (Fig 5.3). The project had two main objectives: on the one hand, to illustrate a soldier's life in a fort; on the other, to enable visitors to experience in three dimensions the full scale and monumentality of Roman military architecture. The positive impact on visitors of such unusual 1:1 reconstructions has been observed on numerous occasions (Seeher 2011).

The archaeological basis for the reconstruction was provided by excavations on the previous fort occupied by Ala II Flavia at Heidenheim (Scholz 2009, 107–12) that provided clear archaeological evidence for double barracks 84m long and 24m wide. This evidence was used as the basis for a reconstruction which could be used in both the virtual display and the 1:1 physical replica at the Aalen museum. The physical replica was built by a team of archaeologists, architects and carpenters working together. Since no archaeological sources other than the ground plan are known, many architectural details had to be formulated on the basis of modern technical experience. The methods used and decisions made are explained to visitors by information panels at the site.

Owing to limitations of space and budget the reconstruction was restricted to three *contubernia*. The building was constructed on a clearly visible concrete platform. It is therefore clear to the visitor that the building is a replica and forms part of the museum's exhibition space. The first *contubernium* contains full-size replicas of a cavalry soldier and his horse. The second and third *contubernia* have been constructed as a metal workshop, where military metalworking techniques are demonstrated for educational purposes.

An important objective of the overall interpretation concept was that the virtual reconstruction and the 1:1 scale replica should complement each other, producing different sensory perceptions in the minds of visitors that would leave a lasting impression. Feedback since completion of the project shows that the complementary approaches used have succeeded in creating a memorable experience for visitors, identifying the cavalry fort of Aalen as a unique and special place with impressive buildings, and as part of the World Heritage Site.

THE MULTILINGUAL AUDIO-GUIDE FOR THE MUSEUM AND ARCHAEOLOGICAL PARK

The various interpretation media described above are complemented by an audio-guide which intensifies and adds value to the visitor's visual experience. The visitor is provided with additional verbal information about the function of the buildings and the lives of soldiers and civilians. The soundtrack includes both factual information and imagined stories based on the evidence, which enables the visitor to engage with the lives of people from the past.

FILM PRODUCTION: *THE EDGE OF EMPIRE – ROME'S BORDER WITH THE BARBARIANS*

The final element of the museum's varied and integrated approach to presentation is a 20-minute animated film shown at the museum cinema (Cebulla *et al* 2008). The virtual reconstructions form part of the film, giving an overview of the history and function of the Limes and of Roman rule in the border provinces. In contrast to the rather factual approach adopted elsewhere in the museum, the film features emotive and thrilling stories and scenes. The film rounds off the visitor experience within the museum as a whole by placing the archaeological evidence and the virtual and physical reconstructions in a broader context, offering more complex perspectives.

ASSESSMENT

Assessment of public reaction to the new approaches to presentation has shown that they have achieved their objectives. Annually, the Limes Museum at Aalen welcomes around 45,000 visitors, 35% of whom are schoolchildren. Visitors leave the museum with a clear impression of the appearance and size of Roman Aalen, despite the fact that only a small fraction of the site is visible. The combination of different reconstruction techniques, ranging from the table model through 1:1 replicas to virtual reconstructions, helps to intensify and to reinforce the impressions of each visitor. Similar results have been obtained through the use of varied reconstruction techniques at other Roman military sites not visible above ground, for example at Ruffenhofen, Xanten and Nijmegen (Pausch 2010; Otten 2011; Peterse and van Enckevort 2011).

We would recommend applying the approaches used at the Limes Museum to presenting other parts of the often invisible Limes monument. At selected sites with significant tourism potential, both virtual and 1:1 physical reconstructions would be appropriate. In other locations it might be more appropriate to develop internet-based information systems using mobile phone technology.

A major challenge is that of linking the archaeological monument of the Limes with its associated museums, as these are the key places where the public can engage with the World Heritage Site in its broader context. Only in museums is it possible for visitors to have an intensive and interactive experience with the Limes, from the detailed presentation of evidence from geo-magnetics or laser scanning to the transformation of that evidence into virtual reality. Museums have the potential to enable visitors to reconstruct the Roman past of a site or of an entire region themselves.

VIRTUAL LIMES WORLDS

The first virtual presentation of the monument was completed in 2009 and called Virtual Limes Worlds, an interactive media production based on survey data collected by laser scanning. The presentation documents and virtually reconstructs the course of the Limes for approximately 60km in the Rems-Murr-district between Welzheim and Jagsthausen (Landratsamt Rems-Murr-Kreis 2010). Visitors can also operate an interactive animation in real time at a watchtower and a small fort, enabling them to experience the daily life of soldiers along the Limes. It is intended to make the presentation available to all communities along the 60km section and to provide a permanent installation in the museum of Welzheim.

For the Limes Museum in Aalen, it is proposed to develop a similar interactive presentation for the whole of the Limes in Baden-Württemberg, to celebrate the 50th anniversary of the Museum in 2014.

RESULTS

The protection of the Limes as an archaeological monument and the realisation of its potential and significance for tourism and as an element of the landscape depends to a great extent on public awareness – on public appreciation of its appearance and function and the associated acceptance of the Limes as a unique archaeological monument. To achieve this aim, it is necessary to create more places along the Limes, such as the Limes Museum at Aalen, where the visitor can engage with the World Heritage Site and understand its significance both as an archaeological monument and as an exemplar of UNESCO's World Heritage aspirations. This requires approaches to presentation that bring to life the original appearance of the monument, using multimedia alongside traditional models and drawings. The displays at Aalen represent best practice in the complementary use of virtual reconstructions and 1:1 scale replicas.

BIBLIOGRAPHY AND REFERENCES

Cebulla, F, Kemkes, M, and Würfel, M, 2008 *Der Limes – Römer in Germanien. Animationsfilme und Unterrichtsmaterialien* [DVD-ROM], Westermann, Braunschweig

Kemkes, M, 2008 Der Limes als Vermittlungsaufgabe, in *Der Limes als UNESCO-Welterbe, Beiträge zum Welterbe Limes 1* (ed A Thiel), Theiss, Stuttgart, 54–67

Kemkes, M, Scheuerbrandt, J, and Willburger, N, 2006 *Der Limes. Grenze Roms zu den Barbaren*, 2 edn, Thorbecke, Ostfildern

Landratsamt Rems-Murr-Kreis, 2010 *Virtuelle Limeswelten* [online], available from: http://www.limeswelten. net [7 August 2011]

Otten, T, 2011 Neue Konzepte der Präsentation archäologischer Stätten in Nordrhein-Westfalen, in *Schutzbauten und Rekonstruktionen in der Archäologie. Xantener Berichte 19* (eds M Müller, T Otten and U Wulf-Rheidt), Phillip von Zabern, Mainz, 49–54

Pausch, M, 2010 Möglichkeiten und Erfahrungen der Visualisierung im Kastell Ruffenhofen, in *Perspektiven der Limesforschung, Beiträge zum Welterbe Limes 5* (ed P Henrich), Theiss, Stuttgart, 191–200

Peterse, K, and van Enckevort, H, 2011 Rekonstruktion und Visualisierung des römischen Nijmegen, in *Schutzbauten und Rekonstruktionen in der Archäologie. Xantener Berichte 19* (eds M Müller, Th Otten and U Wulf-Rheidt), Phillip von Zabern, Mainz, 79–85

Scholz, M, 2009 Das Römische Reiterkastell Aquileia/Heidenheim. Die Ergebnisse der Ausgrabungen 2000–2004, *Forschungen und Berichte zur Vor- und Frühgeschichte in Baden-Württemberg*, Theiss, Stuttgart

Seeher, J, 2011 Die visuelle Macht der Baurekonstruktion. Überlegungen zur Wiedererrichtung von antiken Bauwerken am Beispiel der Lehmziegel-Stadtmauer von Hattusa, in *Schutzbauten und Rekonstruktionen in der Archäologie. Xantener Berichte 19* (eds M Müller, T Otten and U Wulf-Rheidt), Phillip von Zabern, Mainz, 461–73

6

Vindonissa: Changing Presentations of a Roman Legionary Fortress

Jürgen Trumm and Matthias Flück

Introduction

The protection and presentation of archaeological structures is a century-long tradition in Vindonissa. Whereas older models and reconstructions tried to recreate the ancient situation as closely as possible, current approaches to presentation work consciously with abstraction and schematising. They invite the viewer to experience the process and methods of presentation and do not presume to offer definitive solutions. They attempt, rather, to entice the viewer into antiquity for a moment, to stimulate the imagination. Knowing the subjectivity of all history writing, the viewer is allowed, to a large extent, to create his own history of Roman Vindonissa.

The *Via et Porta Praetoria* Archaeological Site

At Vindonissa, a legionary fort in northern Switzerland, systematic field research began at the end of the 19th century when, in 1897, the amphitheatre was rediscovered and, shortly after, restored and presented to the public (Frei-Stolba *et al* 2011). The amphitheatre marks not only the beginning of systematic excavation, but also the beginning of preservation and presentation of Roman ruins at this important site on the Roman frontier. It is interesting to note that since the beginning of field archaeology at Vindonissa, the restored Roman remains have been used for different purposes including theatrical performances and even church services.

In 1906, the northern gate (*porta decumana*) of the legionary camp was discovered and excavated by Hans Dragendorff. Shortly after his excavation the poorly preserved remains of the foundations were restored up to around half a metre above ground level. As a consequence, the northern gate today illustrates how Roman remains were presented at the beginning of the 20th century. The same is true for the western gate (*porta principalis dextra*) of the legionary camp, discovered in 1919 by Samuel Heuberger. Like the northern gate, it was restored immediately after excavation to around half a metre in height. A few years later, in 1921, the southern gate (*porta praetoria*) was discovered by Samuel Heuberger; however, conservation and on-site presentation were not possible as the whole area was privately owned. The excavator was forced to rebury the imposing ruins.

As well as presentation through *in situ* remains, the Roman archaeology of the legionary fort has been displayed in the Vindonissa Museum, inaugurated in 1912, with the help of drawings and plaster models (Herzig 1946/47).

Since 1919, no further *in situ* presentation of Roman remains had been realised inside the

FIG 6.1. VINDONISSA/WINDISCH (SWITZERLAND). THE ARCHAEOLOGICAL SITE *VIA ET PORTA PRAETORIA*
WITH THE OUTLINED SOUTHERN GATE OF THE LEGIONARY FORTRESS LOOKING NORTH.

fort of Vindonissa. However, outside the fortress a short stretch of an intact Roman water pipe
(*aquaeductus* or *rivus*) was restored in 1966, as well as a public bath (*balneum*) near the eastern
side of the legionary fort, partly preserved under a modern construction between 1970 and 1974.

New approaches to presentation did not appear until 2003 when the southern gate, the *porta
praetoria*, came into focus again. Due to the planned construction of four apartment blocks,
a major rescue excavation around the monument became necessary (Trumm 2009b; Trumm
and Flück forthcoming). At the beginning of the project a simple and traditional presentation
of the Roman gate was envisaged: restoration of the foundations inside a lawn or playground,
surrounded by the new apartment blocks. Shortly after the onset of fieldwork we realised that
the Roman structures were in extraordinarily good condition. As a result, the government of the
Aargau Canton accepted responsibility for this important part of its historical heritage. A part
of the area under construction, the *via et porta praetoria*, was purchased by the state in 2007 in
order to protect and present the Roman remains to the public.

The *via et porta praetoria* archaeological site is an important station on the new Path of the
Legionary visitor route which links the dispersed Roman remains of ancient Windisch using a
fresh and modern approach (Trumm and Pauli-Gabi 2008). This new approach to presentation
of the archaeological site was based on three principles:

First, maximum preservation and protection of the Roman remains above and below ground;
Second, representation of ancient forms and volumes using only modern materials;
Third, open and free access for all visitors.

FIG 6.2. VINDONISSA/WINDISCH (SWITZERLAND). THE ARCHAEOLOGICAL SITE *VIA ET PORTA PRAETORIA* WITH THE CONSERVED SECTION OF THE VIA PRAETORIA AND THE RECONSTRUCTED PORTICO LOOKING SOUTH.

The approach to representing the ancient forms and volumes of the gate and the portico was to use rusty steel grids (Fig 6.1) suspended from a framework of polished steel. Only this framework, resting on 14 pillars, was allowed to touch the intact Roman remains under the ground. All the other Roman remains were untouched by modern construction. In this way, the *via et porta praetoria* archaeological site functions as an open-air museum as well as a protected area for future field research.

After two years of planning and construction, the archaeological site was opened in autumn 2007. When visitors enter the site today, they first pass the outline of the Roman gate which is 12 metres high. In front of the gate they see the Roman road, the *via praetoria*, preserved *in situ* under a glass case. On both sides of the reconstructed portico, fibreglass panels display illustrated information about Vindonissa and the Roman army. The text is in four languages: German, French, Italian and English – with the title always in Latin. On the north side of the gate, a conserved section of the *via praetoria* is open on all four sides protected by a large glass case (Fig 6.2). Opposite, an life-size photograph shows a section through two and a half metres of stratigraphy, representing 2000 years of history.

To combine modern architecture with ancient views, two pairs of stereo binoculars offer a glimpse into the past (Figs 6.3 and 6.4). One pair in front of the gate shows a virtual view to the *porta praetoria*. Another pair inside the portico looks towards the north gate of the legionary fortress. These virtual reconstructions are based on on-site archaeological data gathered during the excavations of 2003–2006, complemented by off-site data from other legionary forts such

Fig 6.3. Vindonissa/Windisch (Switzerland). The archaeological site *VIA ET PORTA PRAETORIA* with a virtual view to the southern gate of the legionary fortress.

Fig 6.4. Vindonissa/Windisch (Switzerland). The archaeological site *VIA ET PORTA PRAETORIA* with a virtual view to the via praetoria looking north.

as León in Spain, Mirebeau in France, Regensburg in Germany, and Chester and Wroxeter in the UK.

In summary, the *via et porta praetoria* archaeological site offers a new and careful approach to full-scale visualisation of Roman remains. Unlike other sites with reconstructed Roman gates such as at Saalburg, Welzheim and Weissenburg in Germany, South Shields in the UK or Buciumi in Romania, we wished to avoid presenting our visualisation as if it were entirely accurate and factual. We preferred instead to suggest different perspectives on antiquity.

A NEW MODEL OF VINDONISSA

Scale models fascinate children and adults alike. They allow the viewer to engage directly with the scene depicted . The viewer can choose his or her own vantage point and observe the situation from an infinite number of perspectives. A model is able to convey the results of scientific research to the general public in a vivid and simple way. Science is made tangible.

In the wake of the extensive archaeological excavations in the first half of the 20th century, many scale models and reconstructions were designed for Vindonissa. During this period reconstruction drawings and, especially, scale models were made of several buildings; both drawings and models were intended to form part of the displays in the Vindonissa Museum which opened in 1912 (Fellmann and Wertenschlag 2009). The models in question were of the amphitheatre, built before 1941; the baths of the legionary fort, built by Zentralmuseum in Mainz (see Eckinger 1933/34, 8); the hospital or *valetudinarium*, built by E Wehrle from Zurich to a scale of 1:100 (see Laur-Belart 1938/39, fig 1; Herzig 1944/45, 40–42); a storage building near the northern gate with an arsenal, also built by E Wehrle from Zurich to a scale of 1:100 (see Herzig 1945/46, 40–47); and the *principia* (Fellmann 1956/57a, 62, fig 33). C Simonett, the museum director at that time, wrote the following on the design of these models by the architect H Herzig from Brugg and on his donation of them to the museum: 'We cannot thank Mr Herzig enough, for showing so much commitment not only towards the visualisation but also towards the scientific issues for the task at hand' (Simonett 1945/46, 48–9). The stone fortifications of the legionary fort, particularly the gates discovered between 1911 and 1922, were also reconstructed in 2D drawings and 3D models (Herzig 1946/47, 52–72; Simonett 1946/47, 86).

One particular model deserves special mention. In 1921/22, E Wehrle from Zurich created an exact scale model of the foundation remains of the southern camp-gate as they were discovered (Simonett 1940/41, 5, fig 2–3; Kielholz 1946/47, 44). In 1946/47, the architect H Herzig drew a reconstruction of the whole settlement of Vindonissa including the topographical setting with the plateau and the rivers (Herzig 1946/47, 68, fig 9). He wrote of his work: 'My aim was to depict the size, the buildings and the vicinity of the camp as impressively as possible. From the environmental perspective, the military and topographical situation was accentuated' (Herzig 1946/47, 67).

As early as 1956, on the back of R Fellmann's initiative, the Vindonissa Museum was home to a model of the whole legionary fort on a scale of 1:200 (Fellmann 1956/57b, 75; 1957/58, 183). This model, made in traditional manner of plaster cast and wood, displayed the legionary camp on a green base.

In 2008, as part of the design of a new permanent exhibition in the Vindonissa Museum, a decision was made to build a new model (Figs 6.5 and 6.6). This was to be based on up-to-date archaeological information and to use state-of-the-art production techniques. One of the

FIG 6.5. DETAILED VIEW OF THE EASTERN CIVIL SETTLEMENT ON THE NEW MODEL OF VINDONISSA. IN THE BACKGROUND THE LEGIONARY CAMP OF THE 1ST CENT IS VISIBLE ON THE HIGH PLATEAU.

aims was to allow for a contemporary perspective, thus enabling the visitor to locate the Roman remains within the modern settlement landscape.

Thanks to the clear representation of the physical geography of the region with the rivers Aare and Reuss, the new model enables the visitor to orientate themselves quickly. The projection of a modern map onto the model allows the visitor to compare today's situation with that of the past (Fig 6.6). The modern communities of Brugg and Windisch are undergoing structural upheaval (Trumm 2009a, 126, fig 3), and the new model helps local people identify their own living space as well as displaying similarities between the Roman period and today. For example, the viewer can discover that the course of the main street of modern Windisch corresponds to a large extent with the course of the *via principalis* of the Roman legionary fort, and that the hitherto largely untouched open space of the so-called *Fehlmannmatte* is in fact the courtyard of the former *campus* of Roman Vindonissa (Trumm 2009a, 134–5).

MODEL-BUILDING WITH NEW TECHNOLOGIES

Well-substantiated scientific research has made it possible to give the model a high level of detail, thus giving maximum plausibility to the visualisation of the situation around AD 90. As opposed to the old model of the fort presented in the Vindonissa Museum from 1956 to 2007, the new version now displays the whole surroundings of Vindonissa and not just the legionary fort. The new model shows well over 500 buildings on a surface of 3.20 × 2.32m at a scale of

FIG 6.6. OVERVIEW OF THE MODEL WITH THE PROJECTION OF THE MODERN MAP ONTO THE MODEL.
IN THE FOREGROUND: THE *CAMPUS*. NOTE THE HITHERTO LARGELY UNTOUCHED OPEN SPACE IN THE
COURTYARD OF THE ROMAN BUILDING.

1:450. Archaeological evidence informed the research and the reconstruction of the buildings (Pauli-Gabi 2006; Trumm 2010). The unexplored areas of the legionary fort were reconstructed by analogy with other forts of the late first century AD. The functioning of the legionary fort, the spatial relationships, logistical details, water supply, waste management, security and even the emissions of craft workshops were all taken into account.

The civil settlement areas surrounding the fort were represented in the same way. Here the archaeological evidence defines the minimum surface area of the settlement of Vindonissa while comparison with other small Roman towns of the late first century AD helps construct a plausible settlement structure, set harmoniously into the known topography.

A conscious decision was made to reduce the use of colour and surface texture so as not to let individual details get in the way of the whole picture (Fig 6.5). A high level of detail would also suggest an in-depth knowledge of the site which, in many cases, simply does not exist. Other parts of the new exhibition deal with particular themes and with the material culture of Roman Vindonissa, illustrated with finds. The model offers a visualisation of how the settlement may have looked at a specific point in time. The visitor is able to understand that this visualisation is not based purely on the contemporary state of knowledge but is also influenced by modern ideas about presentation.

State-of-the-art technology has been used in presenting the settlement of Vindonissa, in the design process and in the final displays. The physical geography is based on a 3D digital CAD model. From the digital CAD data, the buildings were printed out directly on a 3D printer. This method of 3D printing is fascinating, as it shows how digital data is transformed into real objects. In a process of layered construction, a powder-of-plaster cast is printed in 0.10mm steps – from the foundations up to the rooftops. One of the advantages of this method is that the buildings can be printed in the desired colour. A final hardening with epoxy applied by the model-maker gives the buildings the necessary stability. The terrain is cut out of the plastic using a CNC method. The museum displays are highlighted and enlivened by themed projections from an overhead projector.

A PIONEERING PROJECT

The complexity and size of the model of Vindonissa is without peer in Switzerland. Outside Switzerland such models are rare. They appeal to a wide audience, not only those with an archaeological interest; the combination of 3D printing technology with precision production makes the Vindonissa model a point of reference and an educational resource for architecture, product design, industrial design or engine building.

The realisation of the new model of Vindonissa is an example of successful cooperation between state institutions (Cantonal Archaeology Service of Aargau, Aargau Geographic Information System AGIS), Colleges (University of Basel, University of Applied Sciences Northwestern Switzerland, University of Applied Sciences Basel Cantons) and private companies (Digitale Archäologie Freiburg i. Br., R Zanini Formenbau Menziken, Visual Data Systems VDS Arlesheim, I-Art Interactive Basel).

Further projects for a 4D visualisation of the Vindonissa model (Living Vindonissa) and an online version of the 3D model are currently in the pipeline in cooperation with the institute for 4D technologies of the University of Applied Sciences Northwestern Switzerland (Flück 2011).[1]

BIBLIOGRAPHY AND REFERENCES

Eckinger, T, 1933/34 Thermenmodell, *Jahresbericht der Gesellschaft Pro Vindonissa*, 8

Fellmann, R, 1956/57a Die Principia des Legionslagers Vindonissa, *Jahresbericht der Gesellschaft Pro Vindonissa*, 5–69

— 1956/57b Museum. Arbeitsbericht des Konservators, *Jahresbericht der Gesellschaft Pro Vindonissa*, 75–6

— 1957/58 Museum. Arbeitsbericht des Konservators, *Jahresbericht der Gesellschaft Pro Vindonissa*, 183

Fellmann Brogli, R, and Wertenschlag, N, 2009 Das Vindonissa-Museum um 1912 – ein Haus im Spannungsfeld zwischen Wissenschaft und Vermittlung, *Jahresbericht der Gesellschaft Pro Vindonissa*, 97–115

---

[1]   A television broadcast about the realisation of the new model of Vindonissa can be viewed at: http://www.sendungen.sf.tv/einstein/Sendungen/Einstein/Archiv/Sendung-vom-14.05.2009 [20 August 2012].

Flück, M, 2011 The printed legionary camp of Vindonissa. The development of a new digital and physical model of Vindonissa, *Proceedings of International Conference on Cultural Heritage and New Technologies, Workshop 15, November 15–17, 2010,* Vienna, 333–47

Frei-Stolba, R, Hänggi, J, Hänggi, R, Matter, G, Trumm, J, Tschudin, W, and Zemp, I, 2011 *The Amphitheatre in Vindonissa Windisch-Brugg*, Schweizerischer Kunstführer Serie 89, Nr. 885, Bern

Herzig, H, 1944/45, Das neue Modell des Lager-Spitals, *Jahresbericht der Gesellschaft Pro Vindonissa*, 40–2

— 1945/46 Die Rekonstruktion von Zeughaus und Getreidemagazin in Vindonissa, *Jahresbericht der Gesellschaft Pro Vindonissa*, 40–7

— 1946/7 Versuch einer Rekonstruktion der Tore, Türme und Umwallung von Vindonissa, *Jahresbericht der Gesellschaft Pro Vindonissa*, 52–72

Kielholz, A, 1946/47 Die Gesellschaft Pro Vindonissa 1897–1946. Aus der Chronik des halben Jahrhunderts ihrer Geschichte, *Jahresbericht der Gesellschaft Pro Vindonissa*, 1–51

Laur-Belart, R, 1938/39 Jahresbericht 1938/39, *Jahresbericht der Gesellschaft Pro Vindonissa*, 1–15

Pauli-Gabi, T, 2006 Vindonissa, in *Reallexikon Germanischen Altertumskunde* (eds H Beck, D Geuenich and H Steuer), de Gruyter, Berlin, 427–30

Simonett, C, 1940/41 Das Museum, *Jahresbericht der Gesellschaft Pro Vindonissa*, 3–8

— 1945/46 Das Museum, *Jahresbericht der Gesellschaft Pro Vindonissa*, 48–9

— 1946/47 Das Museum. Arbeitsbericht des Konservators, *Jahresbericht der Gesellschaft Pro Vindonissa*, 85–7

Trumm, J, 2009a Ausgrabungen in Vindonissa im Jahr 2009, *Jahresbericht der Gesellschaft Pro Vindonissa*, 123–41

— 2009b *Vindonissa* – intra muros, extra muros. Ausgrabungen 2003–2006 im Süden des Legionslagers Windisch, in *LIMES XX. Estudios sobre la frontera romana*, Gladius Anejos 13/3 (eds A Morillo, N Hancl and E Martin), Madrid, 1371–82

— 2010 Vindonissa. Stand der Erforschung, *Jahresbericht der Gesellschaft Pro Vindonissa*, 37–54

Trumm, J, and Flück, M, forthcoming Vindonissa. Via et porta praetoria. Neue Grabungen und Forschungen zu den Steinbauten im Süden des Legionslagers, *Veröffentlichungen der Gesellschaft Pro Vindonissa 22*, Brugg

Trumm, J, and Pauli-Gabi, Th, 2008 Im Bannkreis von Vindonissa. Auf neuen Wegen zum römischen Legionslager, *Heimat am Hochrhein 33*, 63–8

Via et porta praetoria, 2007 *Via et Porta Praetoria, Vindonissa. Archäologiestätte Windisch* (eds Kanton Aargau, Departement Finanzen und Ressourcen, Abt Hochbau), Projektdokumentation No 10, Aarau

7

Bringing to Life the Ancient City
of Viminacium on the Danube

Snežana Golubović and Miomir Korać

Introduction

The present-day territories of the villages of Stari Kostolac and Drmno, situated about 95km south-east of Belgrade, lie within the limits of the urban territory of the ancient city of Viminacium, the capital of the Roman province Moesia Superior, named Moesia Prima in the late Empire. The ancient Roman city and military fort (covering an area of over 450ha of the wider city region and 220ha of the inner city) are now located under cultivated fields, across which artefacts and fragments of objects from Roman times are scattered. Exploration of the Viminacium cemeteries was undertaken during construction of the Kostolac thermal power plant and operation of the Drmno opencast mine.

The necropolis of Viminacium was explored during the last three decades of the 20th century and over 13,500 graves discovered, along with more than 30,000 archaeological artefacts. Excavation of the southern part of the Viminacium cemetery offered valuable data about burial rites from the fourth century BC (Jovanović 1984; 1985), over the whole Roman period, through the first to the fourth centuries AD (Zotović and Jordović 1990; Korać *et al* 2009) to the period of the Great Migration (Zotović 1980; Ivanišević *et al* 2006). The finds were displayed at the national museum in Požarevac, a town situated 12km from the site itself. With nothing visible at the site, visitors were unable to obtain a real impression of the necropolis, the city or the military fort. The outlines of the fort and the city were marked on maps made by the early explorers of Viminacium: Count Marsigli, Felix Kanitz, Mihailo Valtrović and Miloje Vasić (Korać and Golubović 2009, 7). However, at the beginning of the 21st century, no Roman remains were visible or presented at the site itself.

A new impetus to the exploration and subsequent presentation of Viminacium was given by a multidisciplinary team of young researchers headed by Miomir Korać from the Archaeological Institute in Belgrade. They applied modern research methods including remote sensing, geo-electrical and geo-radar and were subsequently involved in conserving and presenting features within a proposed archaeological park. Mathematicians, electrical engineers, geophysicists, geologists and researchers participated in the Viminacium project, working alongside archaeologists, and were involved in remote detection, 3D modelling and recognition of forms, as well as in artificial intelligence. Aerial photos, geo-radar and geomagnetic surveys of the site offered an accurate picture of the fort with its defensive walls, gates, towers and an administrative building (*praetoria*) lying beneath the fertile farmlands of Stig.

This research was initiated through the Itinerarium Romanum Serbiae project, organised by the Archaeological Institute from Belgrade, the Ministry of Science, the Ministry of Culture and the Serbian Tourism agency. The project aims to link research, cultural tourism, engagement of local people and regeneration under the theme of reviving and reconnecting ancient Roman roads. Viminacium was seen as both the key archaeological site for the project and as a test case for exploring approaches and techniques for protection, presentation and management.

THE AQUEDUCT

The most successful application of geo-radar research was in detecting the position of an important aqueduct supplying water to Viminacium, of which about 1.5km was excavated. The aqueduct dates from the first century AD; it was built of stone bound with lime mortar. The sides of the aqueduct were also covered with lime mortar, while the bottom was covered with waterproof mortar. The underside was built of fired bricks bearing the stamps of the Roman legions '*LEGIO IIII FLAVIA FELIX*' and '*LEGIO VII CLAUDIA PIA FIDELIS*', who built it. The aqueduct was covered with massive floor tiles and was destroyed in the first half of the fifth century AD during the invasion of the Huns.

This was the first time that archaeologists at Viminacium have had the opportunity to examine the aqueduct in its integral form with all its constructional elements. Geophysical research revealed another 1800m of the aqueduct, while remote detection traced a further 1350m of it; the total length was about 10km. The aqueduct brought fresh water to the ancient city and to the military fort of Viminacium. It was a unique feat of construction and engineering. Its gradient from the water source to the Roman city and military fort measured 1‰ to 2‰. The names of two craftsmen (Claudius and Tiberius) who built it were found inscribed in several places.

In 2003 part of the aqueduct was moved as it had been endangered by the opencast coal mine. Sections of the aqueduct were transferred to the other side of the road, next to the eastern edge of the mine. In the meantime, the archaeological park was established approximately 10km away in a protected zone next to the western edge of the mine. It was decided to move the sections of the aqueduct a second time so that they could form part of the archaeological park and be more easily accessible to visitors. The transfer took place in autumn 2009 along with a complete Roman water tower that had been excavated in the intervening period and was also endangered by the mine. The various parts of the aqueduct and the water tower were cut very precisely into smaller segments and transferred in specially constructed steel crates to the protected zone. They are now finally located within the protected zone of the archaeological park where the intention is to display them properly.

THE ARCHAEOLOGICAL PARK

The excavation of several thousand Roman graves in the necropolis prompted a systematic review of how best to present the remains of the city and the military fort, bringing to life for visitors what was once the biggest city of Moesia Superior. Several buildings and features discovered over the past ten years are presented within the archaeological park. The task was to work out how best to present the recently discovered and impressively preserved features in original ways, allowing visitors to appreciate their scale and quality whilst at the same time ensuring their long-term conservation.

Four features are currently open to the public and another three are being prepared (Fig 7.1). These are described below:

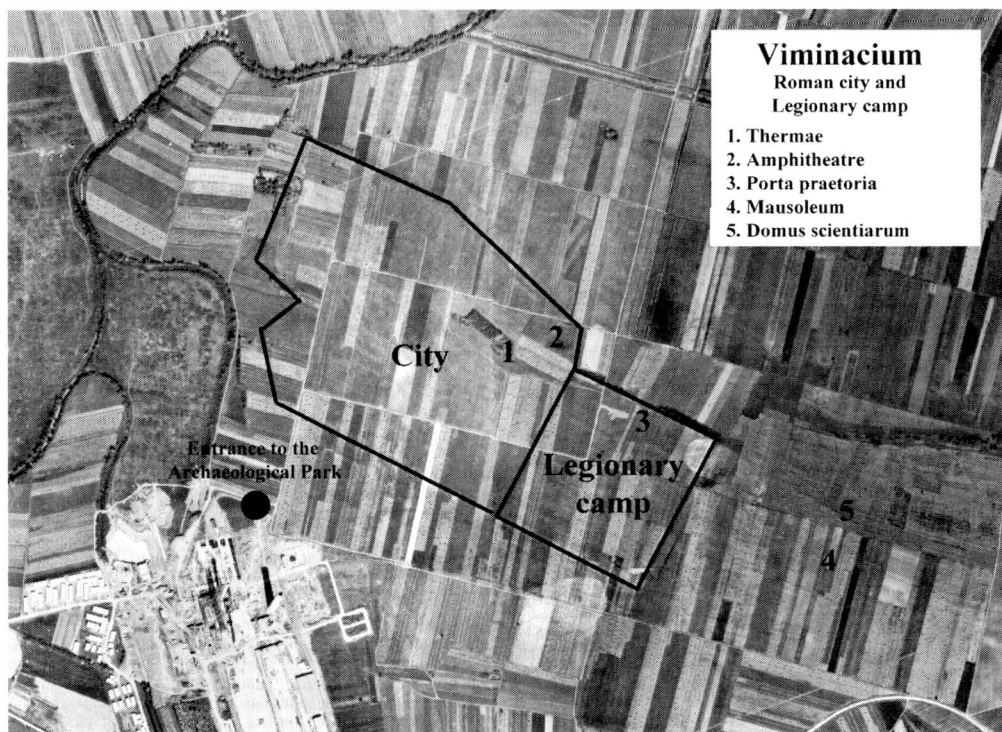

FIG 7.1. VIMINACIUM SHOWING THE SITES CONTAINED WITHIN THE ARCHAEOLOGICAL PARK.

Thermae

The baths (*thermae*) were excavated between 1973 and 1975, when they were also partly protected and conserved. Unfortunately the structure was not maintained properly and over the course of 30 years had become overgrown. In 2003, the site was re-excavated with the intention of conserving the areas already investigated and excavating new areas which would make presentation of the whole site possible.

The Viminacium baths are distinguished not only by their luxury but also by their architectural design. The long period during which they remained in use (from the first to the fourth centuries) makes it possible to trace the individual stages in their construction. Archaeological excavations have shown that there were five apses, four of which were the so-called *tepidaria* (warm rooms) and the fifth was a *frigidarium* (cold room).

The baths are preserved to the level of the hypocaust and show evidence of several construction phases. The floor of the older baths, once resting on short brick-built pillars, was covered with a mosaic. The remains of frescos testify to the luxury of the establishment.

It was decided to construct a roofing structure to protect the remains and that the use of wooden materials would be most appropriate, both aesthetically and for economic reasons. Following consultation with experts from the Faculty of Architecture in Belgrade, who already had experience in constructing such facilities (Kujundžić *et al* 2004), the project was designed and then implemented in 2004 and 2005.

FIG 7.2. THE ARCHAEOLOGICAL PARK AND OPENCAST COAL MINE.

The roof comprises a light lamellar structure with a special sheet covering. This structure makes it possible to bridge large spans without any supports impacting the monument itself, thereby preventing damage to underlying archaeology. Specially designed curtains at the sides provide good ventilation during summer. The protective roof enables visitors to access the site and at the same time permits continued excavation of the remaining, unexcavated areas throughout the year, independent of weather conditions. Underneath the roof, some minor conservation work has been done to the exposed walls to prevent decay.

This approach represented an important innovation for the future management of archaeological sites and monuments in Serbia; that certain important sites such as the baths at Viminacium should be afforded appropriate protection to enable them to be made publicly accessible. Following the opening of the archaeological park five years ago, several hundred thousand people have visited the baths (Fig 7.2). At present the visit encompasses the whole site. However, due to the extent of the site, it is intended in future to construct several viewing platforms to allow a better appreciation of the various elements.

Porta Praetoria

The Roman fort of Viminacium was built in the early decades of the first century AD. The approximate dimensions of the fort were 443 × 387m. Historical sources state that Viminacium was a significant military fort in which the Roman legion VII *Claudia Pia Fidelis* was stationed. The north gate of the fort, the *Porta Praetoria*, was uncovered during systematic excavations carried out in 2002 and 2003. The remains include massive paving slabs, a *cloaca* and richly

FIG 7.3. THE DOMUS SCIENTIARUM AND MAUSOLEUM.

decorated architectural elements, all of which demonstrate the importance of this major defensive site on the Empire's northern frontier. It was decided to protect the site and open it to the public using the same protective structure as had been developed for the baths. This made it possible to excavate the site throughout the year. Unfortunately this site is of lesser interest to visitors since only the foundations of the towers are preserved, while the pavement and the sewer are only partially preserved. Information panels display images of early Viminacium excavations and describe the Roman fortification system, but a human guide is needed to bring the fort to life for visitors. It is hoped at some stage in the future to put up a screen on the other side of the gate, for the projection of an appropriate film, but current circumstances do not allow this.

Mausoleum

The mausoleum has been the focus of the most innovative and imaginative approaches to public access (Fig 7.3). Its plan is square, measuring 20 × 20m and it is built of stone and ashlar blocks and decorated with columns. The main structure is located in the centre of the mausoleum. Its dimensions are 5 × 5m and it is built of green schist bonded with plaster. At its centre is a tomb. The deceased person was laid on a wooden support and cremated on the spot with all the associated grave goods. After the burial a thin layer of earth was cast over the remains and then the entire space was closed with stone and lime plaster. This form of burial, known as *bustum*, is generally very rare and it was quite exceptional during the period to which the mausoleum belongs. The individual cremated and buried in this place must have been a person of great distinction in the Roman hierarchy. The graves found around the central *bustum* were

FIG 7.4. EXCAVATION OF AMPHITHEATRE.

quite rich in grave goods: 17 gold items were found. Copies of some of these items were made during 2005.

To protect the site and to allow public access, a roof was constructed using a different design from that of the baths and the north gate. The roof comprises supports made of bonded lamellate wood. The basic structure has eight curved and four straight wooden supports. Other elements of the structure are made of bonded lamellate and solid wood, with a metal framework anchored between the wooden supports. The solid wood components which form the pyramidal apex of the structure are joined with metal connectors. The curved supports have a span of 20m and their base is square with rounded angles. The structure covers an area of 32 × 32m and rests on concrete foundation walls which enclose the underlying area.

The roof reflects the form of the space it covers: the cemetery space is square in shape and has several concrete extensions for large graves. The biggest, central grave in the cemetery is lit directly through the apex of the structure, thus highlighting the central spot in the cemetery.

Visitors to the mausoleum area also have an opportunity to see some fine late Roman funerary frescoes. More than 20 tombs decorated with frescoes were excavated during the 1980s, the distinctive style pointing to the existence of an outstanding fresco workshop in Viminacium during the fourth century (Korać 2007, 142). This workshop exported its products beyond the Province, as did several other craft workshops established in Viminacium.

Three of these tombs have been made accessible to visitors; one, the so-called Cupid Tomb excavated recently, is *in situ* while the other two tombs found during the 1980s have been moved and rebuilt. Access has been created by constructing a 20-metre-long tunnel along the northern outer wall of the mausoleum and removing some of the bricks in the floors of the tombs so that visitors can observe the frescoes inside.

The scenes, and the techniques used to depict them, are extraordinary and without parallel in late antiquity. The practice of burying Christians and pagans side by side, found commonly at Viminacium and at other urban centres, is reflected in the frescoes which combine classical and Christian elements. One of the tombs presented alongside the *in situ* Cupid Tomb has Christ's monogram depicted on its western side, defining the tomb as Christian. Scenes of earthly and heavenly hunting and the Garden of Eden are depicted on the other sides (Korać 2007, 49). The second tomb has on its western side a portrait of a young woman who was buried inside the tomb (Korać 2007, 69). The beauty of the portrait and the quality of the painting technique are outstanding and have been the subject of many different studies. The young woman's portrait has been the inspiration for an art film and she has become known as the Lady of Viminacium or the Mona Lisa of Viminacium.

Amphitheatre

Investigation of the amphitheatre at Viminacium began in 2003 with a combination of geo-physical research, landscape analysis and comparison with reliefs on Trajan's column. This research led to identification of the amphitheatre. Subsequent excavation has revealed that it was built of stone blocks and rubble bound with mortar. Over the past four years the area around the arena has been revealed, with passages on the eastern, southern, western and northern side (Fig 7.4). Around three quarters of the amphitheatre have been explored so far, allowing the estimate that it could have held up to 12,000 spectators. Once the excavation is finished it is intended to partially reconstruct the building to allow a variety of performance events to take place, for example, classical concerts, plays, folk music etc.

Research Centre

The Viminacium scientific and research centre is a multipurpose facility designed in the shape of a Roman *villa rustica*. The upper level consists of a set of *atria*, around which there are workshops, laboratories, offices and accommodation for professional teams as well as for visitors. Adjacent to these rooms is the library with a reading room, documentation centre, a kitchen, a dining room and a replica of a Roman *thermae*, which is to be used as a small spa centre. The lower level is intended for storage of museum collections and archives and has increased security and strict climatic control.

The intention is to make it possible for scientists from Serbia and elsewhere to use the centre for research, workshops, summer schools, conferences and meetings. It will also be used as accommodation for the increasing number of tourists visiting Viminacium (Korać 2010, 23). Although not fully finished, the research centre has been operational since 2008 and has hosted a variety of research groups, workshops, concerts and events.

Itinerarium Romanum Serbiae

In a wider context, Viminacium is the leading archaeological site in the Itinerarium Romanum Serbiae project, organised by the Archaeological Institute of Belgrade, the Ministry of Science, the Ministry of Culture and the Serbian tourism agency. The project aims to revive and reconnect ancient roads which in many cases run parallel to modern motorways. It has been designed as a multi-level international project with combined scientific and cultural aims using modern methods of research, conservation and presentation. A network of tourist accommodation and facilities is planned, designed as replicas of Roman buildings including villas (*villa rustica*), resting places (*mutatio*) and hotels (*mansio*). The intention is to construct 100 villas (*villa rustica*) located along ancient Roman roads at intervals of between 5 and 10km. The villas will be sited in the countryside (in forests, fields or pastures), mostly along the rivers Sava, Danube, Morava and Timok.

CONCLUSION

Since 2006, when the Viminacium archaeological park was opened, the number of visitors has increased progressively to almost 100,000 in 2009. Viminacium has become an important historical and cultural destination for schools, students and tourists. Feedback from these users will be used to inform future developments.

Viminacium has become a model for the combined scientific and cultural development of archaeological sites, while the project Itinerarium Romanum Serbiae, for which Viminacium is the centrepiece, has been identified as a project of national significance for the preservation and presentation of cultural heritage. Based on the Viminacium experience we suggest that the best way to protect any archaeological site is to revive it and develop it as a tourist attraction. At Viminacium, development of the site as a tourist attraction alongside scientific research has helped protect the site from illicit excavation and building development and has raised awareness amongst local people of the significance of their local heritage, motivating them to assist in its protection. Viminacium is also an example of how cultural heritage can be used as a basis for economic and regional development. It is planned to use the approach developed at Viminacium as a model for the development of other sites within the Itinerarium Romanum Serbiae project.

BIBLIOGRAPHY AND REFERENCES

Ivanišević, V, Kazanski, M, and Mastykova, A, 2006 *Les nécropoles de Viminacium à l'époque des Grandes Migrations*, Collège de France – CNRS, Paris

Jovanović, B, 1984 Les sépulture de la nécropole celtique de Pećine près de Kostolac (Serbie du nord), *Études Celtiques* 21, 63–93

— 1985 Nekropola na Pećinama i starije gvozdeno doba Podunavlja, *Starinar* 36, 13–17

Korać, M, 2007 *Slikarstvo Viminacijuma*, Centar za nove tehnologije – Viminacium, Beograd

— 2010 *Viminacium: Fasti Romanae 2011/2012*, Centar za nove tehnologije – Viminacium, Beograd

Korać, M, and Golubović, S, 2009 *Viminacium – Više Grobalja 281–530 (kremacija) 268–560 (inhumacija)*, Tom II, Arheološki institut – Centar za nove tehnologije, Beograd

Korać, M, Golubović, S, and Mrđić, N, 2009 *ITINERARIUM ROMANUM SERBIAE, Road of Roman Emperors in Serbia*, Center for New Technologies Viminacium, Beograd

Kujundžić, V, Tekić, Ž, and Djordjević, S, 2004 *Savremeni sistemi drvenih konstrukcija, Arhitektonski fakultet Univerzitea u Beogradu*, Beograd

Zotović, Lj, 1980 Nekropola iz vremena seobe naroda sa uže gradske teritorije Viminacijuma, *Starinar* 31, 95–115

Zotović, Lj, Jordović, Č, 1990 *Viminacivm I, nekropola Više Grobalja*, Arheološki institut – Republički zavod za zaštitu spomenika culture, Beograd

8

An International View of Reconstruction

CHRISTOPHER YOUNG

INTRODUCTION

This chapter focuses on the issues surrounding reconstruction of UNESCO World Heritage properties, principally archaeological sites. It is written from the perspective of a national heritage body rather than from that of UNESCO itself, though the author has considerable experience of working with the UNESCO World Heritage Centre and the advisory bodies to the World Heritage Convention. The chapter attempts to interpret UNESCO guidance within the context of national policy and practice in the UK in particular, and of international guidance in general. Given the context in which it was originally delivered, as a paper at the 2009 Limes Congress, there is also a focus on the reconstruction of Roman military sites, which often appears to be a particular ambition of their managers.

The terminology in this field can be confusing, particularly since the same words are frequently given differing meanings by different practitioners. For the avoidance of doubt, and possibly in imitation of Humpty Dumpty, who said 'When I use a word, it means just what I choose it to mean, neither more nor less' (Carroll 1871), this chapter uses the definitions set out in the 2001 English Heritage statement on reconstruction of archaeological sites including ruins:

> *Restoration* means returning the existing fabric of a place to a known earlier state by removing accretions or by reassembling existing components without the introduction of new material
>
> *Reconstruction* means returning a place to a known earlier state and is distinguished from restoration by the introduction of new material into the fabric
>
> *Re-creation* means speculative creation of a presumed earlier state on the basis of surviving evidence from that place and other sites and on deductions drawn from that evidence, using new materials
>
> *Replication* means the construction of a copy of a structure or building, usually on another site or nearby. (English Heritage 2001, paragraph 5)

The first two definitions are taken from the Burra Charter (Australia ICOMOS 1999) while the second two were developed specifically for the English Heritage guidance.

RESTORATION AND RECONSTRUCTION: FOR AND AGAINST

While some restoration causes no problems, more generally restoration and reconstruction have been problematic since the development of the concept of conservation in Europe in the 19th century. The strongest statements came from England in reaction to the wholesale reconstruction of churches to a (generally) imagined ideal medieval state. They can be summarised in John Ruskin's famous phrase 'Do not let us talk of Restoration. The thing is a lie from beginning to end' (Ruskin 1889, 196).

A more reasoned statement of the case is contained in the Manifesto of the Society for the Protection of Ancient Buildings, written by William Morris in 1877:

> But those who make the changes wrought in our day under the name of Restoration, while professing to bring back a building to the best time of its history, have no guide but each his own individual whim to point out to them what is admirable and what is contemptible; while the very nature of their tasks compels them to destroy something and to supply the gap by imagining what the earlier builders should or might have done. Moreover, in the course of this double process of destruction and addition the whole surface of the building is necessarily tampered with; so that the appearance of antiquity is taken away from such old parts of the fabric as are left, and there is no laying to rest in the spectator the suspicion of what may have been lost; and in short, a feeble and lifeless forgery is the final result of all the wasted labour.
>
> (SPAB 1877)

The cases for and against reconstruction have been strongly argued ever since. Restoration and reconstruction continue to arouse strong opinion and emotions among conservationists. This is despite the fact that wholesale reconstruction is only ever proposed for a very small number of sites (Stanley Price 2009).

The case against is summarised at its most elegant in the quotation above from the SPAB Manifesto. For archaeological sites the strongest argument is that their value is primarily evidential and that reconstruction damages that evidence, both above and below ground. Reconstruction can also damage the aesthetic values of buildings or their settings and may present a misleading impression of the site to the public. It will also never be entirely accurate. Reconstructions very often have higher maintenance costs than those of an unaltered site.

The arguments for restoration or reconstruction tend to focus on the presentational and educational aspects of a site. There can be considerable educational and interpretive benefit from being able to show complete rather than fragmentary structures. Reconstruction, if carried out using traditional methods, can also add to our understanding of construction techniques used in the past. More intangibly, restorations or reconstructions can make a contribution to the sense of place of a site, or even to sense of national or local identity (the argument for the reconstruction of the Old Town of Warsaw). A complete structure may also attract more visitors than a ruin or a buried site and so have economic benefit.

A further factor is the public attitude towards restoration, which tends to be favourable. As conservation becomes more transparent and less the preserve of the professional and the official, so public attitudes will need to be taken more into account in decision-making. This could become a powerful factor in the future.

It is in any case a myth that structures can be preserved totally unchanged. A degree of change is inevitable in the permanent preservation and display of structures that have been buried. Masonry will need to be repointed to be weatherproof and it may be necessary to reshape the profile of the masonry to shed water easily. In the display of any archaeological site, too, it is quite normal to excavate fully negative features such as ditches and to display them to the public. This is a form of restoration. Replacement of missing roofs and floors in standing ruins is also relatively common for reasons of both structural stability and access.

Roman military remains seem to be a prime target for reconstruction or, technically, for recreation or replication since it is almost impossible to be certain of the original form of Roman structures. Clearance and display of ditches is common but there is also actual reconstruction or recreation of either wooden or stone structures. The so-called Clayton Wall is a drystone partial reconstruction of Hadrian's Wall, but not to full height. It is possible that the actual height of the Clayton Wall was governed by the need to have a sheep-proof barrier along its line, which is often a boundary between different agricultural holdings.

Full-scale recreation of Roman military structures is common and longstanding, the most notable example being the Saalburg fort on the Upper German Limes, reconstructed at the behest of Kaiser Wilhelm II at the end of the 19th century. Since then many Roman forts, towers and defences have been recreated in various places around the Roman Empire, including in the UK. The reasons for this are unclear but may relate to the fact that so few Roman military structures are complete or near-complete. The desire to reconstruct or recreate Roman military structures continues, as is evidenced by the recent Culture 2000 volume on Roman frontiers (Breeze and Jilek 2008).

National and International Policy and Guidance

Clearly, different countries will have differing approaches to reconstruction. However, World Heritage properties are also subject to the guidance and rules of the UNESCO World Heritage Committee as set out in its Operational Guidelines (UNESCO 2011) and other guidance. This guidance is based in part on the experience of the Committee and its advisory bodies, ICOMOS (the International Council on Monuments and Sites) and ICCROM (the International Centre for the Study of the Preservation and Restoration of Cultural Property), and in part on international guidance. In the management of the current parts of the Frontiers of the Roman Empire World Heritage Site, and also of future extensions to the property, it is necessary to take this, as well as national guidance, into account. The World Heritage Committee has also adopted a specific decision relating to reconstruction of the Frontiers of the Roman Empire.

UK official policy has followed the general line established by Ruskin and SPAB, though in practice the boundaries have sometimes been blurred and examples of partial reconstruction can be found in many places, particularly of half-timbered buildings. Most recently, English Heritage published guidance on the reconstruction of archaeological sites, including ruins, in 2001 (English Heritage 2001). This recognised that there could be circumstances in which restoration and reconstruction could be acceptable provided that what was done was in no way speculative, that the impact on the significance of the site was acceptable, and that any proposals were also acceptable in terms of impact on the site's setting. The guidance also made the point that long-term requirements and costs for maintenance were an important consideration (English Heritage 2001, paragraphs 30–37).

In 2008, English Heritage published *Conservation Principles, Policies and Guidance* which set out the framework within which English Heritage will make judgements in its casework. It re-states our general policy on restoration for all aspects of the historic environment:

Restoration to a significant place should normally be acceptable if:
a. the heritage values of the elements that would be restored decisively outweigh the values of those that would be lost;

    b. the work proposed is justified by compelling evidence of the evolution of the place, and is executed in accordance with that evidence;

    c. the form in which the place currently exists is not the result of an historically-significant event;

    d. the work proposed respects previous forms of the place;

    e. the maintenance implications of the proposed restoration are considered to be sustainable
(English Heritage 2008, paragraphs 126–137)

International guidance, particularly within the wider European context, effectively begins with the 1964 Venice Charter (Venice Charter 1964). This states very clearly that speculative reconstruction should not be permitted, saying (Article 9) that '[restoration] must stop at the point where conjecture begins'. On archaeological sites it is even clearer:

> … All reconstruction work should however be ruled out *a priori*. Only anastylosis, that is to say, the reassembling of existing but dismembered parts can be permitted. The material used for integration should always be recognisable and its use should be the least that will ensure the conservation of a monument and the reinstatement of its form.
>
> (Venice Charter 1964, Article 15)

Since then, there have been a number of other doctrinal documents which provide further guidance. The *ICOMOS Lausanne Charter for the Protection and Management of the Archaeological Heritage* (ICOMOS 1990) takes a more liberal view. Recognising that reconstructions can be valuable for both experimental research and interpretation, Article 7 of the Charter says:

> [reconstructions] should … be carried out with great caution, so as to avoid disturbing any archaeological evidence, and they should take account of evidence from all sources in order to achieve authenticity. Where possible and appropriate, reconstructions should not be built immediately on the archaeological remains, and should be identifiable as such.

The reconstructed Roman bath house at Segedunum (Wallsend) on Hadrian's Wall is a good example of this approach. Based on careful research of all possible sources, including surviving remains elsewhere along Hadrian's Wall, the bath house is sited close to the fort but is not in the same location as the original fort bath house. Built as a working replica, it has provided useful information on how these buildings functioned as well as being a major interpretive tool.

The Riga Charter is a regional guidance document produced in 2000 which addressed the particular issues of reconstructing buildings destroyed during the Soviet period in Eastern Europe. It recognises that in some circumstances, subject to many caveats, reconstruction can be acceptable when the building that is being restored 'has outstanding artistic, symbolic, or environmental … significance for regional history and cultures' (Stovel 2001, 239).

Documents such as these represent a move away from the absolute certainties of the Venice Charter and also, perhaps, a move away from the belief that the value and significance of places and monuments lie entirely in their fabric. This reflects the more nuanced approach to authenticity evidenced in the 1994 Nara Declaration which has been incorporated into the World Heritage Operational Guidelines (UNESCO 2011, Annex 4).

The Nara Declaration was, to some extent, developed in reaction to a perceived European emphasis on the importance of fabric. It recognises the diversity of heritage alongside the need to respect international norms and guidance. It defines authenticity as being about the credibility of the evidence of the values of a place, and it places great weight on the need to understand the values for which heritage is preserved. If values are not necessarily related to fabric, then a more flexible approach to reconstruction may be acceptable in some circumstances. This approach allows, for example, for the Japanese approach to conservation of religious buildings by periodic dismantling and reconstruction.

Apart from its recognition of the need to respect cultural diversity, the Nara Declaration was also an important stage in the recognition that managing and conserving cultural heritage should be based on a full understanding of why a place is significant and that places should be managed to protect their significance. This has been foreshadowed in the World Heritage Convention with its emphasis on Outstanding Universal Value, as well as in the Burra Charter, and is now widely accepted (see English Heritage 2008 for one example of this approach). Values can be classified in various different ways, but all systems recognise that value need not lie just in the original fabric. If the primary significance is aesthetic, for example, it may be appropriate to restore missing elements of an architectural masterpiece.

Linked to this recognition that values should be properly analysed and described is the realisation that the process of defining value needs to be accessible to the public. It is no longer possible for decisions to be taken just within a closed group of professionals, if indeed it ever was. One consequence of this is the need to give some weight to the views of the public in coming to decisions on conservation, including restoration or reconstruction. This could include views on whether or not reconstruction might be appropriate, particularly when, as noted above in the context of the Riga Charter, the decision on reconstruction is in some way political, in that it reverses some action of a previous regime.

This was the reason for the inscription in 1980 of the wholly reconstructed Historic Centre of Warsaw on the World Heritage List. Much of the significance of the property lay in its role as a symbol of national identity and the demonstration of this by its restoration. At the same session, the Committee adopted changes to the Operational Guidelines, saying 'reconstruction is only acceptable if it is carried out on the basis of complete and detailed documentation on the original and to no extent on conjecture' (UNESCO 1980, paragraph 18b). In terms of Warsaw, this was indeed the case since the level of documentation for the Old Town was exceptional.

Similar wording has been maintained ever since and the Operational Guidelines currently say: 'In relation to authenticity, the reconstruction of archaeological remains or historic buildings or districts is justifiable only in exceptional circumstances. Reconstruction is acceptable only on the basis of complete and detailed documentation and to no extent on conjecture' (UNESCO 2011, paragraph 86).

There have been exceptional cases where reconstruction has been allowed, for example the Mostar Bridge, inscribed in 2005 for its symbolic meaning 'as an exceptional and universal symbol of coexistence of communities from diverse cultural, ethnic and religious backgrounds' (UNESCO 2005). In practice, too, the Nara Declaration's emphasis that responsibility for cultural heritage rests first with the community that created it, and then with that which now sustains it, means that restoration may be appropriate in some circumstances. Normally, however, reconstruction has not been supported.

FRONTIERS OF THE ROMAN EMPIRE WHS

In the context of Roman military archaeology, the views of the UNESCO World Heritage Committee are important because of the moves to develop the Frontiers of the Roman Empire WHS. As conceived a decade ago, this property could eventually include the entire surviving remains of the Roman frontiers in around 20 countries in Europe, Asia and Africa. Transnational World Heritage properties such as this are regarded by the World Heritage Committee as single entities which need to have a common approach to management and conservation. Overall management of the Frontiers of the Roman Empire WHS is coordinated by the Intergovernmental Committee of States Parties who have part of the property on their territory (so far Germany and the United Kingdom). There is also a wider scientific advisory group, known as the Bratislava Group. This has expert members from States Parties containing inscribed or potential parts of the World Heritage Site. The Bratislava Group aims to share knowledge and experience of Roman frontiers and their identification, protection, conservation, management and presentation, leading to the distillation of a common viewpoint. More recently a site managers' group, known as the Hexham Group, has been established to be primarily responsible for developing and coordinating common approaches and sharing best practice in the management and presentation of inscribed parts of the Frontiers of the Roman Empire WHS.

So far the Frontiers of the Roman Empire WHS consists of the artificial barriers of Hadrian's Wall and the Antonine Wall in the United Kingdom and of the Upper German-Raetian Limes in Germany. Proposals are in hand for nominating parts of the riverine frontiers along both the Rhine and the Danube. The issue of reconstruction is of high importance because of the penchant among many Roman military archaeologists for reconstruction of Roman military sites. The problem has already been considered by the World Heritage Committee. In the case of the Frontiers of the Roman Empire WHS, reconstructions later than 1965 (ie after the Venice Charter) were specifically excluded from the German Limes when it was added to the World Heritage property. This means that the Saalburg fort can be included in the inscription except for the most recent additions.

This decision applied only to the German section of the Frontiers of the Roman Empire WHS. If applied to Hadrian's Wall, it would mean that the stretches of the Wall partially reconstructed by John Clayton in the 19th century would be part of the World Heritage Site but that the reconstructed buildings at Arbeia would not. Should the property be further extended to include the Roman Rhine frontier, the reconstructed elements of the legionary fortress at Xanten would presumably have to be excluded from it.

Taken at face value, therefore, the World Heritage Committee's policy on reconstruction of Roman military sites which are, or might become, parts of the Frontiers of the Roman Empire WHS seems absolutely clear – reconstructions later than 1965 cannot be part of the property and must be treated as part of a buffer zone. However, in the world of World Heritage it sometimes seems that in practice there are few absolute certainties. Despite the very clear guidance in the Operational Guidelines since 1979, it is possible to point to various cases where reconstruction or restoration has occurred. Warsaw and Mostar have already been discussed. In both those cases, special circumstances certainly applied.

There are, however, other cases which have been considered by the World Heritage Committee or its advisers which show that different treatments are possible. When the Historic Monuments of Ancient Nara were inscribed on the World Heritage List in 1998, reconstruction was an issue since parts of the palace – a purely archaeological site with no upstanding remains and covering 120ha – had been reconstructed. The reconstructed elements are the Suzaku Gate, the East Palace Garden and (still in progress) the First Imperial Audience Hall. In many ways, the situation here seems similar to that of buried Roman remains known from excavation except that there is probably more evidence from elsewhere of the appearance of Japanese buildings of this period.

ICOMOS, in their evaluation, did not regard this as an obstacle to inscription, observing that: 'There has been some *in situ* reconstruction on the Nara Palace Site. The continuity of traditional architecture in Japan and the substantial amount of data recovered by archaeological excavation has ensured that the reconstructed buildings have a high level of authenticity in design and materials' (ICOMOS 1998, 38).

The evaluation did not recommend that such reconstruction should cease. Nor did the Committee exclude reconstructions from the inscribed property. There was no suggestion that they should be treated as vertical buffer zones, as was the case for the German Limes.

Subsequent Committee decisions have merely asked for submission of full details of proposed reconstruction for their consideration before work began. Work on the reconstruction of the First Imperial Audience Hall has continued on the basis of excavation evidence and Japanese buildings elsewhere. Plans to reconstruct other parts of this compound of the palace exist.

ICOMOS also do not seem to have been concerned that the reconstruction of the East Palace Garden at Nara is based only on the archaeological evidence from the site, which means that there is inevitably some degree of conjecture in what has been done. Similarly, the recently inscribed Pure Land Buddhism landscape at Hiraizumi, also in Japan, contains four gardens, two of which have been reconstructed from rice paddy fields, and two of which are planned to be. Although this has not created an obstacle to their inclusion in the property and future reconstruction has not been ruled out, the Japanese authorities have been asked to submit proposals for the Committee's consideration before undertaking this work.

Another case is the proposal to replicate the main Tsogchin temple of the Buddhist monastery of Erden Zuu in the Orkhon Valley Cultural Landscape in Mongolia. The temple was destroyed during the Communist purge of Buddhism in the 1930s and the remains of the monastery were preserved as a museum. Following the collapse of Communism and the revival of Buddhism in the past two decades, the monastery is now used again for religious purposes and there is a demand to recreate this temple. A small amount of archaeological evidence and a few photographs exist of the temple before it was destroyed and these are considered to provide sufficient evidence for reconstruction. Because part of the Outstanding Universal Value of this cultural landscape is the continuing nomadic culture, with an emphasis on its religious element, ICOMOS seem inclined to agree the proposal in principle, provided that it is carried out to the highest standard. The recent reconstruction of another Buddhist shrine within the Orkhon Valley, the Tuvhkun monastery, was not an obstacle to inscription.

It has been argued that, in fact, reconstruction has happened within many World Heritage properties (Dushkina 2009). On the other hand, Bagrati Cathedral in Georgia was placed on the World Heritage in Danger List in 2010 because of works to restore it. The World Heritage Committee requested that the project stop immediately and that the reconstruction which has been carried out should be reversed within one to two years.

These are only a few examples of differing approaches within the application of the World Heritage Convention. In each case, the circumstances have differed greatly but it is clear that in some circumstances it is possible to accept reconstruction or even replication within a World

Heritage property of structures known primarily from archaeological evidence. In each case, the decisions of the World Heritage Committee or its advisers have been influenced by the definition of the property's Outstanding Universal Value and by the nature of the surviving evidence.

What, then, are the implications for the Frontiers of the Roman Empire WHS? Reconstruction or replication of some of its features will clearly continue to be an issue since there is obviously a continuing desire in some quarters to carry out such works. At present, the situation is anomalous since reconstructions built later than 1965 have been excluded from one part of the property but tacitly included in another. The West Gate at Arbeia was already there when Hadrian's Wall was inscribed in 1986, and two further buildings have been added subsequently. It would be helpful to have a consistent approach across the whole property since the World Heritage Operational Guidelines require such an approach. There could also be a risk to the status of the World Heritage property as a whole from reconstructions outside the guidance of the World Heritage Committee, since actions deemed damaging in one place could put the whole property at risk, according to its rules. This could, for example, have been the case with the most recent reconstructions at the Saalburg fort.

This suggests that there is a need to explore, with the UNESCO World Heritage Committee via consultations with ICOMOS and the World Heritage Centre, whether there is any potential for latitude in this area and whether ground rules on reconstruction and replication can be established which could be applied to all existing and potential elements of the Frontiers of the Roman Empire WHS and which would be acceptable to all stakeholders. It is fortunate that the Frontiers of the Roman Empire WHS has the Bratislava Group established as a scientific advisory group within an agreed management structure. This is unusual for a World Heritage property, but potentially very useful in this instance. Reconstruction is the sort of issue on which the Bratislava Group could collect evidence and develop proposals which could form the basis for discussion with ICOMOS and the World Heritage Centre. The eventual outcome of such discussions may not be predictable, but they should at least lead to firm guidance for the future that could be applied to all parts of the Frontiers of the Roman Empire WHS. In the meantime, no major plans for reconstruction should be implemented without agreement from the Intergovernmental Committee for the property.

BIBLIOGRAPHY AND REFERENCES

Australia ICOMOS, 1999 *The Burra Charter (The Australia ICOMOS Charter for Places of Cultural Significance)*, available from: http://australia.icomos.org/publications/charters/ [21 June 2012]

Breeze, D J, and Jilek, S, 2008 *Frontiers of the Roman Empire: The European Dimension of a World Heritage Site*, Historic Scotland, Edinburgh

Carroll, L, 1871 *Through the Looking-Glass, and What Alice Found There*, Macmillan, London

Dushkina, N, 2009 Historic reconstruction: prospects for heritage preservation or metamorphoses of theory?, in *Conserving the authentic: essays in honour of Jukka Jukilehto* (eds N Stanley-Price and J King), ICCROM Conservation Studies 10, ICCROM, Rome

English Heritage, 2001 *English Heritage Policy Statement on Restoration, Reconstruction, and Speculative Recreation of Archaeological Sites including Ruins*, English Heritage, London

— 2008 *Conservation Principles, Policies and Guidance for the Sustainable Management of the Historic Environment*, English Heritage, London

ICOMOS, 1990 *Charter for the Protection and Management of the Archaeological Heritage*, ICOMOS, Paris

— 1998 *Evaluation of Cultural Properties (WHC-98.CONF.203 INF.11)*, available from: http://whc.unesco.org/en/decisions/514 [21 June 2012]

Ruskin, J, 1889 (1849) *The Seven Lamps of Architecture*, 6 edn, George Allen, Orpington

Society for the Protection of Ancient Buildings (SPAB), 1877 *The Manifesto* (London), available from: http://www.spab.org.uk/what-is-spab-/the-manifesto/ [21 June 2012]

Stanley Price, N, 2009 The Reconstruction of Ruins: Principles and Practice, in *Conservation: Principles, Dilemmas and Uncomfortable Truths* (eds A Richmond and A Bracker), Butterworth-Heinemann with Victoria and Albert Museum, London

Stovel, H, 2001 Conference Report on The Riga Charter on Authenticity and Historical Reconstruction in Relationship to Cultural Heritage, *Conservation and Management of Archaeological Sites* 4, 239–40

UNESCO, 1980 *Operational Guidelines for the Implementation of the World Heritage Convention*, UNESCO, Paris

— 2005 *Decision WHC-05/ COM 8B.49*, available from: http://whc.unesco.org/en/decisions/514 [21 June 2012]

— 2011 *Operational Guidelines for the Implementation of the World Heritage Convention*, UNESCO, Paris

Venice Charter, 1964 *International Charter for the Conservation and Restoration of Monuments and Sites (The Venice Charter 1964)*, available from: http://www.icomos.org/charters/venice_e.pdf [21 June 2012]

9

A Roman Museum for Vienna

Michaela Kronberger

Introduction

Until very recently, Vienna's best preserved Roman remains were difficult for visitors to find. The Roman Ruins, as this Wien Museum site was called, are six feet below ground, directly underneath the Hoher Markt square. The remains were discovered in 1948 during work on the city sewers and comprise remnants of officers' houses. Two inconspicuous city council signs pointed the way through a restaurant to reach stairs that led down to the excavations.

Despite poor signage, approximately 15,000 visitors found their way to the museum each year. An outing to the museum is a fixed date in the schedule for Vienna's schools whenever it comes to the Romans' turn in the curriculum. However, access around the remains was so narrow that a modern approach to presenting the remains of Roman Vindobona was impossible. For pupils and teachers, who account for more than half of all visitors, the absence of any visitor infrastructure (especially toilets) was a major inconvenience. Acknowledgment of this problem was a catalyst for the train of events that led to the opening of a new Roman Museum in early May 2008.

When it became known in spring 2007 that the premises above the excavations would be available to let, the Wien Museum management team seized the opportunity to modify the building and implement a state-of-the-art museum concept. Families, those interested in Vienna's history and tourists were all identified, alongside school children, as key target audiences.

Architects from Querkraft were brought in for the innovative redesign of the building which had been erected in 1956. The construction programme involved several modifications to the building which were implemented over a period of time. So as to include existing features rather than cover them over, the decision was taken to sheath the facade of the building with metal springs that resemble tesserae or ashlars. This decision has given the Roman Museum a physical presence on the exterior of the building whilst retaining the building's integrity (Fig 9.1).

It was much more difficult to create generous exhibition areas from the long and narrow interior space, which contained a conspicuous staircase and numerous small rooms. The solution lay in moving the stairs onto one longitudinal wall, thereby creating a vertical opening spanning three floors, from the excavations in the cellar up to the first floor. As well as creating a dramatic space, this design resulted in a massive wall measuring 26 feet at its highest point which could be used for presentation and display. The banisters were designed to include display cases, enabling linkage between displays in the main exhibition area and the huge concept wall (Figs 9.2, 9.3 and 9.4).

FIG 9.1. THE FACADE OF THE ROMAN MUSEUM AT HOHER MARKT 3.

FIG 9.2. THE UPPER FLOOR OF THE ROMAN MUSEUM. THE DISPLAY BOXES ALONG THE HANDRAILS ARE ARRANGED IN CONTEXT WITH INFORMATION ON THE WALL.

VINDOBONA AND THE HISTORY OF THE CITY OF VIENNA

The main aim in designing the new Roman Museum was to enable the visitor to experience the history of the city: on the one hand to be able to relate the ancient topography to that of today; on the other hand to engage with the people who lived here long ago.

Almost every route taken daily by Viennese people in the central districts of their city overlies layers of earth that reveal Vienna's rich history. Many know that the legionary fortress of Vindobona, founded at the end of the first century AD, was located somewhere in the first district. Some streets and place names, such as the Graben, provide clues to the past through their

FIG 9.3. THE EXHIBITION'S GRAPHICS ARE SHADED FOR EMPHASIS. ON THE RIGHT IS THE STAIRCASE DOWN
TO THE EXCAVATION SITE.

names or through their alignment. An example of the latter is the Naglergasse, which follows
the line of the former defensive walls, although the actual topographical relationship is poorly
understood. Outside a small circle of scientists and archaeological enthusiasts with specialist
knowledge, few are aware of the large garrison settlement outside the fortress that developed
in a semi-circle around it and was home to merchants, craftsmen, families of the soldiers, inn-
keepers, prostitutes and so on. Likewise little is known about the civil town, with its mainly
native population, or the rural settlements located in the surroundings of Vienna, important for
supplying the urban centres.

The selection of objects for display in the new museum was determined not only by their
intrinsic interest as objects (value, interest, visual impact, age etc) but also by the stories they
could illustrate. These stories included the process of manufacture, how and when they were used
and by whom, how they were buried and how they were rediscovered after nearly 2000 years.
These objects are often the best link to the lives of the people who once owned them, given the
paucity of literary sources.

Our knowledge of the fortress site of Vindobona and its surroundings has improved considerably in recent years through intensive research, new excavations, and the Vienna Museum inven-

tory project.[1] The approach to the interpretation of this research for visitors involved identifying specific questions felt to be of interest to a wide audience, including:

- Where were the settlement centres?
- Who lived in Vindobona before the Romans?
- What did the buildings look like? Who lived in them?
- Did the local people really prefer to settle in the civil town?
- Did soldiers also have families?
- What did the legionaries do during peacetime?
- Who built the aqueduct of Vindobona?
- Did all Romans come from Italy?
- What did the inhabitants of Vindobona eat?

The selected questions and their answers provide the basic structure around which the exhibition was built. Due to space limitations the exhibition concentrates on the growth of Vindobona from around the middle of the second to the middle of the third centuries AD.

ARCHITECTURE, GRAPHICS AND CONCEPT: A HOLISTIC AND INTERDISCIPLINARY APPROACH

A long and intensive discussion process between the graphic artist, the team of architects and the curators to develop a conceptual approach to presentation preceded the implementation of the project. The common goal was to create an exhibition which would make often complex scientific content accessible to a wide range of audiences. At the same time there was the clear commitment to impart knowledge. The long-standing belief that archaeological artefacts can speak for themselves without being placed in context was rejected. The approach taken was to divide interpretation into distinct chapters with their own content, summary texts in appropriate font size and graphic information. The latter in particular was useful in replacing long paragraphs of text. Selection of each exhibition object involved an assessment of its cultural–historical background and its role in the context of the story being told. As a consequence, many inconspicuous everyday items are presented in the museum alongside high quality works of art.

The discussion regarding the exhibition's architecture was especially interesting. One issue was that the exhibition space was broken up by numerous metal supports. This problem was solved by covering the walls of the exhibition room with a variegated surface, allowing displays to be individually adapted to different themes. Large objects, such as architectural elements, were mounted so that their original setting and function could be registered at a glance. Graphic illustrations were also used to enable better understanding. Structural elements were emphasised by shading designed to provide an impression of the original size and/or position in the architectural structure (Fig 9.3).

One special challenge was the design of the huge staircase wall. It provided the opportunity to link the different elements of Roman Vienna through a large graphic display. From a central image of present-day Vienna overlain with the settlement centres of antiquity and positioned directly in the visitors' line of sight, lines were drawn over three floors connecting the various

---

[1] Information about archaeological research on Roman Vienna is available in the publication series of the Stadtarchäologie Wien, available from: http://www.wien.gv.at/archaeologie/publikationen/index.html [20 August 2012].

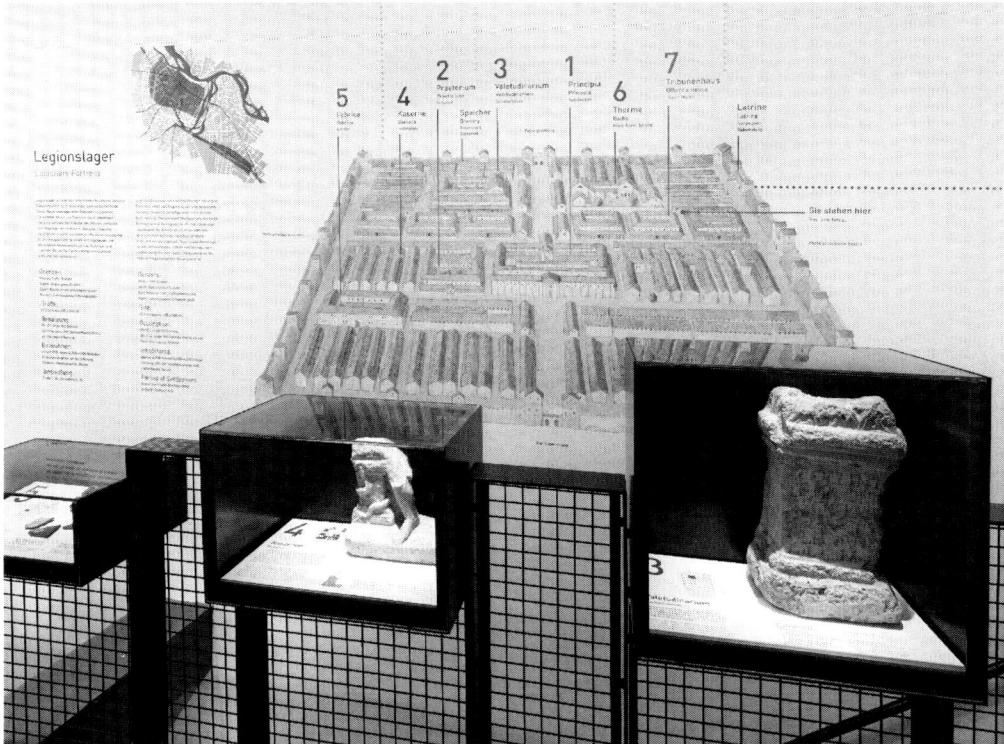

FIG 9.4. IMMEDIATELY UPON ENTRY, VISITORS SHOULD BE MADE FAMILIAR WITH THE TOPOGRAPHY OF ROMAN VINDOBONA AND HOW IT RELATES TO THE VIENNA OF TODAY.

topographic chapters of Roman Vienna (legionary fortress, civil town, urban settlement outside the fortress, rural settlement and graveyard). For example, one line leads to the legionary fortress which is depicted by a graphic illustration. On the same level, separated from the illustration by the staircase, is the area of the permanent exhibition that focuses on this topic. In the handrail leading to the stairs is a series of display cases, each one dedicated to one of the central buildings of the legionary fortress. The captions in the display cases and the artefacts on display are closely related to the wall graphic (Fig 9.4).

ILLUSTRATION, RECONSTRUCTION, ANIMATION

Visualising buildings or whole settlements is one of the most controversial topics in archaeology and this project proved to be no exception. Given the target audiences that the Wien Museum identified for the new Roman Museum, it was clear from the outset that an important requirement was to provide families and non-specialist visitors with a visual impression of how Vindobona may have looked.

However, it is difficult to achieve complete scientific accuracy in depicting building development spanning nearly 1900 years in a densely populated urban area. As in examples elsewhere, the archaeological evidence from the site has to be used alongside comparable evidence from other places to reconstruct the likely appearance of buildings in Vindobona. So as not to mislead visitors into believing Vindobona looked exactly the same as presented in the displays, two different visual approaches were adopted.

The first approach was to use graphic illustrations in the style used in children's books, mounted directly on to the wall. These illustrations intuitively convey the idea that the images represent an imaginative reconstruction. The layout of the buildings and the evolution of the settlement depicted in the illustrations were nonetheless based on the latest scientific evidence. The colour pigments of the graphics were obtained from soil unearthed during excavations in Vienna.

The second approach was through computer-animated film. A particular priority was to include ways of depicting spatial relationships and building elevations that presented slight variations on the solutions chosen for the graphic illustrations. It was felt that, in this way, visitors might understand that there is more than one way of depicting the buildings and layouts and that there is scope to use one's imagination.

LOOKING IS JUST NOT ENOUGH!

Adult visitors as well as children have the urge to touch objects. Understanding is achieved through sensory means as well as by the transfer of knowledge in written or visual form. Special attention was devoted to children in the design of the exhibits. A variety of interactive elements were integrated into the exhibition to place exhibits (objects and text) in context. This decision was made so as not to create an isolated peripheral zone for younger visitors, but instead granting them space as an integral part of the exhibition. Additionally, a number of handling replicas were made and included amongst the exhibits. Three computer stations distributed throughout the Museum encourage visitors to undertake further research. Two stations offer opportunities to find out more about the excavations in Vienna. A third station traces the long process and the many steps that archaeological finds have to go through, from excavation to storage or presentation in a museum. One of the museum's main attractions – a *mortarium* dating from the second century AD – can be seen in an adjacent display case and can be reconstructed through a 3D puzzle.

AT THE HEART OF RESEARCH ABOUT VIENNA

The Roman Museum includes a small exhibition area intended for temporary displays. This is envisaged primarily as a platform for the various institutions concerned with Vienna's Roman past to present their latest research and finds. The intention is for the Roman Museum to provide a meeting point for all those involved with the archaeology of Vienna. Since the opening of the Roman Museum, the results of four important excavations have been presented by the Stadtarchaeologie Wien, the Austrian Federal Office for the Care of Monuments (Bundesdenkmalamt) and the Archäologie Service.

VIDEO GUIDE

A multimedia video guide has been available for visitors since 2009. It offers information additional to the exhibitions in English, German and, for the first time, in sign language. The project was promoted by the city of Vienna, together with the Schulungs- und BeratungsGmbH Equalizent, the NOUS company, and the Museum of Modern Art Stiftung Ludwig Wien and was implemented during the course of the project.

ACCESS FOR VISITORS WITH DISABILITIES

For visitors with impaired mobility a wheelchair-accessible stairclimber provides access to all three floors of the museum and the display cases were designed to enable exhibits to be viewed comfortably by wheelchair users. As noted above, the exhibition contains objects that can be touched and the plan is to make the exhibition fully accessible for the visually impaired and blind.

Vistors with learning disabilities have also been catered for with a view to making the museum fully free of barriers. Text information was carefully kept short, concise and simple to understand and complemented by numerous illustrative graphics. Visitors should be able to gain an impression of ancient Vindobona without reference to the text.

REVIEW AND CONCLUSION

In retrospect, the five years of running the new outpost of the Vienna Museum can be looked back on with satisfaction. The marked increase in visitors (an average of 21,000 a year) and the numerous positive entries in the visitors' book attest to the success of the Roman Museum, as does the award of Austrian Museum of the Year Prize for 2009, a distinctive award by the Austrian Federal Ministry for Education, Arts and Culture.[2]

FACTS AND FIGURES

Architecture: Querkraft Architekten (http://www.querkraft.at).
Graphics: Larissa Cerny.
Concept and Curatorial Implementation: Michaela Kronberger, Kristina Adler-Woelfl.
Curatorial Assistance: Sandro Fasching, Constanze Sarbiak, Roman Skomorowski.
Animated Films: Medienagentur 7reasons (http://www.limes.co.at).
Illustrated Paintings: Bernhard Muenzenmayer-Stipanits (www.b-muenzenmayer.com).
Interactive Games: Walter Pehn (http://www.upgrade.cc).

[2] For visitors' information about the Roman Museum, please see: http://www.wienmuseum.at [20 August 2012].

10

Woerden – Hoochwoert (Dutch Limes): Showing the Invisible

Tom Hazenberg

Introduction

In the Dutch city of Woerden, civil servants, local authorities, developers, enthusiastic citizens and archaeologists have succeeded, by working together, in revealing to the general public the city's invisible Roman past. There are several reasons for this success. The aim of bringing the Roman past to life through visual display was an integral aspect of an archaeological heritage management programme, and served a range of purposes (social, historical, educational and commercial). The framework that was built for presenting the city's Roman history concerned not only the hardware (pictures, displays etc) but also the people who use it, such as guides and teachers. All of this amounts to a considerable advance in bringing the invisible Roman past to life and in highlighting the importance and value of archaeology to the city. This chapter looks back on the path taken to realising the vision of Roman Woerden, paying special attention to the process and to key decisions made along the way.

The Woerden – Hoochwoert Project: Development, Research and Storytelling

Work has been ongoing since the 1990s to develop a new shopping complex around a yet-to-be-constructed square by the Church of St Peter (Petruskerk) in the centre of the typical Dutch fortified city of Woerden. The development included an underground car park designed to hold 560 cars. Thanks to years of archaeological research it was known that the *castellum Laurium* had to be somewhere in the neighbourhood of this church, but its exact location was not determined until 1999. The design of the planned car park was adjusted to ensure the almost total *in situ* preservation of the *castellum*. The final large excavation campaigns of 2002 to 2004 focused mainly on the enormous construction pit of the car park, later dubbed the Castellumgarage. Only a few trenches were excavated within the *castellum* itself.

For the 2002–2004 excavations, an integrated approach was formulated to plan and monitor all aspects of the archaeological heritage management programme (Hazenberg 2003). Four objectives were defined in this integrated masterplan:

1. protect the castellum
2. carry out high-end research into the Roman era in Woerden, focusing on the following main elements: the castellum, the vicus, the infrastructure and the Rhine
3. organise activities for the general public during the excavations
4. place the excavation results in the public domain and present them to the inhabitants of, and visitors to, Woerden.

We can now look back on the end result with pride and satisfaction. The *castellum* has been mostly preserved and is currently at the centre of a legal process which should ensure its legal protection (objective 1). The excavations were carried out by an enthusiastic and experienced team of archaeologists on the basis of a Project Outline (Programma van Eisen) produced by the Dutch National Service for Cultural Heritage (Rijksdienst voor het Cultureel Erfgoed). Publication was achieved within the deadline in parallel with dissemination of information concerning the more significant discoveries to an international audience (Hazenberg and Vos 2010; Vos *et al* 2011). Results of the analysis of the wood from the Roman ship Woerden 7 gave rise to doctoral research on comparable Roman ships found in The Netherlands (objective 2). The overall results of the excavation programme are presented briefly below.

Considerable attention was devoted to informing the general public during the course of the excavations. This was accomplished by means of an extensive promotional package comprising newsletters, a website, tours, educational programmes, regular press conferences and an on-site viewing tower. Around 15,000 people visited the exhibition of the Roman ship Woerden 7 (objective 3).

The final aim, of placing the archaeological results in the public domain and presenting them for the benefit of local people and visitors (objective 4), is the main subject of this chapter.

THE ARCHAEOLOGICAL EVIDENCE

As mentioned earlier, the 2002–2004 excavation programme can be regarded as the conclusion of 30 years' research in Woerden's city centre. The first 25 years' research was carried out by the Radbout University in Nijmegen, under the direction of professors Jules Bogaers and Jan-Kees Haalebos. Professor Haalebos assisted staff of ADC ArcheoProjecten in setting up the final programme, but was unable to witness the outcome, owing to his unexpected death. Wouter Vos and Edwin Blom directed the major excavations of the 2002–2004 programme and published a new overview of Roman Woerden (Blom and Vos 2008; Vos *et al* 2010).

The earliest feature of Roman Woerden is the Roman fort, possibly constructed around the time that Caligula was preparing an invasion of Britannia. This fort, Woerden I, may have formed part of a pre-Limes phase which is thought to have existed, based on information derived from recent research in Utrecht-De Leidsche Rijn, Alphen aan den Rijn and Valkenburg (province of Zuid-Holland). Woerden I was in use for only a brief period of time. Upon creation of the Limes by the emperor Claudius, a new location in the vicinity of Woerden I was selected for the construction of a true frontier fortification, Woerden II. The development of the *castellum* can be tracked up to construction phase Woerden IV, by which time it was either partially or entirely built of stone.

Only limited research was carried out on the *castellum* as it was under little threat from development. The main information came from the stratigraphy of the defensive ditches and a number of small excavation trenches in the interior that revealed foundations of barracks-like structures. A significant find was that of a foundation supporting a low-standing wall which, from its location, was probably the southern wall of the *principia*.

Much was expected of the *vicus* that was supposed to lie between the *castellum* and the Rhine. However, as is so often the case in Dutch Limes research, this excavation failed to yield a clear overview of a military *vicus*. The finds assemblage indicates that the *vicus* appeared at the end of the first century and was used intensively up to the beginning of the third century. Several strip houses were identified from the soil features and the existence of a public bathhouse is suspected nearby. Two rows of large stone blocks may represent the foundations of a boathouse.

In contrast to the disappointing evidence from the *vicus*, the shipwrecks of Woerden are major highlights, not just for Woerden but on a national and international level. The remains of no fewer than seven ships have been found in Woerden since 1978. Unfortunately, just three ships (Woerden 1, Woerden 7 and a rafter of Woerden 8) have been documented by means of excavation. The others are known through a written source (Woerden 4) and through rescue operations ensuing after accidental discoveries (Woerden 2/6, Woerden 3 and Woerden 5). An overview of the Roman ships is provided below (Table 10.1):

Table 10.1: Roman shipwrecks, discovered in Woerden (NL)

Woerden 1	1978	barge laden with Belgian grain
Woerden 2/6	1988 / 1998	barge
Woerden 3	1988	woodcut canoe
Woerden 4	1576	barge?
Woerden 5	1998	woodcut canoe
Woerden 7	2003	barge with rowing rig, constructed from 'German' and 'Dutch' wood
Woerden 8	2003	galley

Both excavated barges have yielded valuable information. Woerden 1 sank along with its cargo of grain from what is now Belgium, providing a good insight into the supply routes of food destined for the Limes troops. Woerden 7 (Fig 10.1) revealed two major new pieces of evidence. First, archaeologists discovered a rowing rig on the starboard side of the transom. This was the first evidence of rowers on a barge of the Zwammerdam type, raising the possibility of an additional method of propelling such vessels. Subsequently a rowing rig was discovered on one of the Zwammerdam vessels, Zwammerdam 6, which is of comparable design in other respects also. Another discovery was equally remarkable: Woerden 7 turned out to have been constructed not only from oak from the Eiffel, but also from local wood. This fact, coupled with the great similarities in construction to Zwammerdam 6, gives rise to the proposition that these ships were constructed locally – the earliest evidence of shipbuilding in the area.

Besides yielding information on the general picture of *castellum*, *vicus* and shipping, the excavations also produced numerous attractive finds: a frog-shaped fibula, a Germanic sword, four gems and many metal objects. All of this information and evidence was included in some form in the visual displays and publications intended for the general public.

PRESENTING THE ROMANS IN WOERDEN – AIMS AND BEGINNINGS

Although the programme for archaeological heritage management was designed to integrate protection, research and public presentation, the development of permanent presentation was not tackled as a distinct major project. However, despite the fact that development and decision-making for this aspect of the programme occurred in a rather *ad hoc* way, the integrated approach nonetheless created a framework for success. Right from the very start of the Woerden–Hooch-woert project in 2002, decisions were made to ensure that once the research had been concluded

FIG 10.1. EXCAVATION OF THE WOERDEN 7 BOAT.

there would be money available to realise the ultimate aim of public presentation. The municipality of Woerden set money aside at the start of the programme and was later able to use this as
match funding to draw on other sources of finance, including the developer Multi Development,
Reaal and the province of Utrecht. An important conclusion is that astute decisions made right
at the start of the programme to set aside funds for public presentation led to an increase in
capacity for public outreach.

There was no predetermined plan for how to go about presenting Roman Woerden, nor had
any solid public opinion survey been undertaken to inform presentation. During the research
phase of the programme the general public was, however, asked to participate in thinking about
possible ways of presenting the information to the public. This included Archeologie Actueel
Live, an event in Woerden's City Hall for local people and archaeologists, organised by alderman
Wim Groeneweg. These ideas were subsequently included in the presentation designs. Additionally, the designers were able to draw on extensive knowledge of Roman Woerden resulting
from the excavations, and on experience of communicating this information to a wide range
of audiences including passers-by, archaeologists and schoolchildren while the excavations were
in progress. The same approaches that were adopted in catering to all these different audiences
during the excavations were applied in the permanent displays.

Analysing the process of producing the permanent displays reveals a formula for success: an
historic framework for, by and about people. Through communication and events, the history
of the location has been displayed and brought to life. Through their active participation in
the process of developing the permanent displays, the Roman history of Woerden appeals to

many different audiences and enhances the role of Woerden–Hoochwoert as a meeting place and attractive shopping centre.

Several key principles were applied in designing the permanent displays. The displays must be attractive to people hastening past them on their way to the shops, yet also be informative for those who want to know more about Roman Woerden. Some people come to Woerden especially to see them. A layered approach enables people to be informed according to their level of interest. Different archaeological viewpoints and uncertain interpretations of evidence are also shared at varying levels of detail, designed for groups of schoolchildren as well as historically-minded visitors.

The stories and images of Roman Woerden were developed by the same archaeologists who carried out the excavations and published the results. It was also these archaeologists who helped draw the general public into the world of their discoveries during the excavations. This was a two-way process with archaeologists and the public engaging with each other and exploring their respective ways of seeing the world around them. As a result, there was no question of any tension between academic and public archaeology in this project. Such a shared experience offers a fertile breeding ground for open discussion between the general public and archaeologists.

Another principle applied extensively was that of *lieux de mémoire*: signposting the exact locations where Roman remains were discovered. Examples are the *castellum* wall, the Roman shipping waterway, the Woerden 7 ship profiles and the stratigraphy of *castellum* Laurium. This approach helps the inhabitants of Woerden to realise that they are part of the rich history of their city.

During the design phase, various attempts were made to utilise professional designers. This failed time and again, mainly due to the archaeologists' and designers' misunderstanding of each other – a clash between storytelling and form. The decision not to use professional designers resulted in highly informative, simply designed presentations of the Roman past. A deliberate decision was also made to utilise tried and tested materials and techniques of presentation. Only in a few instances were more innovative methods employed. The most innovative achievement was in implementing an archaeological heritage management programme in such an integrated and holistic way, using simple techniques on a moderate budget.

The results can be divided into the physical infrastructure of presenting Roman Woerden – the hardware – on the one hand and the peopling and animation of this infrastructure – the software – on the other.

THE HARDWARE: AN INFRASTRUCTURE FOR PRESENTING WOERDEN'S ROMAN HISTORY

Walking through Woerden, one sees physical reminders of Roman history in many places. Visitors to and inhabitants of Woerden are exposed to the archaeological discoveries of the city in public spaces above and below the ground. They can also encounter them in the Stadsmuseum Woerden and in a book that is accessible to all. A schematic overview of the physical historical infrastructure of Roman Woerden follows below (Table 10.2).

As mentioned above, proven methods of display were used including enlargements of attractive finds and traditional reconstruction drawings, all printed on indestructible dibond. Other traditional methods include granite plaques that delimit the *castellum*, attractive but simple information panels and a beautiful but standard full-colour book. Some artist's impressions of Woerden in Roman times were produced specifically for the book (see Fig 10.2). Only a few

Table 10.2: The physical historical infrastructure of Roman Woerden (NL)

Object/find/theme	Location	Location type	Interpretive media
Border of the *castellum*	Kerkplein, Havenstraat, Hogewoerd	street	Granite strip
Roman Strip Cartoon	Kerkplein	street	History in words and picture engraved granite strip cartoon
Roman Ship Tour	Passim	street	Information panels at find locations of Roman Ships
Frog-shaped fibula	Entrance Kerkplein	parking	Display of the real object
Time Travel	Elevators	parking	Lightbox that leads the visitor through the Middle Ages and into Roman times
Archaeological excavation	Level -2	parking	Photo gallery
Special finds	Level -2	parking	Pictures of metal finds and gems
Vicus	Level -2	parking	Reconstruction: view from the gate of the *castellum* towards the *vicus* and the river Rhine
Victor and Titullinus	Level -1	parking	Children's game
Woerden 7 findspot	Level -1	parking	Exact location of Woerden 7, displayed as a 1:1 scale picture and technical drawing
Laurium – the Roman settlement	Level -1	parking	Reconstruction: view from the Rhine toward the harbour, *vicus* and *castellum Laurium*
Woerden 7 display	Level -1	parking	Diorama of the remains of Woerden 7 combined with two models of children at play set against a bank of the Rhine, with the *castellum* in the background
Roman Woerden	Stadsmuseum Woerden	Museum	Simple exhibition of the most important Roman finds of Woerden
Romeinen in Woerden		Book	Popular scientific full-colour book, 240 pages, 600 illustrations

elements of the displays used more innovative techniques. One example is the original frog-shaped fibula displayed beside the pay station of the car park, protected by thick glass. Another example is the remains of the Woerden 7 ship. These remains have been outstandingly preserved by the Museum für Antike Schiffahrt and are displayed behind glass but without additional preservation facilities. This is the first time that such a large part of a Roman barge has been displayed without using expensive preservation methods. This accessible approach allows the Dutch general public to become acquainted with such boats.

A conscious decision was made not to make use of audiovisual techniques or modern mobile data media. Audiovisual techniques were avoided for fear of high maintenance costs. Modern media have not yet been utilised but can be easily incorporated in due course. The lightbox in the elevators that transport the visitor into Roman times and back to the present is the only display in Woerden that includes a technical component: jumping lights which signal each new floor.

FIG 10.2. COLOURING PICTURE OF WOERDEN IN ROMAN TIMES.

THE SOFTWARE: GUIDES, PUBLIC AND EVENTS

During the development of Roman Woerden, the creators learned that an infrastructure without users cannot last very long. These users are visitors, of course, and being accompanied by experienced local guides allows them to enjoy Roman Woerden all the more. As well as providing guided tours, the guides also ensure that the physical infrastructure of Roman Woerden is maintained and repaired as required. It is also vital that large events take place regularly around Roman Woerden, so that the Roman past retains its prominent position within the branding and destination marketing of the city of Woerden. The guides and events are the heart and soul of Roman Woerden's infrastructure and represent the driving force behind the public's perception of Roman Woerden.

Effective cooperation had developed between archaeologists and municipal officers on the one hand and two groups of guides on the other as part of the public engagement activities during the 2002–2004 excavations. One of the groups of guides was the Gilde, a group of enthusiastic inhabitants of Woerden accustomed to providing historical walks. This group took it upon itself to incorporate the excavations into its story of the city, expanding it with Roman history. While the excavations were in progress, the group delivered guided tours drawing on up-to-date information provided by the archaeologists. The Gilde now forms a central group that makes extensive use of the physical display infrastructure; all tours provided through the tourist information office are organised by the Gilde.

FIG 10.3. TEACHING SCHOOLCHILDREN IN THE CASTELLUMGARAGE.

Another guide group is the KUVO-CEC foundation which organises cultural education for all schools in the Woerden region, commissioned by the municipality. It too organised Roman-themed classes focused around the 2002–2004 excavations. From 2007 onwards, the group transformed these classes into a permanent programme of Roman-themed learning activities, both on the streets and in the Castellumgarage (Fig 10.3). After talks with the managers of the Castellumgarage, it was agreed to keep a section of the car park free of cars twice a week for the duration of one of the activities: the Victor and Titullinus game. This is safer for children... and for the cars.

The success of Roman Woerden has prompted other initiatives. Since 2009, a replica of the Roman ship De Meern 1, also excavated in 2003, has been sailing around Woerden. The ship is under the control of the Romeins Schip foundation. Its berth and a share of the start-up costs were facilitated by the municipality, but it is now wholly managed by volunteers and has grown into a great public attraction. Visitors to this attraction are also shown around Roman Woerden.

When the municipality announced the completion of the Woerden–Hoochwoert project in April 2011, the volunteer groups, in cooperation with the local historical society, declared 2011 and 2012 to be Years of the Romans and introduced a whole range of related events. This illustrates that Roman Woerden's physical infrastructure, issuing from various professional disciplines, has been wholly adopted by the general public, creating a platform through which further to explore, safeguard and present the city's Roman past.

RESULTS AND EVALUATION

In Woerden, the cooperative efforts of many different groups of people, civil servants, local authorities, developers, citizens and archaeologists have resulted in a type of visitor and educational infrastructure for Roman archaeology and history that is rare in the Netherlands. That infrastructure includes walking routes, displays, fine reconstruction drawings of Roman Woerden, boat rides on a Roman ship and a museum. Everything is managed and animated by enthusiastic and knowledgeable guides. Those who seek further information can read more in an attractive book.

It is unsurprising that Woerden has won prizes for its efforts. After being nominated for the European Association of Archaeologists' Archaeological Heritage Prize, Woerden won the Dutch Ym van der Werff prize for Cultural Heritage in 2007. In 2008, the Castellumgarage was nominated for the VexPan prize for most attractive multi-storey car park. The city's most welcome prize, however, is the enthusiasm displayed by an increasing number of visitors to Roman Woerden. It would be fair to cautiously conclude that the Romans have had a positive impact on tourism in Woerden. Roman Woerden offers interested parties an effective and innovative display infrastructure through which a compelling story is told, combined with the memorable experience of inland navigation through Roman times in a replica Roman ship.

The site's educational impact has also been considerable. All schoolchildren in Woerden and its surrounding area take the full Roman tour at least once during their school lives, supplemented by special classes at school. Taken as a whole, Roman Woerden is a rather remarkable achievement for the Dutch Limes, where literally not a single remnant visibly recalls the Roman era. It is a fine example of displaying the invisible!

The reasons for this achievement are diverse. A key factor was the desire to display and bring to life the Roman past that formed part of an integrated archaeological heritage management programme. An important lesson to take from the Woerden example is that limiting the research budget and making provision for public display at the start of the project resulted in an even greater benefit for the city's Roman heritage than could have been provided by research alone, leading as it did to greater public understanding and engagement. Following the research phase, archaeology has successfully served further purposes: a social purpose in strengthening the volunteer community through the creation of a Roman display infrastructure; an educational purpose by allowing citizens and school pupils to become acquainted with the history of the place in which they live and work; and a commercial purpose by stimulating cultural tourism and by enhancing the feeling of safety in the Castellumgarage. The seeds of success were sown in the realism of the planning phase and in the decision to engage people in animating the Roman display infrastructure.

There is one final observation of great importance. During the entire duration of the project, from 2002 to 2011, the core team consisted mainly of the same people and the early successes of the excavations fed into a widely-held desire to return the Roman past to the inhabitants of Woerden, engaging them as active participants in the process of displaying and animating their city's Roman past. At the end of the day, it is people who accomplish things, and the city and its inhabitants have received the reward that they deserve.

BIBLIOGRAPHY AND REFERENCES

Blom, E, and Vos, W K (eds), 2008 *Woerden – Hoochwoert. De opgravingen 2002–2004 in het Romeinse castellum Laurium, de vicus en van het schip de 'Woerden 7'*, Amersfoort, ADC Monografie 2

Hazenberg, T, 2003 *Totaalplan archeologie Kerkplein en omgeving: gemeente Woerden*, Hazenberg AMZ Publicatie 2003 – 1, Leiden

Hazenberg, T, and Vos, W K, 2010 An extraordinary sword from Roman Woerden (NL), in *Waffen in Aktion. Akten der 16. Internationalen Roman Military Equipment Conference (ROMEC), Xanten* (eds H-J Schalles/A W Busch), 13–16 June 2007 (Xantener Berichte 16), 217–21

Vos, W K, Blom, E, and Hazenberg, T, 2010 *Romeinen in Woerden. Het archeologische onderzoek naar de militaire bezetting en de scheepvaart van Laurium*, Hazenberg Archeologie, Leiden

Vos, W K, Morel, J, and Hazenberg, T, 2011 The Woerden 7: an oar-powered Roman barge built in the Netherlands – details on the excavation at the Nieuwe Markt in Woerden (Hoochwoert), *Archäologisches Korrespondenzblatt* 41/1, 101–18

11

Mainlimes Mobil: Presenting Archaeology and Museums with the Help of Smartphones

Erik Dobat, Sandra Walkshofer and Christof Flügel

The Development of an Idea

Our special interest is the presentation of archaeological information to the public using modern technologies and moving images (Walkshofer and Dobat 2005). At the Limes Congress in Newcastle in 2009 we presented the film *The Limes on the River Main*. This film was designed to present the different forts of the Main Limes and its archaeological remains through the website www.museen-mainlimes.de. The challenge was to create a short 13-minute film that could be watched in sequences so that web designers could link a specific archaeological site directly to the corresponding sequence in the film.

Based on that project we developed the idea of presenting film sequences at the archaeological sites themselves, using mobile phones. The Landesstelle für die nichtstaatlichen Museen and the Bayerische Sparkassenstiftung agreed to initiate a prototype project for the Limes in Bavaria to explore the possibilities of this new technology. We had been experimenting with video on mobile phones for as long as we had been interested in the project, but, in terms of user experience, the quality of video on the small colour displays available at that time was poor. However, the idea that in the near future the viewer would have in their pocket the hardware to view multimedia content anywhere was constantly on our minds.

The development of smartphones in the last few years has turned that idea into reality. It is now possible to present high quality videos, audio sequences, stills and text-based information on mobile devices. Based on our experience with documentary films, we can distribute video content to audiences in new ways using smartphone technology. It is now possible to produce interactive documentaries, but we also have to develop new narrative techniques and explore the capabilities of the new technology (Walkshofer and Dobat 2006, 125). Most smartphones today provide GPS navigation and have an integrated compass. This enables us to navigate users to archaeological sites in the landscape and provide high quality information, right on the spot, through their own mobile devices. Archaeology provides the perfect data and content to explore this new potential: it is possible to link an archaeological site with museum collections and vice versa. These new location-based services can provide new experiences for users. It is no longer necessary to rent technical devices from a museum or other institution – instead it is possible to upload the information to your mobile device and use it for as long as you wish; and you can obtain the information about a site when you are at the site.

ARCHAEOLOGICAL CONTENT: FRONTIERS OF THE ROMAN EMPIRE WORLD HERITAGE SITE

Defining a Test Region

In 2009 we started developing the idea of providing an archaeological information system that would be accessible through a mobile device. We started to think about platforms and technical requirements, but the most important need was to find a test region in which to develop a prototype. Together with the Landesstelle für nichtstaatliche Museen in Bayern and the CHC – Research Group for Archaeometry and Cultural Heritage Computing of the University of Salzburg (Austria), we worked on media content for the innovative web-based project, www. museen-mainlimes.de. Through this project, archaeological information concerning the *Frontiers of the Roman Empire: Upper German-Raetian Limes World Heritage Site* in the region of the River Main has been gathered into a complex web database. The web interface enables easy access to content and information. Because of the advanced database behind the interface, the content is always displayed in a unique way and there are also many cross references between different archaeological sites of the region (Schaller and Flügel 2010).

The project provided us with a great deal of information about the Main Limes and we had already created a lot of footage for the media section of the website (Flügel *et al* 2011b). The Main Limes is a relatively small and clearly defined region and therefore perfectly suited for development of a prototype (Fig 11.1). We decided to concentrate on the Bavarian part of the Main Limes, excluding the two northernmost forts at Seligenstadt and Großkrotzenburg in Hesse.

THE ARCHAEOLOGY OF THE LIMES ALONG THE RIVER MAIN

In 2005 the Upper German-Raetian Limes became part of the Frontiers of the Roman Empire World Heritage Site as designated by UNESCO. The Limes in the region of the river Main (Main Limes) is part of the Upper German Limes. From Miltenberg in Bavaria to Großkrotzenburg in Hesse, the River Main marks the frontier of the Roman Empire. Between the Odenwald forest and the Spessart forest the river runs for approximately 50km from south to north.

Late in the reign of the emperor Antoninus Pius (AD 138 – AD 161), the final course of the Limes was set in the Main region. The so-called Odenwald Limes was abandoned and the Main Limes was extended either from the fort of Obernburg or the fort of Wörth to Miltenberg. From Miltenberg the new artificial frontier line ran for approximately 80km straight to the south where the Upper German Limes met the Raetian Limes in the Rotenbach valley next to Lorch.

The Main Limes was controlled by nine forts. Two of these, the fort of Großkrotzenburg in Hesse and the fort of Miltenberg-Bürgstadt (Ostkastell) guarded the transition from the artificial frontier over land to the river frontier line along the River Main. Six forts were occupied by regular *cohortes* (Großkrotzenburg, Seligenstadt, Stockstadt, Obernburg, Miltenberg-Altstadtkastell), while three smaller forts were occupied by so-called *numeri* (Steidl 2008).

In general it is difficult to present the remains of the World Heritage Site along the Main Limes. At present only two watchtowers have been discovered along the river frontier, located just to the south of Obernburg; most of the remains of watchtowers have probably been destroyed by flooding. Where archaeology is known it is usually not visible on the ground. In many cases modern towns have been built on top of the Roman forts and nothing can be seen today. There are only a few sites where some archaeological remains are visible. At the so-called Altstadtkastell of Miltenberg, for example, the remains of the stone wall of the fort can be seen in an orchard

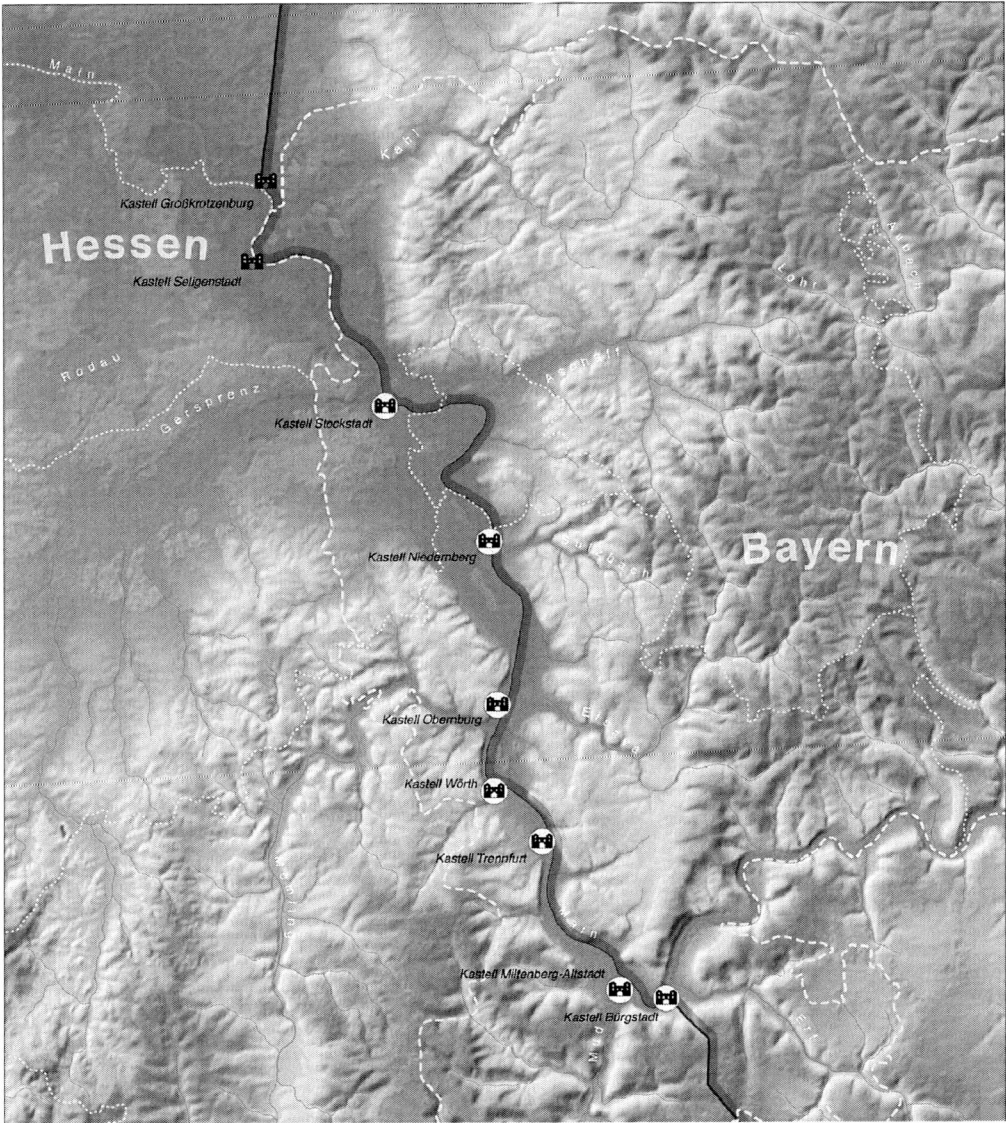

FIG 11.1. THE MAIN LIMES.

and the remains of the bathhouse of the fort have been preserved. The *principia* of the fort itself is not visible, but the remains of a medieval church built on top of the *principia* can still be seen.

The forts of Stockstadt, Niedernberg, Obernburg and Miltenberg-Bürgstadt have been built over: the fort of Stockstadt has been destroyed by the construction of a modern factory on top of the Roman remains; the *numerus* fort of Miltenberg-Bürgstadt lies beneath a residential complex; and the forts of Niedernberg and Obernburg underlie the centres of the modern town and village. Even today, the streets of these settlements follow the Roman layout and by walking through them it is still possible to experience the dimensions of the Roman forts. The archaeology of Obernburg is especially interesting. Here a station for a unit of *beneficiarii* has been discovered and extensive archaeological excavations have revealed the ground plan, many finds and inscriptions. Obernburg is the best researched *beneficiarii* station in the whole Roman Empire. Of special interest are the inscriptions left by the *beneficiarii* that allow us to reconstruct a vivid picture of the Roman past in the region (Steidl 2008, 108–13). Many inscriptions and finds are on display in the local Roman Museum and the Bavarian State Archaeological Collection in Munich (see below).

The *numerus* forts of Wörth and Trennfurt are not built over; they are located in a field and in an orchard. Nothing is visible above ground. The fort of Wörth is of special interest because the north-western stone wall of the fort collapsed into the ditch complete, enabling the archaeologists to reconstruct accurately the height of the fort wall as approximately 6.35 metres. The forts of Seligenstadt and Großkrotzenburg in Hesse are located in the centres of the villages (Baatz and Herrmann 2002, 325, 477).

MUSEUMS IN THE REGION

There are five museums with Roman collections in the region. The museums of Wörth, Stockstadt and Großkrotzenburg are small museums which only open once a week or on special request. The Roman Museum of Obernburg displays the epigraphic inscriptions of the *beneficiarii* and other finds from the fort of Obernburg. The city museum of Miltenberg is currently the region's most important museum. A collection of Roman artefacts is displayed on two floors and includes finds from the two forts in the region and from the Limes.

The museums of the Main region are key to presenting the World Heritage Site to the public. They display original artefacts from the region, enabling local people to identify with their history and archaeology (Flügel 2008). The *Museums and Communications Plan for the Limes World Heritage Site in Bavaria*[1] recommends the establishment of a central Main Limes Museum at an appropriate location on the Bavarian Lower Main.

The archaeological information system we are developing aims to link the archaeological site with the finds from it that are usually located in the museum. The objective is to provide the user with instant access to information about finds in the landscape, at the locations where they were discovered. At the same time the user can obtain information about where the original artefact is displayed. We envisage that the museums will also provide services such as Wi-Fi connections to enable applications to be downloaded within the area.

---

[1]   http://www.limes-oesterreich.at/FRE_DOWNLOADS/LimesMusEntwicklung_BY.pdf [28 August 2012].

Technological Requirements and Distribution

At the start of the project we had to decide on the platform upon which to develop the application. There are two principal operating systems for smartphones that seem likely to dominate the future in this field. On the one hand is the innovative Apple iOS and on the other is the open source platform Android, promoted by Google.

For our prototype we chose Apple iOS. The reasons for that decision were:

- easy distribution through the App Store;
- limited hardware versions;
- many users.

The application is optimised for the iPhone, but it also runs on the iPod Touch and the iPad. All functions including GPS navigation are available on the iPhone. Therefore the iPhone is recommended for the best user experience. The potential for migration to other platforms is also important. Currently the optimal solution seems to be a production for both Apple iOS and for Android: about 50–60% of smartphone users could then access the application (using both platforms) with the likelihood that there will be an increasing number of users for these two operating systems.

We also decided that it was important for the application to work offline. The Limes sometimes run through remote regions and it is important therefore that internet connection is not essential. Videos and audio sequences in particular need a high-speed internet connection to guarantee a good user experience. Consequently we integrated the content in the application to ensure good video and audio quality everywhere. This is important for international users too, as data roaming costs in the EU are often very high. If there is an active internet connection the user will have access to additional content through the web click button at the top right which provides access to the web database: www.museen-mainlimes.de (see above).

Realisation: Development of the Content

Even when using the most recent and exciting technology available on the market, the content should remain the most important concern. The technological devices are simply vehicles to communicate archaeological content to audiences. However, the technology also provides opportunities to adapt or change narrative techniques and for users to access the information in different ways and in different locations such as in a cafe or within the landscape. Content development therefore needs to be very carefully considered. This is especially true for multimedia devices such as smartphones, where it is possible to wrap content in a video file, an audio sequence or text-picture information. Selection of the best media to communicate key messages needs to be carefully thought through in each case (Flügel *et al* 2011a).

Cost is another important consideration. Text-picture information is cheaper to produce than an audio sequence and high quality video sequences are the most expensive. For video sequences, an animated 3D model is more expensive than, for instance, a landscape shot involving simply panning or tilting in different directions.

Our starting point was therefore to define what we wanted to achieve with the application. We defined our primary aim as enabling the user to access useful and interesting archaeological information when visiting an archaeological site in the landscape. GPS navigation should help

FIG 11.2.   GPS ORIENTATION.

the user to verify the location of a Roman fort or other site in the landscape even when the remains are not visible (Fig 11.2).

We defined 48 hotspots along the Bavarian part of the Main Limes from Miltenberg to Stockstadt, each one relating to an archaeological site or find, or providing important historical or epigraphical information. We then had to define the best medium to communicate the information for each hotspot. An example is the fort of Wörth which is located in a field and where nothing is visible on the ground surface. The decision was taken to implement an animated 3D reconstruction as a video sequence. The user stands next to the field and through the 3D model he is able to envisage the Roman fort in the landscape. Another interesting example is a hotspot in Obernburg. House number 41 has a Roman inscription in its wall. The Latin inscription is at eye level and can easily be seen and read by a visitor. A simple audio sequence seemed the best way to convey the required information, avoiding the unnecessary and distracting use of video or text information.

The 48 hotspots of the Mainlimes Mobil application include:

- 16 video sequences (approx length: 01:00 – 03:00 min)
- 14 audio sequences
- 18 text-/picture-information

A second aim was that the 48 hotspots would collectively describe the World Heritage Site and

FIG 11.3.   'HOTSPOTS' OF THE MAINLIMES MOBIL APPLICATION.

the functioning of the frontier system. Each of the hotspots therefore focuses on a different aspect of the frontier system. Together the hotspots create an overall picture of the Main Limes which enables the user to understand the function of this Roman frontier system on the basis of current evidence.

TECHNICAL IMPLEMENTATION

Content production is already demanding, especially if you include video and audio; technical development of the content into the application adds another level of complexity.

First we had to solve the problem of real-world navigation using the application. Geo-referenced maps provide the main means of accessing the content. An overview map shows the whole region and several more detailed maps enable the content to be accessed. The maps are zoomable (pinch and zoom) and clickable. By choosing the fort of Wörth on the overview map, for instance, the user gains access to a detailed map of the city of Wörth. On this map various hotspots are available. By clicking on a hotspot the user gains direct access to content related to that hotspot. If the user has an iPhone, they can turn on GPS navigation. A blue spot marks their position on the map; it is now possible for the user to explore the Roman archaeology in the vicinity of Wörth. When a user comes within a 15-metre radius of a hotspot, an alert with a sound signal is triggered. The user can then decide whether they are interested in that particular information (Fig 11.3). An alternative means of navigation through a tabular view is also available for each town or village. This provides instant access and an effective overview of all the hotspots. Each hotspot is geo-referenced to guarantee accurate navigation and a correct alert.

WEB TOOL

The Web Tool allowed us to gather all the information and connect the content with the maps and hotspots. The correct longitude and latitude was needed for each hotspot to enable it to be connected to the correct map. The content was then attached to the hotspot and the programmers were able to create the application. The application needed a lot of testing. Correct location of the hotspots was the most difficult task involving a lot of trial and error, especially when hotspots were quite close together (less than 20m).

The Web Tool also allows us to keep the application up-to-date as it is quite straightforward to update the application once the geo-referenced hotspots are connected with the map and the content. New results from scientific research can be integrated at reasonable cost. For example, we can envisage the text-picture information within the application as mobile wall charts which can be updated quite easily, in contrast to fixed on-site information panels. In the future a combination of information panels and text-picture information might be the best way to present a monument using content that is best matched to the respective media.

A third aim of the project was that content should be available in different languages. From the beginning, content was planned in German and English and the Web Tool gave us the opportunity to record both languages at the same time. There are now two versions of the application available.

FUTURE DEVELOPMENTS

The archaeological information system Main Limes Mobil provides information about archaeological sites and finds in the region. It brings the museum and its finds into the landscape and it can also bring the landscape into the museum. An integrated GPS-based alert system automatically informs the user that they are approaching an interesting site with information available.

The integration of different languages is very important within the European Union and we incorporated many languages into earlier multimedia projects (Walkshofer and Dobat 2008). The mobile information systems on smartphones enable us to use different languages and to promote archaeological monuments to an international audience.

We are including a riddle in our application. If you are able to solve it, you will receive a DVD about the Frontiers of the Roman Empire (Breeze 2011, 76). The idea of the riddle is based on the popular geo-caching activity and can only be solved by visiting the sites. The next step will be the integration of this geo-caching riddle into the navigation element of the application, enabling users to monitor their progress in solving the riddle. This feature is targeted especially at families spending a day or two in the landscape, discovering archaeological sites, solving a riddle and in so doing learning more about the World Heritage Site.

Another important feature in future projects will be the implementation of augmented reality technology, through which it will be possible to bring to life archaeological monuments through real-time viewing using smartphone cameras. These new features are planned for other parts of the World Heritage Site and other locations. We recently completed an extended version of the application with augmented reality technology for the Raetian Limes in Middle Franconia (Bavaria). This application is now (since March 2013) available for Android and Apple iOS.

The Mainlimes Mobil application was launched in July 2011 by the Bavarian Minister of Science and Culture, Dr W Heubisch, by the Bayerische Sparkassenstiftung and by the Landesstelle für nichtstaatliche Museen in Bavaria and is now available through the iTunes App Store. The English version can be downloaded for free at: http://itunes.apple.com/de/app/main-limes-mobile/id446660434?mt=8.

Bibliography and References

Baatz, D, and Herrmann, F R, 2002 *Die Römer in Hessen*, Nikol Verlagsgesellschaft mbH & Co KG, Hamburg

Breeze, D J, 2011 The Antonine Wall, in *Xantener Berichte Band 19* (eds M Müller, T H Otten and U Wulf-Rheidt), Philip von Zabern Verlag, Darmstadt, 71–8

Breeze, D J, and Jilek, S, 2008 The Culture 2000 Project 'Frontiers of the Roman Empire', in *Frontiers of the Roman Empire – The European Dimension of a World Heritage Site* (eds D J Breeze and S Jilek), Historic Scotland, Edinburgh, 7–14

Dobat, E, 2009 The Gask 'system' in Perthshire: the first artificial frontier line of the Roman empire?, in *First Contact – Rome and Northern Britain* (eds D J Breeze, L M Thoms and D W Hall), TAFAC, Mongraph 7, 39–48

Flügel, C, 2008 The World Heritage Site 'Frontiers of the Roman Empire', in *Frontiers of the Roman Empire – The European Dimension of a World Heritage Site* (eds D J Breeze and S Jilek), Historic Scotland, Edinburgh, 175–8

Flügel, C, Dobat, E, and Walkshofer, S, 2011a Mainlimes Mobil - Ein mobiles Informationssystem für das Welterbe, in *Nachrichtenblatt der Deutschen Limeskommission – Der Limes* (ed P Henrich), 5. Jahrgang, Heft 2, 32–3

— 2011b Mainlimes Mobil - Ein mobiles archäologisches Informationssystem für das Welterbe, in *Museum heute 40 – Fakten, Tendenzen, Hilfen* (ed W Stäbler), Landesstelle für die nichtstaatlichen Museen beim Bayerischen Landesamt für Denkmalpflege, München, 90–2

Schaller, K, Egger, J, and Uhlir, C, 2009 Archäologische Museen vernetzt. An Information System for the Archaeological Museums in Bavaria, in *Proceedings of SCCH09 – Scientific Computing & Cultural Heritage*, November 16th-18th, Heidelberg, Germany, available from: http://www.museen-mainlimes.de/user_uploads/MainlimesWebsite.pdf [12 June 2012]

Schaller, K, and Flügel, C, 2010 *Museen am Mainlimes* [online], available from: http://www.museen-main-limes.de/ [12 June 2012]

Steidl, B, 2008 *Welterbe Limes – Roms Grenze am Main*, Logo Verlag Eric Erfurt, Obernburg am Main

Walkshofer, S, and Dobat, E, 2005 *Weltkulturerbe Limes* [DVD Video], Konrad Theiss Verlag, Stuttgart

— 2006 Praktische Filmarbeit mit Schülern, in *Geschichte im Film – Beiträge zur Förderung historischer Kompetenz* (eds W Schreiber and A Wenzl), Themenhefte Geschichte 7, Neuried, 122–8

— 2008 From Scotland to the Black Sea – Making the DVD 'Frontiers of the Roman Empire', in *Frontiers of the Roman Empire – The European Dimension of a World Heritage Site* (eds D J Breeze and S Jilek), Historic Scotland, Edinburgh, 163–5

12

Voices from the Past: Presenting (re)Constructed Environments through Multimedia Technologies

Jim Devine

Many visitors (and would-be visitors) to the Antonine Wall World Heritage Site find the task of interpreting and understanding the visible archaeological remains somewhat challenging. Over a number of years in the role of Head of Multimedia in the Hunterian Museum, and as an Associate Lecturer with the School of Computing Science at the University of Glasgow, the author has been exploring ways of addressing this issue. Multimedia technologies have the potential to aid in the presentation and interpretation of archaeological sites, and their associated artefacts held in local museums collections, for a wide range of public audiences.

The coming of age of interactive digital information and communication technologies has provided cultural heritage organisations with a range of opportunities to utilise these ever more flexible digital technologies to provide access to their cultural resources in increasingly innovative ways. The advent of the World Wide Web, over 20 years ago now, presented heritage organisations with a unique opportunity to provide access to their resources to a truly global audience. Resources which hitherto were only available to those fortunate enough to live within travelling distance of archaeological sites or museum collections were suddenly accessible via the then new medium of web technology. Moreover, many museums around the world saw the potential to turn this new medium into additional virtual display space in which to reveal many artefacts that had been languishing in storage or in reserve collections. The earliest cultural heritage websites, although brave first steps into what was for most heritage professionals very new territory, were often little more than web versions of printed information leaflets and brochures. It was not long, however, before many museums recognised the potential this new medium had to revolutionise the way in which we presented our collections to our new virtual visitors.

We have come a long way since then. Computer-generated 3D reconstructions of Roman archaeological sites and monuments are now fairly commonplace, although still rather expensive to produce. The author has spent considerable time and effort focusing on how to incorporate the best technology solutions for the interpretation of heritage sites, whilst remaining aware of the budgetary constraints within which the vast majority of heritage organisations must operate. To this end the collaborative ventures forged by the author between the heritage industry and academia have produced some interesting examples of how we, as heritage professionals, academics and commercial interpretation developers, may work together to obtain the maximum benefit to the heritage organisations and their public audiences, from the ever more limited financial resources available.

Having secured a modest grant from Museums Galleries Scotland, and incorporating Glasgow Computing Science students on academically assessed project work, we set out to develop a

3D reconstruction of the Roman fort at Bar Hill on the Antonine Wall based upon archaeo-logical excavation reports, and with the benefit of input from Professor Lawrence Keppie, one of the authors of the reports (Robertson *et al* 1975). The resulting 3D model, whilst in itself both interesting and informative, was, however, only the starting point for a series of further experiments. These aimed to take the interpretation and presentation of the site to a new level of understanding and appreciation for the visitor, and hopefully to engage the audience in the process of viewing associated museum artefacts in the context of the sites from which they were excavated.

The first approach was to further enhance the Bar Hill fort 3D reconstruction model by the introduction of a live-action Guide within the computer-generated imagery (CGI). This live action-CGI technique has been used extensively in the film industry for several years, but we believe that this was the first time that it had been employed in the cultural heritage industry. It has certainly proved to be a popular and innovative approach for the presentation of the Anto-nine Wall. Our subject for the Guide was taken from the Hunterian Museum Roman collection from the Antonine Wall. This includes the gravestone of a female named Verecunda which was found near Bar Hill. We know nothing of Verecunda's life beyond her name and the fact that she lived and died on the Antonine Wall. The absence of anything other than a *praenomen* on her gravestone suggests that she may have been a slave. This provided us with an opportunity to bring our audience group into the development process. The author runs a Junior Archaeologists' Club for children aged 8 to 16, and has been working with local primary and secondary schools to generate interest in the Antonine Wall World Heritage Site. These groups were recruited to come to the Museum and discuss what life might have been like for this person living on the Antonine Wall in the second century AD. This proved to be a very popular way of getting young people actively engaged with an artefact and its provenance that they might otherwise have regarded as being rather uninteresting, or even boring.

We thus recreated a life for Verecunda and have used her as a guide to the Roman fort for our present-day visitors. In developing the project we made every effort to retain historical accu-racy, whilst allowing a degree of creative licence in the development of our character in order to enhance audience engagement, both in the children's recreation of the character and in allowing the character of Verecunda to engage virtually with visitors. Having worked together with the young people to build a story around the life of Verecunda, we then needed to find someone to play out the role for us in front of the camera. One of the Junior Archaeologists stepped up to the mark and we got the camera rolling with her acting out some simple directions in front of a green screen. The live action sequences were subsequently composited with the CGI model of the Roman fort to produce a series of short introductions to various parts of the fort, and brief explanations of what each building within the fort was used for.

This experiment led to a wider study with two local Glasgow schools. With support – and some limited financial assistance – from Historic Scotland and Glasgow City Council, we teamed a group of senior sixth-year pupils from Bellahouston Academy with a class of primary year 5/6 pupils from Glendale Primary School. The author provided each group with a background framework from the archaeological and historical perspective and, using the model developed in the Verecunda scenario, provided the pupils and their teachers with a selection of characters drawn from the Roman inscribed stones in the Hunterian collection, along with a bare outline sketch of who each person was. The Glendale Primary pupils then developed their own stories around their characters, with the Bellahouston Academy pupils acting as mentors to the younger children. The budget from Historic Scotland also allowed for the input of a professional story-teller to help the children plan out their storylines.

The outcome was an unparalleled success, culminating in the pupils from both schools giving a presentation on their project – which included multimedia elements and a live performance from the reconstructed Roman characters – to the Hexham Group of archaeologists and heritage professionals from the Frontiers of the Roman Empire World Heritage Site who were gathering in Scotland for their international meeting. This presentation formed the highlight of the minis-terial reception for the Hexham Group in the Queen's Hall of Edinburgh Castle, in the presence of Fiona Hyslop MSP, the Scottish Government's Cabinet Secretary for Culture and External Affairs. The overwhelming view of the heritage professionals, the education specialists, the politi-cians and, most importantly of all the pupils and their teachers, was that the project's focus on using museum artefacts to draw on real people from the past and place them in their archaeo-logical and historical contexts provided learning opportunities that were highly engaging for the pupils, raising their awareness of the importance of the archaeological sites and heritage collec-tions on their doorsteps to a level at which they felt a personal sense of ownership and pride.

The next stage was to look at how we might maintain the momentum of what we had achieved in generating an interest in the Antonine Wall among school pupils and teachers and, through them, parents and colleagues. The experimental content developed for Bar Hill fort using the live action-CGI techniques had been produced primarily with kiosk-based visual displays for museums and heritage centres in mind. However we now wanted to shift our emphasis to providing resources to enhance the interpretation and understanding of the archaeological sites by enabling visitors to access learning and informational resources *in situ*.

This led to discussions with collaborators in the School of Computing Science at the Univer-sity of Glasgow, and in particular with Professor Stephen Brewster and Dr David McGookin, who had been conducting research, funded by the European Union and the Engineering and Physical Sciences Research Council, into Human Computer Interaction (HCI) in the area of Information Interfaces and Presentation for mobile devices (McGookin *et al* 2011). We very quickly established a symbiotic collaborative partnership whereby the concepts and the content from the Bar Hill project being developed by the heritage, education, and multimedia profes-sionals provided the perfect range of media and presentational challenges for the experimental software solutions being developed by the computing scientists.

The group worked together to produce a smartphone application based around Bar Hill fort. This incorporates a virtual excavator which allows schoolchildren and family groups visiting the site to interact with a variety of media to interpret the site, including audio descriptions and arte-facts from the site held by nearby museums, which can be 'excavated' at their original findspots on the site of the fort, utilising the smartphone's on-board sensors: global positioning system (GPS), gyroscope and magnetometer, to locate artefacts by audio direction finding. Once the findspot has been accurately identified the visitor can shake the smartphone to 'excavate' what lies beneath, revealing an image of the artefact at its original findspot (see Figs 12.1 and 12.2), along with information about the artefact and the local museum in which it can be seen.

The feedback on the Bar Hill smartphone application from the primary and secondary schools and from the Junior Archaeologists' family group was extremely positive. Demonstra-tions to various professional conferences and meetings have also elicited a high level of interest in this approach to delivering interpretive information on archaeological and historical sites (see Fig 12.3). The next steps for the project are to secure funding to develop the concept further

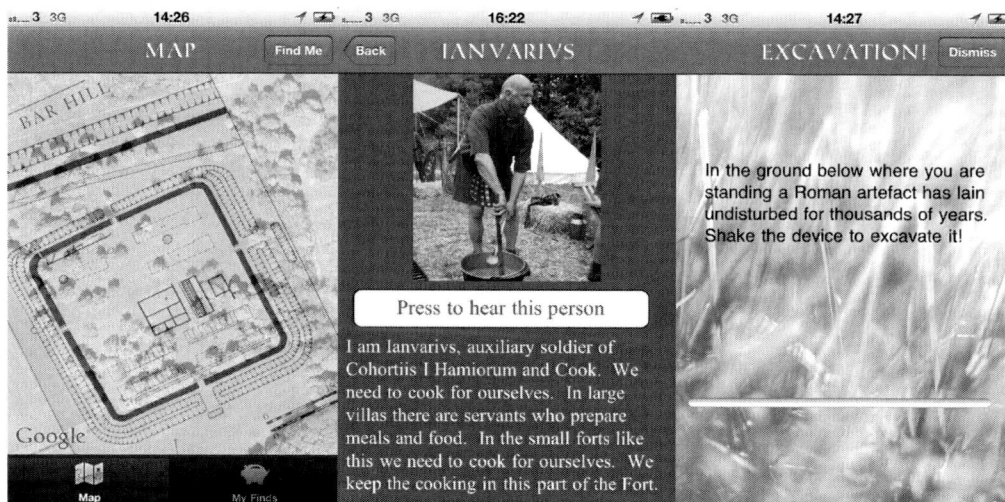

FIG 12.1. SMARTPHONE APP SCREENSHOTS SHOWING (LEFT TO RIGHT): MAP OVERLAY, AUDIO CLIP AND VIRTUAL EXCAVATOR.

FIG 12.2. SMARTPHONE APP SCREENSHOTS SHOWING (LEFT TO RIGHT): EXCAVATED FIND, FIND MARKER FLAG, AND MY FINDS COLLECTION.

FIG 12.3. VIRTUAL EXCAVATORS: GLENDALE PRIMARY SCHOOL PUPILS SITE TEST THE SMARTPHONE APPLICATION.

and to look at linking sites to provide discovery trails, connecting multi-period archaeological and historical sites in the same localities and across neighbouring locations. To this end, the author's multimedia company (Interpretive Media Limited), in partnership with the School of Computing Science at Glasgow University and other partners from the academic, local authority and commercial sectors, has submitted a funding application to take forward the concept under the Scottish Informatics and Computer Science Alliance (SICSA) Smart Tourism Project. The MINERVA Project will seek to address the SICSA Smart Tourism goal of delivering 'innovative approaches and technology solutions to enhance the Scottish Tourism sector's technology base' (SICSA 2011), whilst providing a proof of concept of this technology for the heritage agencies and local authorities tasked with the promotion and interpretation of the Antonine Wall World Heritage Site.

BIBLIOGRAPHY AND REFERENCES

McGookin, D K, Vazquez-Alvarez, Y, Brewster, S A, and Bergstrom-Lehtovirta, J, 2011 Digitally Glueing the Past: Multimodal Interaction for Un-Stewarded Historical and Archaeological Sites, Proceedings of *Digital Engagement*, 15–17 November 2011, Newcastle

Robertson, A, Scott, M, and Keppie, L, 1975 *Bar Hill: A Roman fort and its finds*, British Archeological Reports, volume 14, Oxford

SICSA, 2011 *Smart Tourism* [online], available from: http://www.smarttourism.org/ [8 June 2012]

13

Digital Reconstruction and the Public Interpretation of Frontiers

R Michael Spearman

Constructive Partnerships

The study and description of history is fundamentally a process of reconstructing the past: piecing together fragments of documents, buildings and artefacts to create a believable story or illustration of people, events and places. For heritage professionals this process and its associated debate is the stuff of history. For exhibition interpreters it is less the debate and more the conclusions that matter. For the majority of the public it is the story. Balancing these sometimes very different levels of interest has never been easy. An acceptable level of accuracy for one group can be a source of obfuscation for another. The successful combination of these different approaches is, nevertheless, essential if we are to make accessible the processes and results of historical debate to the wider public. By doing so we can hope to enrich public consciousness with accurate and accessible reconstructions of our past.

Just 15 years ago historical reconstructions were most often presented via the pages of a book – academic tome or romantic fiction. This format normally required a significant reduction and simplification of the evidence. There were constraints on word count and number of illustrations that we had all grown used to. Today, with the proliferation of digital publication and interpretation centres, the volume of information we present to the public, consciously or subconsciously, can be very large indeed. In particular 2D and now 3D visual reconstructions are often so detailed and realistic that they routinely challenge our understanding of the evidence upon which the visual reconstruction itself is based. This explosion in the use and availability of information is resulting in some fundamental changes to how we research, manage and present our heritage.

To create believable illustrations of people, events and places today requires new and diverse skill sets. The balance of interpretive effort has been moving from the written word to animated digital spaces. Digital reconstructions have become an aid to archaeological investigation. Different structural and artefact options can now be modelled with relative ease. Reconstructions for public interpretation are making ever-increasing use of audio and visual technology. The textures within digitally created models are achieving photo-realistic quality. Interactive audio guides have the presence of radio plays. 3D digital technology is now bursting upon us with new and exciting tools. There is procedural modelling, where building elements are easily cloned to produce visually appealing cityscapes. Crowd simulations can animate realistically where and how individuals or groups of people move around purposefully within 3D reconstructions. The impetus for much of this work is not human history but the film, television and game indus-

FIG 13.1. RECONSTRUCTION OF MILE CASTLE FROM *EAGLES EYE* FILM – INCLUDES FIGURES TO GIVE SCALE.

tries. As a result, many of the reconstruction teams entering the heritage debate are not heritage trained or motivated. New people with new skills are looking afresh at the evidence gathered from excavation, survey and museum studies. They bring with them new and different views of what is fit for public consumption. In many respects this is a positive addition to the process of public engagement with human history – even if at times heritage professionals feel there ought to be a warning about some or all of these additions.

The established processes of generating and reviewing the hard evidence for reconstructions means that technical reconstructions will be more readily engaged with professionally than some of the more dramatic or extrapolated models intended for media use or general illustration. But it is important, as the 2009 Limes conference and this volume indicates, that academic engagement with the emerging world of digital reconstruction is constantly expanded and kept under review. The heritage sector needs to engage at all levels with the technical sector, and vice versa. Only then can we hope to enhance the quality, and therefore public value, of what is reconstructed – or indeed constructed. There are many areas where this can and does happen. One of particular import is the world of exhibition display and interpretation. This is one of the main areas where heritage organisations are market facing and as a result have access to somewhat larger resources and skills. Such partnerships can be very fruitful for both heritage and technical members of the display teams; witness the *Eagles Eye* film shown in the Roman Army Museum at Carvoran fort (Fig 13.1).

Different Perspectives

No frontier is passive, least of all one that is imposed on semi-subjugated people and includes a substantial man-made barrier. Whether they are ancient history or current affairs, the creation of a physical frontier between communities is normally a very significant political event. Such physical barriers involve the full military and political authority of at least one of the boundary states. It is not possible to arrive at a modern reconstruction of Rome's northern frontiers without addressing the issues of their purpose and effect on both the included and the excluded populations. We therefore have to add to the detailed work of accurate physical reconstruction the even more challenging task of reconstructing political and social intent and consequence. This is, and always has been, difficult history. It is the study of past, present and future conflict. There will be no one correct view – even with the perspective of centuries.

There will always be at least two sides to the story of any frontier, if not indeed a multiplicity of perspectives that change over time. To have any chance of reconstructing the political and social impact of a frontier, it is necessary to examine all the available evidence and to reconstruct as multiperspectival a model of that frontier as possible. If we reconstruct something as partial as, for instance, Life on the Roman Frontier, we will have already constrained public access to the views of *the other* and *the self*. In reconstructing and presenting frontiers we need to be clear that there is no one authorised history (see Figs 13.2 and 13.3). This is especially necessary when the documentary and archaeological evidence is far more complete for one side than it is for the other.

In teaching the history of 20th-century Europe, historians and teachers have developed very sophisticated techniques for debating and reviewing recent conflicts and new frontiers. When faced with pupils and parents for whom the events being taught are very far from being of purely historical interest, teachers in Jerusalem, Nicosia, Belfast or Belgrade have stepped up to very serious social and educational challenges. The work of the Council of Europe in this area has been significant and includes Robert Stradling's *Teaching 20th Century European History* (2001). It is worth referencing three of his guiding aims:

- To gain a more comprehensive and broader understanding of historical events and developments by taking into account the similarities and differences in the accounts and perspectives of all the parties involved;
- To gain a deeper understanding of the historical relationships between nations, or cross-border neighbours, or majorities and minorities within national borders;
- To gain a clear picture of the dynamics of what happened through examining the interaction between the people and groups involved and their interdependence.

(Stradling 2001, 142)

Stradling's language is that of a modern documentary historian but, as we reconstruct, interpret and present ancient frontiers, the application of a similarly open and multiperspectival approach makes fundamental sense. Moreover, only by working at this level can we hope to provide comparatively safe ancient models for those teaching or caught up in events that urgently need greater perspective than is yet available.

Fig 13.2. Cartoon by Barry Hunau depicting a Palestinian suicide bomber climbing the West Bank Barrier.

Fig 13.3. Cartoon by Carlos Latuff: 'IsraHell's concentration camp'.

Working Models

The truth is that no reconstruction of a human history scene is complete without people. To reconstruct an historic set without people is to build a stage without actors, and yet a significant number of 2D and 3D reconstructions do just that. Putting in the people is, it seems, difficult to do well. Until recently, putting figures in to 3D digital models could also be very expensive. But we need people in our reconstructions, both to prove them technically and to give them a range of historical perspectives. Where are the children, the women and the men? Where are the plants and animals? Where is the light? Where are the voices, the sounds of life? How did these spaces work for people? These questions are too many and too important for our reconstructions to be left unpopulated.

We have become used to testing a 3D model of an archaeological structure for its historical or engineering validity. We now need to test models routinely with different artefacts and above all with humans, to consider, map and demonstrate their circulation patterns and functionality. Other disciplines model crowd simulation to demonstrate the safe evacuation of buildings, or the flow of people through a pedestrian precinct. Why do we not model activity within a Roman fort or Iron Age village? Other disciplines script, costume and animate digital actors for film, television and computer games. Why do we not populate our interpretations of the past with scripted characters? In the world of physical reconstructions this is nothing new; many interpretation centres have been populating buildings and spaces with live re-enactors for years. But no matter how good the actor, and many are very good indeed, their day-to-day numbers are normally limited and the opportunity for multiperspectivity therefore restricted. Some interpretation teams have got round this by using audio and video characters to extend the range of views expressed and the variety of human activity illustrated. Visitors themselves sometimes help to populate reconstructed spaces, especially if there are artefacts and furniture to help create a sense of function. Many visitors are happy, or are entrapped, to help bring this together by interacting with re-enactors, props and digital media – often with pleasantly surprising results.

In the past, cost undoubtedly constrained what could be done to populate models of ancient sites, buildings and towns. Believable digital actors were for big-budget film and games, not the academic study of reconstructions. But with better and cheaper software it is time to let our structural modellers team link up with digital animators to create realistic heritage figures that can be programmed to move and interact in meaningful ways. It is time to pay real attention to the human form, costume and action. Experimental archaeologists have long investigated past farming, manufacturing and building techniques. If the results of their work were now combined with digital systems for recording human movement and manipulation, we would have new evidence-based mechanisms to investigate and digitally illustrate the use of ancient buildings and spaces. On the software side of this equation, the modelling of people and their actions is very advanced and becoming more available and affordable by the year. We need to begin capturing data on the movement and activities of ancient people ready to populate our digital 3D reconstructions; we need people in our models to test their usability, communicate ideas, provide different perspectives, handle artefacts, humanise the past and to relate to.

Spoken Words

Whether the people we place in our models are live re-enactors, audio ghosts or digital avatars, we need to provide them with things to do and even to say. To be able to sketch the character

of an ordinary person in history is a rare event. To even find a person's name in the archaeological record is an exceptional event. Populating reconstructions with characters as opposed to
animatrons is never going to be easy, but it is something scriptwriters do all the time. Making
characters believable is something actors do all the time. Once again we discover the need to
extend our team if we are successfully to deliver reconstructions that inform and change professional and public perceptions of the past. This is not easy work. Docudramas, historical plays,
fantasy movies – all have their established genera that go back decades. But they are not first
and foremost about accurate reconstruction. They are not normally charged with delivering a
trustworthy picture of our past. They do not normally need to be multiperspectival in their plots.
The world of reconstruction is different: it has to be evidence led. It cannot mis-sell itself. Its
users have to know when they have moved genera. When viewing the modern world, most of us
are exceptionally skilled at distinguishing between fact and fiction. When viewing professionally
reconstructed ancient worlds, most will need assistance to see where the lines between black,
white and grey have been drawn.

Not surprisingly, when it is possible to bring named people and places together reconstructors
want to make the most of any named individuals. In the context of societies with a written and
inscribed record, as with at least the Roman side of the frontier's history, they will want to use
people for whom we have some contextual information. Discoveries such as the writing tablets
from Vindolanda provide exceptional opportunities for scripted reconstructions. For instance,
just by focusing on the character and time of Flavius Cerialis we can learn much about his family,
friends and military correspondents:

Table 13.1

Character	Position/ Relationship	Location	Period	Tablets
Flavius Cerialis	Prefect CO of the Ninth Cohort of Batavians	Vindolanda	From c. AD 101 until the Regiment left Vindolanda in early AD 105	622, 233, 244, 247, 248, 261, 227, 265, 118, 234, 225, 618, 242, 250, 628
Sulpicia Lepidina	Wife of Flavius Cerialis	Vindolanda	As above	291, 292, 294
Aelius Brocchus	Correspondent of Flavius – Also a Prefect?	Unknown – Nearby Fort?	As above	622, 233, 244, 247, 248
Claudia Severa	Wife of Aelius Brocchus, Correspondent of Sulpicia Lepidina	Unknown – Nearby Fort?	As above	291, 292
Felicio	Centurion of Flavius Cerialis	Vindolanda?	As above	242, 193
Slave (name unknown)	Slave/Various servile members of Cerialis' household	Vindolanda	As above	194, 197, 191, 196, 190, 616, 632, 581, 596
Others	Various recipients of Cerialis' correspondence	Outwith Vindolanda	As above	234, 248, 225, 618, 250, 628

Researched from: A K Bowman, *Life & Letters on the Roman Frontier* (1998). See also Vindolanda Tablets
Online, available from: http://www.kcl.ac.uk/artshums/depts/classics/research/proj/vindo.aspx

From these and other sources there is much upon which to base a reconstruction of both the practical and emotional attitudes to life on the Wall, at least for the Roman military community. The survival of such remarkable sources from one side of the Wall may help to explain in part why modern Europeans see themselves as in some way the inheritors of the mantle of Rome. Europeans have a curiously ingrained belief in the benefits of romanisation and therefore a less than open perspective on what Rome's frontiers meant for native communities. Simply because we do not have equivalent voices and precious few of the sites and artefacts to reflect the views of the occupied population, our modern world has passed them by. To the victor goes not only the spoils but also the historical record. Not perhaps a reality that makes the work of teachers in conflict zones any easier. Multiperspectivity can come, however, in different forms.

Perhaps the most striking approach to multiperspectivity is a remarkable historical precedent for inventing characters and even for putting words in their mouths. In his *Agricola*, Tacitus brings forward: 'a man of outstanding valour and nobility named Calgacus ... who is reported to have said (amongst a great deal else): "To robbery, butchery and rapine they give the lying name of government; they create a desolation and call it peace"' (Tacitus, Agricola, 29–30 Penguin Classic 1970 edition).

Tacitus' purposes in reporting the words of Calgacus are certainly different from ours, but as the aims of multiperspectivity noted above indicate, the fact that he did so is an important addition to the modern discussion of frontiers.

We can, indeed we ought, also to approach the issue of ancient frontiers from the study of modern examples. As studying Tacitus indicates, the realities of conquest or occupation have changed little. Frontier walls continue to be imposed by states upon societies and their modern nicknames, such as the Wall of Divide and Rule in Bagdad, or Peace Walls between communities in Belfast or just The Wall through the West Bank, tell their own story. Contrast this with the top-down perspective of generals today. There seems little doubt that the imposers and imposed along the Roman frontier would have understood the doctrine of rapid dominance that came to be known during the 2003 Gulf War as Shock and Awe. In the debate over NATO's involvement and tactics in Afghanistan, General Petraeus and others have described them as a mix of 'clear, hold, build' and 'clear and leave'. Tactics and sentiments that Calgacus or Tacitus would have understood only too well, especially when the emphasis is on *clear*.

Reaching Audiences

The uses for archaeological reconstructions are extremely varied. The information incorporated in them can be equally so. Their role in both understanding and presenting archaeological monuments is on the increase. Data capture for 3D reconstruction is becoming an increasing part of excavation and survey methodology. But in many respects the leading use of 3D reconstruction has remained with excavation and monument-based interpretation centres. Since Jorvik opened in 1984 on the site of the Coppergate excavations in York, populated, authoritative, evidence-based 3D reconstructions created for public audiences have been a popular and standard interpretation device. The advent of digital 3D recording and modelling has made the flow of information from excavation record to such interpretation devices much easier. Now with the advent of affordable 3D projection systems the considerable cost of physical reconstruction can be avoided and a suite of new visitor experiences made available.

New audio and visual tools that can appeal to and attract modern audiences are, of course, of great benefit. But with such powerful interpretation tools the careful selection of the right content and how and where we choose to deliver content to visitors becomes critical. Content, tool and visitor have to come together effortlessly, reliably and in the right place. Within buildings and exhibitions we can support content delivery through control over the visitor's environment: light, ambient effects, etc. The challenges for storytelling outdoors are much more significant, but they are being solved and the benefits of using GPS triggering and portable media players are extraordinary.

The advent of affordable and accurate GPS devices is changing the way in which we present sites. Previously only fixed notices or live interpreters could deliver information at particular points on a site. Now GPS triggered mobile technology can automatically deliver audio and even visual content to the visitor with all the appearance of serendipity. The result is multi-layered storytelling activated by location and direction of travel. These devices open the way to place information and experience into and alongside the landscape. Whether indoors or in the field, the user requirement is the same: a rich, informed and interesting story that is told well and delivered in the right place and at the right time. (No challenge there then.)

SETTING STANDARDS

UNESCO is silent on standards for reconstructing people and their thoughts, but the process needs to be even more rigorous than that for reconstructing buildings and artefacts. People-related content is attractive to and readily absorbed by visitors and is therefore very potent. Like it or not, visitors come able and willing to relate to other people. They have to learn to relate to archaeology or to landscapes. As a result when interpreting antiquities today the trend has been to lead, if at all possible, with stories of the people, not of the artefacts or the structures. Answers to 'what?' 'where?' and 'when?' are all of greater interpretational impact when delivered by or alongside the answer to the all-important question 'who?'.

Visitors expect to be engaged and entertained – which is not to say that their day cannot also be enriched in a wide variety of ways. Nor does it mean that we have to create larger-than-life characters – such as Calgacus – to hold the visitor's attention. Subtle, truthful and authoritative answers can be every bit as powerful if delivered with the right technology and in the right way. To do this all answers need to be researched, documented and authorised for accuracy and balance. They then need to be delivered in ways that are appropriate to the evidence and the context.

It is important to realise that the range of tools at our disposal for researching, interpreting and displaying our 3D heritage is developing rapidly. Technology, particularly in the area of portable technology, is changing not just the way we record excavations but also how we will go on to reconstruct and present our results. In the coming years, presenting results and options will be less and less about the written word and more and more about the 3D visual record and the resulting visual and audio reconstruction. The first phase will be for source material to be illustrated, scripted and recorded to produce an approved archive of media resource and reconstruction options. These resources can then be deployed across a wide range of delivery platforms to provide both consistency and future-proofing. What is critical is that on all platforms and in all stories the content is relevant and credible. The sum of the parts – exhibition, objects, site, landscape – must be believable and accessible. Then when the time comes to put people into this reconstructed theatre stage of history, or indeed pre-history, the framework is strong enough for this to be achieved with just the lightest of touches, as befits the most powerful and difficult interpretation tool available to us.

There can be little doubt that Hadrian's Wall has been interpreted and presented from the moment of its conception. Precisely how the frontier that now bears his name was first presented to the Emperor we do not know. (Was the first model of the Wall the one presented to Hadrian as part of an architectural competition?) Still less do we know how it was presented to those it was to divide. Looking at the Wall today it is difficult to believe that there was not a strong element of shock and awe in the strategy that created it. Critically, as we move further into the era of digital recording, reconstruction and presentation we are able, for really the first time, to escape from the tyranny of only being able to present one view of a reconstruction. Multiple interpretations can now be delivered realistically and authoritatively, not just for visitors to experience, but also as a natural extension of academic research. When dealing with difficult issues in our history – ancient and modern – it is our multiperspectival responsibility to do just this. As Hadrian and his forces must have been well aware, the frontier they cleared, held and built was both strongly appreciated and wholly deplored by the different peoples it affected. Frontiers divide people and places. Even when we reconstruct an ancient frontier, the interpreter's responsibility moves on to a more complex and more significant level.

Bibliography and References

Bowman, A K, 1998 *Life & Letters on the Roman Frontier*, British Museum Press, London

Stradling, R, 2001 *Teaching 20th-century European history*, Council of Europe, Strasbourg

Tacitus, 1970, *Agricola*, Penguin, Harmondsworth

14

Information, Disinformation and Downright Lies: Portraying the Romans

Mike Corbishley

Introduction

It is not difficult to find images of the Romans and information about Ancient Rome in contemporary sources. There are cartoons, picture books for young children, Hollywood films, television comedies, websites, school textbooks and popular histories for the general public, children's toys and violent computer games. This chapter discusses why the Romans and their barbarian enemies have been badly or incorrectly portrayed so often and for so long. In the UK, school textbooks from the 19th century and throughout most of the 20th century have often failed to present what classical texts, archaeologists and historians have revealed. More than that, these early school resources hardly ever presented any evidence for the authors' bold statements of presumed fact. This chapter also discusses the role of information books for children and the use of cartoons in storybooks about the Romans.

Although schools had existed since the early medieval period in Britain there was little opportunity for most children, and especially for girls, to be educated until parish schools became more common in the 17th century. The *Education Act* of 1870 created the opportunity to build secular day schools all over the country. School Boards were established in most districts and built public elementary schools, many of which still survive today as primary schools. Many children were educated at home in the 19th century and this promoted the growth of suitable textbooks for mothers or governesses to use in the home. Several history textbooks were written by women, sometimes using pen names, which demonstrated publishers' understanding of the market available to them.

Accuracy and Prejudice

British textbooks in the 19th century usually dealt exclusively with the history of Britain. They concentrated on the broad story of the past. Textbook writers in the 19th and 20th centuries were often concerned about whether the story about any period, whether historic or prehistoric, was attractive enough to engage the reader or school group. Anderson Graham, writing in 1920 about the handbook to Hadrian's Wall, describes the author, Dr Collingwood Bruce, as 'very far indeed from being a Dryasdust' (1920, 222–3). 'But is history of any use, besides being very entertaining?' asks George in Mrs Markham's textbook *A History of England*, first published in 1819 (1886, 4). This book is written in a chatty style, telling a story which is addressed directly to Mrs Markham's three children, Richard, George and Mary. The book's intentions were to 'relate, with as much detail as might be allowable, the most interesting and important parts of our history' and to avoid 'saying the worst of a character, because few people are in reality so bad as they are often made to appear' (Markham 1886, v). The topic of textbooks will be discussed under these four themes: Prehistory and the Romans; Romans as Conquerors; The Roman Withdrawal; The Use of Evidence.

Prehistory and the Romans

Prehistory has been, and still is, treated badly by school curricula which have been created by some government curriculum authorities and by textbook publishers (Corbishley 2011, 140–4). In Britain, from the 19th century, prehistory was usually defined only in the context of the first Roman invasion. School textbooks about British prehistory often had texts which were simplified to the point of absurdity. Facts were invented. The long story of our prehistoric past was usually condensed into stories about cavemen and Ancient Britons in the Long, Long Ago time. Prehistoric people are often depicted as crude, stupid and uncivilised, for example, 'The Romans were cleverer than the Britons, for they could read and write' (Power c. 1940). Some of the loaded expressions used to describe them were: savages; only natives; barbarians; rough; wild. Charles Dickens, in his *A Child's History of England*, first published in the journal *Household Words* 1851–1853, describes Britons as '… poor savages, going almost naked, or only dressed in the rough skins of beasts … no roads, no bridges, no streets, no houses that you would think deserving of the name. A town was nothing but a collection of straw-covered huts …' (1868, 9–10). Mrs Markham's early Britain was a place where

> … there were neither roads, nor bridges, nor houses, nor churches. The country was nothing but one overgrown forest. The people lived in holes in the ground, or in any miserable huts they could contrive. They had no clothes, except the skins of the animals they killed in the chase; for hunting was their chief employment. (1886, 1)

Lady Callcott, in her 1834 textbook *Little Arthur's History of England*, declares that 'The poor Britons were almost naked, and had very bad swords, and very weak spears and bows and arrows, and small shields, made of basket work covered in leather' (1907, 7). In 1923 R H Scott-Elliot thought, 'Just as we ourselves in India put down the burning of widows on the funeral pyre of their husbands, so the Romans stamped out these horrible human sacrifices, both among the Kelts [sic] and the Gauls', and 'Eolithicus probably believed in some sort of Hunter's Paradise to which he would go after he died, which is very much what the Australian black-fellow thinks' (1923, 160 and 28).

One way of categorising these textbook writers' views of prehistoric peoples is to call them racist. At a UNESCO conference in 1978 on Racism in Children's and School Textbooks, one speaker listed a number of words used in textbooks to describe the indigenous people of Australia: 'tribe, primitive, vernacular, native, uncivilised, coloured, savage, pagan and backward' (Lippmann 1980, 68). Another author asks us to consider, 'Is the group or country presented as having been incapable of developing and maintaining stable societies until instructed in these skills by Europeans?' (Preiswerk 1980, 143); here we could just as easily apply the term group to the late Iron Age peoples in Britain and equate the Europeans to the Roman invaders of Britain.

ROMANS AS CONQUERORS

That the Romans had the right to conquer other peoples was not disputed by early textbook writers because the *savages* clearly needed *civilising*. The Romans brought an ordered society with rules and security. Mrs Cyril Ransome's book *A First History of England* (first published in 1903) assumed that this policy was a success: 'The Britons became so civilised that they grew to be very like the Romans themselves. They spoke Latin, and copied the manners and dress and customs of their conquerors, and learned to live in towns and villas ...' (1915, 9).

In their book *1066 And All That* the humourists Sellar and Yeatman summed up the view with which most children were presented: 'The Roman Conquest was, however, a *Good Thing*, since the Britons were only natives at the time' (1930, 3). At the same time a primary school textbook called *Long Long Ago* informed children that when Claudius invaded, 'This time they settled down to live for a while in our land, and they taught the rough, wild Britons new and better ways of living' (King 1934, 129–30).

The textbook writers in the 19th and early 20th centuries used their accounts of history to emphasise the central role of God in the past and the present. Mrs Markham's answer to George's question, 'But is history of any use ...?' was '... the greatest and best use of it is to show us, by observing events as they follow, the greatness and wisdom of God, and "how wonderfully He ordereth the affairs of men"' (1886, 4). The writers also assumed that the Romans had a God-given right to invade, occupy, rule and civilise native peoples. Lady Callcott wrote, 'You see, therefore, that when God allowed the Romans to conquer the Britons, He made them the means of teaching them a great many useful things; above all to read' (Callcott 1907, 9).

THE ROMAN WITHDRAWAL

'When the Romans quitted Britain, the poor helpless inhabitants were left without leaders, or magistrates, like so many wild animals, without reason and without laws' (Markham 1886, 8–9). The simplistic view that the Romans pulled out of Britain in AD 410 was repeated in almost all school textbooks and popular accounts for the public. Just as the Romans had introduced their version of civilisation to the *British savages*, the assumption was that, once the conquerors had gone, Britain had fallen into rack and ruin: the Dark Ages. Some writers were quite specific: 'In the countries Rome had ruled so well were now no longer towns and laws; the bridges and roads fell to pieces, and men did not know how to build them up again' (Erleigh 1948, 108). The consequences for the northern limits of Roman Britain were serious according to the text-book writers: '... it was no easy matter to keep the savage inhabitants of the hill-country quiet,' (Ransome 1915, 9) and, 'When they were left alone the poor Britons did their best to defend themselves, but it was hard work' (Power c. 1940, 59). It was the 'savage little Picts from the north [who] came swarming like ants across the great wall' (Power c. 1940, 59) who threatened the northern frontier. Textbook authors condemned them as a threat to the civilised Roman province: Hadrian's Wall was 'to keep out the wild Picts who lived in the highlands. They tried to steal animals and attack the farms in the north' (Bareham 1964, 136) (Fig 14.1).

THE USE OF EVIDENCE

The majority of school textbooks were written by authors who did not understand or research evidence about the past. Most authors accepted the firmly-held view that the Romans brought

FIG 14.1. THE PICTS ATTACK HADRIAN'S WALL. THIS ILLUSTRATION FROM A READING SCHEME FOR PRIMARY PUPILS APTLY MAKES THE AUTHOR'S POINT ABOUT THE SAVAGE FEROCIOUS NATURE OF THE ROMANS' ENEMIES IN BRITAIN (BAREHAM 1964, 135).

order where there had been chaos, gravelled roads where there were previously only muddy tracks and baths where there was a distinct lack of personal hygiene in prehistoric times. Any advances the pre-Roman people in Britain had developed were achieved only through invasion by or contact with foreign peoples: 'Most of them were savages, but those who lived near the coast learnt many things from lands across the sea' and the accompanying map has the text 'Savage Britons Lived Inland' and 'Half Savage Britons Lived on the Coast' (Patchett and Rose 1951, 6–7). Many textbook writers tended to make unequivocal statements about the Romans. While this may be understandable in the 19th century, I think there is little excuse in more recent times. A Study Book for 7–11 year olds covering the main areas of National Curriculum History goes in for bold headlines (with underlining). So for the Roman section the children can read: 'Roman Towns Were All Built To The Same Pattern; The Roman Didn't Manage To Conquer Scotland; Hadrian's Wall Protected Britain From The Scots' and the section finishes with 'That's everything you need to learn about the Romans...' (Coordination Group 2003, 26–9).

However, some authors (usually of books intended for secondary school pupils) clearly did do research. A new approach to children's books on history was conceived by Marjorie and C H B Quennell and published after World War I. Their two main series, *Everyday Life in...* (for example, Roman Britain) and *A History of Everyday Things in England* included text and drawings which they produced from research into both archaeological and historic sources. Some other publishers followed suit and used illustrations of objects often taken from British Museum

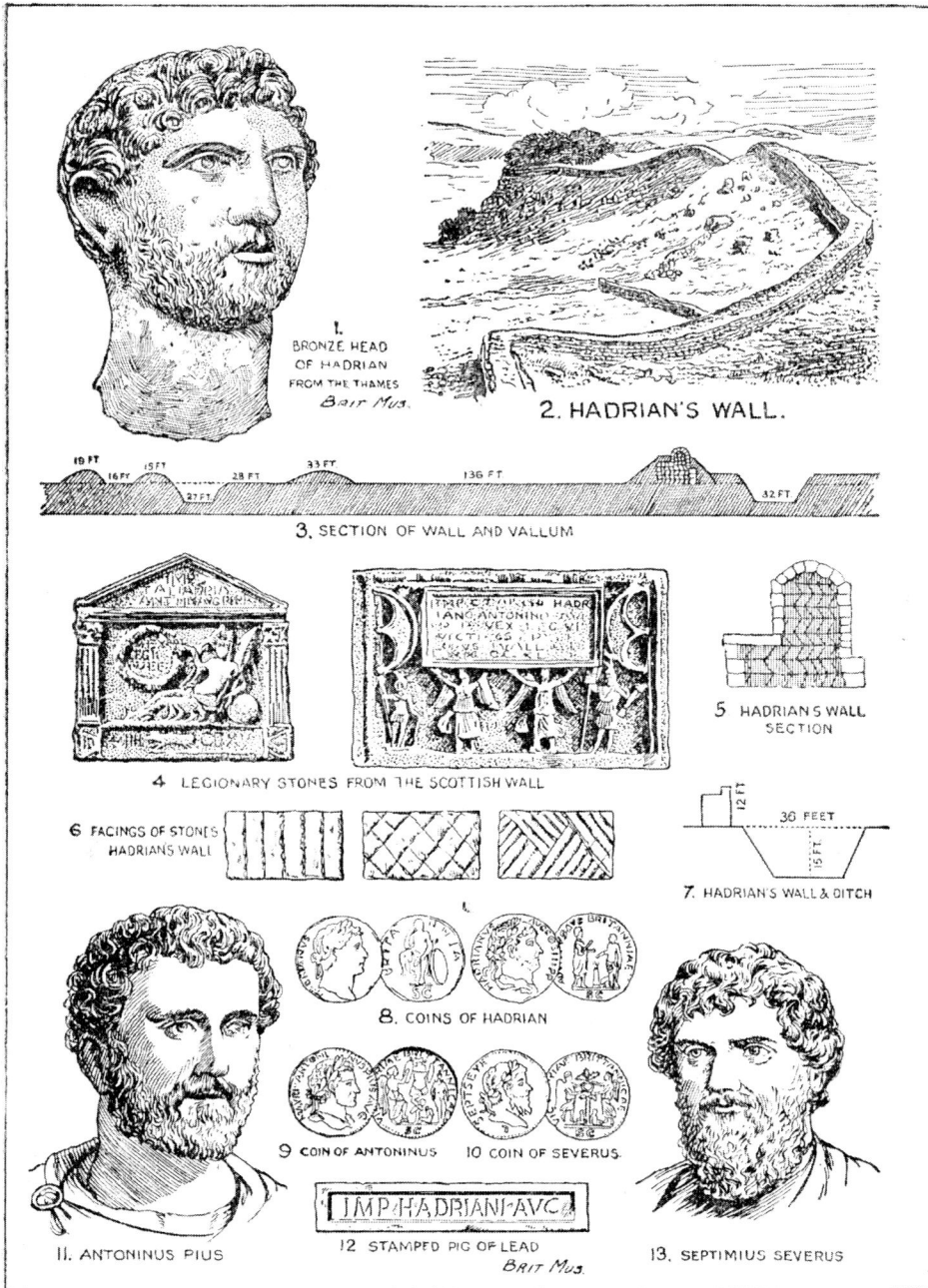

1. BRONZE HEAD OF HADRIAN FROM THE THAMES *Brit Mus.*

2. HADRIAN'S WALL.

3. SECTION OF WALL AND VALLUM

4 LEGIONARY STONES FROM THE SCOTTISH WALL

5 HADRIAN'S WALL SECTION

6 FACINGS OF STONES HADRIANS WALL

7. HADRIAN'S WALL & DITCH

8. COINS OF HADRIAN

9 COIN OF ANTONINUS   10 COIN OF SEVERUS.

11. ANTONINUS PIUS

12 STAMPED PIG OF LEAD *Brit Mus.*

13. SEPTIMIUS SEVERUS

THE NORTHERN WALL. Hadrian's Wall was built about A.D. 120 as a defensive frontier against the Picts. It extends for 70 miles between Bowness, Solway Firth and Wallsend-on-Tyne and was 18 feet high and 8 feet thick.

Fig 14.2. Hadrian's Wall in pictures. Visual information about Hadrian's Wall for educational use, published c. 1935. Some illustrations were provided by the British Museum (Airne 1935, 38).

sources, for example *The Story of Prehistoric and Roman Britain Told in Pictures* (Airne c. 1935) (see Fig 14.2).

But, with very few exceptions, it was not until the 1970s that school history textbooks were written using more up-to-date resources based on primary evidence, whether this was Roman literary sources or archaeological discoveries. School students began to be involved in their own learning and to be asked questions about written source material and photographs of objects, sites or landscapes. The key change probably came with the Schools History Project (SHP 2011) and its publications. It started with the funding in 1972 of a project, History 13–16, and still continues to provide textbooks of a high standard to teach history based on historical and archaeological evidence. One example of a book for this project is the excellent *Hadrian's Wall* which is well-researched and uses sources from Latin literature and objects and sites to pose questions for pupils (Scott 1984). Another good example from the 1980s, for primary schools, is *Ancient Britons*, which constantly poses questions for the reader based on presented evidence in the form of photographs or texts which the author has originated. For example, referring to aerial photographs of Maiden Castle and Alan Sorrell's drawn impression of the Iron Age hillfort at Llanmelin, one of his questions was, 'Which sort of entrance was harder for attackers to reach – the sort at Llanmelin or the sort at Maiden Castle?' (Triggs 1981, 33).

BOOKS FOR CHILDREN

During the 20th century a number of books were published which introduced children to the past. Some of these were designed for children to read for themselves; some formed an extra resource for teachers and parents. These books were usually stories featuring characters which children would be attracted to. Some were historical novels, the best perhaps from Rosemary Sutcliff, though there were several other authors. These are still being published, especially as part of reading schemes in primary schools.

Children should find publications about the past easily accessible. This often means the introduction of a character (dogs and rabbits are popular) and/or a book in cartoon form. A natural progression from the Sesame Street TV series was a cartoon book to introduce children to visiting museums (Alexander 1987). A similar and more recent example from Britain is *Harry and the Dinosaurs at the Museum* in which Harry's older sister wants to visit a museum because she is studying the Romans at school, while Harry is bored and hungry until he discovers the more exciting dinosaurs (Whybrow and Reynolds 2004). Cartoons were used successfully to introduce one of the sites on Hadrian's Wall to children. An activity booklet for children visiting Arbeia Roman fort, written by a Museum Studies student at the University of Leicester on work placement, was subsequently published by Tyne & Wear Museums (Arvanitidi 1996). Richard Brassey's book about Boudica for children is presented in cartoon-style drawings and strips, yet is accurate and offers evidence for all the statements made about the life and times of the queen (Brassey 2006).

Some people (dryasdusts, perhaps?) find the cartoon style incompatible with a learning resource. While it is true that cartoons need to be handled carefully, the format is well-known and understood by children. Not all of the drawings or text about the adventures of Asterix by Goscinny and Uderzo are accurate and cartoon strips and films have a long history of fantastic actions and events which we are not really expected to believe. Think, for example, of the Warner

Write a postcard home

Amaze your friends and relatives – try writing a postcard in Latin the next time you go on holiday! You will find a vocabulary list on your CD-ROM.

FIG 14.3. A ROMAN SOLDIER WRITES HOME. A ROMAN SOLDIER IN A DECKCHAIR WITH SUNGLASSES? THE STYLE OF ILLUSTRATION HERE AND ITS ACCOMPANYING TEXT ARE NOT MEANT TO FOOL THE YOUNG READER INTO THINKING THAT THE ROMANS INVENTED DECKCHAIRS (CORBISHLEY *ET AL* 1999, X).

Brothers' Looney Tunes cartoon character Road Runner: his arch opponent, Wile E Coyote, is often flattened like a sheet of paper and then gets up again.

I turned to a cartoonist to illustrate a series of books for children linked to CDs which contained extra information, games, 360˚ views of three sites (Housesteads, Lullingstone and Wroxeter) and internet connections. In *Real Romans: Digital Time Traveller* the cartoonist Dai Owen and I created cartoon-style maps, and make-your-own activities. The illustration (see Fig 14.3) is an encouragement to the young readers to write some real Latin, which is a feature of the book. The double-page spread which features this drawing is all about Latin words and numbers and the activity is to make a wax writing tablet (Corbishley *et al* 2003, X–XI).

CONCLUSIONS

Writers, whether of textbooks or information books for children, need to make their publications accessible and relevant to the age group or the curriculum they are studying. This does not mean that they have to be boring, or without illustration. It should mean that the resources are based on researched evidence and must be accurate. Children should be exposed to real evidence – accurately-translated quotations from ancient literature and photos or drawings of sites and objects. Accurate artists' impressions may be used to present a view of the past and as a piece of evidence which may be examined and questioned.

Drawing parallels with contemporary events or situations is a well-known and respected educational approach much used by teachers today and in the past. In the 19th and part of the 20th century the most frequent reference was to the creation and management of an empire, for example:

> Just as in our day the first thing we do when we conquer new lands is to make railways and roads, and open up the country … so the Romans in their time made roads and bridged rivers, and succeeded in turning wild savage countries into parts of the civilised world.
>
> (Ransome 1915, 10)

While children were still being taught British history from these early textbooks, such as those by Ransome and Markham, large tracts of the world were being governed by European countries. The British Empire was at its height by the outbreak of World War I. Even after World War II the idea of Britain in control, as it were, of a large portion of the world was evident in books used in schools. The school atlas I used at secondary school in the 1950s showed the world with the Commonwealth countries in pink, the colour favoured for maps of the British Empire (Goodall 1952, 6–7).

Callcott's *Little Arthur's History of England* (first edition published in 1834) has two maps of the British Empire, one showing the Empire at the time of the accession (1837) and the other at the death (1901) of Queen Victoria. Children finding out about the Empire with Lady Callcott were left in no doubt who was in charge: Australia is called 'another Englishman's country' while Canada, Australia and parts of Africa were 'where white men go to make their homes' and 'wherever there is English rule, there is freedom and justice' (Callcott 1907, 281, 285 and 284).

There is still a commonly-held view of the Romans pulling out of the country in AD 410 as if they were an occupying force engaged in a war. If it were true, the nearest parallel might be American troops leaving South Vietnam in 1973. Modern school textbooks generally deal with this period of Romano-British history more sensibly but older generations still tend to see periods of the past with clearly-defined beginnings and endings: battles, invasions or kings and queens, for example. The presentation of evidence and recognition that we do not always have access to facts about the past, only assumptions and ideas, would improve many a television documentary or general book on the subject.

Finally, Hadrian's Wall and the role it played in the Roman occupation of northern Britain is much better known by school students now than it was, and usually features in textbooks which deal with the Roman period in Britain. The Antonine Wall is featured less often. However, they are usually only a small part of the taught story of the Romans and are not dealt with in any detail unless the school wants, and is able, to include a visit as part of its curriculum work. Because of its complexity, size and location, the frontier needs to be part of a residential visit for most non-local schools. Resources for teachers exist but more are needed. Tyne & Wear Archives & Museums provide a range of teaching resources for the sites and museums they manage, from cross-curricular packs to computer games (TWAM 2011). There is a good pack for teachers which puts visits and classroom projects into the context of the National Curriculum (Catling and Rankin 2007). English Heritage used to provide a number of resources for teachers including the excellent *Hadrian's Wall: A teacher's handbook* (Walmsley 2002), now out of print. This is unfortunate as the book promoted the whole of the Wall for curriculum work, not just English Heritage sites in care. English Heritage also produced free booklets for teachers on its Roman museums on the Wall, but the one specially written for vocational students, and the poster pack appear no longer to be available.

Apart from the obvious necessity to provide resources which encourage teachers to visit the frontier sites and museums, there are also opportunities for teachers to use the frontier for cross-curricular studies, as Walmsley showed in his handbook for teachers (2002, 28–39). This is now partly addressed by the Hadrian's Wall Education Forum and its constituent bodies such as the Hadrian's Wall Schools Frontier Network. A list of some of the available resources for teachers can be downloaded (Hadrian's Wall Country 2011). An education pack, or a series of resources, should be published which promote the use of all the frontiers of the Roman Empire, translated into the relevant European languages. Perhaps this will help teachers in Britain to help their pupils understand the Roman frontiers in Holland and Germany and for teachers there to make the two walls in northern Britain part of their curriculum work.

Acknowledgments

Thanks to David Walmsley for his helpful comments on this chapter.

Bibliography and References

Airne, C W, c. 1935 *The Story of Prehistoric and Roman Britain Told in Pictures*, Sankey and Hudson, Manchester

Alexander, L, 1987 *A Visit to the Sesame Street Museum*, Random House, New York

Anderson Graham, P, 1920 *Highways and Byways in Northumbria*, Macmillan, London

Arvanitidi, E, 1996 *Arbeia: Activity Book*, Tyne & Wear Archives & Museums, Newcastle upon Tyne

Bareham, J D, 1964 *Awake to History: Book One, From Caves to Cities*, Pergamon, Oxford

Brassey, R, 2006 *Boudica*, Orion, London

Callcott, Lady, 1907 (1834) *Little Arthur's History of England*, John Murray, London

Catling, J, and Rankin, A, 2007 *This Way to the Northern Frontier, Tribes and Romans in Northern Britain: A Resource for Teachers*, Museum of Antiquities of the University and Society of Antiquities of Newcastle upon Tyne, Newcastle upon Tyne

Coordination Group, 2003 *Key Stage Two History: The Study Book*, Coordination Group Publications, Kirkby in Furness, Cumbria

Corbishley, M, 2011 *Pinning Down the Past: Archaeology, Heritage, and Education Today*, The Boydell Press, Woodbridge

Corbishley, M, Cooper, M, and Owen, D, 2003 *Real Romans: Digital Time Traveller*, TAG Learning and English Heritage, Gravesend and London

Dickens, C, 1868 *A Child's History of England*, Hazel, Watson & Viney, London

Erleigh, E, 1948 *In the beginning: A First History for Little Children*, Heinemann, London

Goodall, G, 1952 *Philip's County Council School Atlas*, George Philip, London

Hadrian's Wall Country, 2011 *Education* [online], available from: http://www.hadrians-wall.org/page.aspx// About-the-World-Heritage-Site/Education [24 June 2011]

King, D, 1934 *Long Long Ago*, Blackie, London and Glasgow

Lippmann, L, 1980 Racism in Australian Children's Books, in *The Slant of the Pen: Racism in Children's Books* (ed R Preiswerk), World Council of Churches, Geneva, 61–71

Markham (Mrs), 1886 *A History of England*, John Murray, London

Patchett, T S, and Rose, R W, 1951 *The Modern School Visual Histories: Book 1 to 1485*, Evans, London

Power, R, c. 1940 *From Early Days to Norman Times*, Evans Brothers, London

Preiswerk, R (ed), 1980 *The Slant of the Pen: Racism in Children's Books*, World Council of Churches, Geneva

Ransome, C, 1915 *A First History of England*, Rivingtons, London

Schools History Project, 2011 *About SHP* [online], available from: http://www.schoolshistoryproject.org.uk/ AboutSHP/index.htm [27 May 2011]

Scott, J, 1984 *Hadrian's Wall*, Holmes McDougall, Edinburgh

Scott-Elliot, G F, 1923 *Stories of Early British Life from the Earliest Times*, Seeley and Service, London

Sellar, W C, and Yeatman, R J, 1930 *1066 And All That: A Memorable History of England, Comprising all the parts you can remember including 103 Good Things, 5 Bad Kings and 2 Genuine Dates*, Methuen, London

Triggs, T D, 1981 *Ancient Britons*, Oliver and Boyd, Edinburgh

Tyne & Wear Archives & Museums, 2011 *Information for schools* [online], available from: http://www. twmuseums.org.uk/schools/home.html [31 May 2011]

Walmsley, D, 2002 *Hadrian's Wall: A teacher's handbook*, English Heritage, London

Whybrow, I, and Reynolds, A, 2004 *Harry and the Dinosaurs at the Museum*, Penguin, London

15

Romanes eunt Domus?

Don Henson

Borders and boundaries are a natural part of every society. We place ourselves behind walls to separate ourselves from others as part of the creation of our identity. These borders can be physical or metaphorical. The most extreme form of border is one where the person looking out from behind the wall assumes a position of superiority over those on the outside. But not all borders have to take this form. Borders which are not physically manifest or only virtual may have a more neutral flavour. Physical proximity is often seen as a threat whereas detached observation at a distance neutralises any threat. Those on the outside then appear as merely exotic rather than as a potential enemy.

Borders were extremely important for the Roman Empire. The later Empire especially was defined by its sense of difference, and superiority, from those on the outside of its borders. In the modern world, our engagement with ancient Rome is as outsiders, beyond the borders now of time. The engagement we have with Rome is complex, since Rome finds its place not only in academic culture but also in the popular arts.

I want here to make a few observations on the use of Rome as a topic for film and television performance through a very particular kind of border: that of the screen. The viewing screen is at once a physical feature but also a mental construct. The screen invites us to enter a virtual space yet, as a border, imposes an act of mental transformation on the viewer if that space is to be crossed. I will restrict myself to English-language media and therefore leave out the rich tradition of Roman portrayal in Italian film and TV. What I have to say is, therefore, culturally specific rather than universal.

When we talk of English-language film and television as seen and heard in the UK, we have to distinguish two different cultural contexts for this: the United States of America and the United Kingdom. There are strong differences between the two in the understanding and uses of Rome. Films of the silent era before 1929 are common, but rarely accessible. Looking only at talking films, we can isolate 32 American and British films made between 1932 and 2007 that have ancient Rome as a primary topic or setting. These fall into various genres. The large-scale epic, expensively shot and dealing with a story against a background of big events, is the commonest of the genres. Filmed versions of the Roman plays of William Shakespeare and George Bernard Shaw are also common. Comedy, overt political commentary and sexploitation have a few examples each, while the list of genres is completed by a musical, a detective drama and myth.

- Epic: *The Sign of the Cross* (1932), *Cleopatra* (1934), *The Last Days of Pompeii* (1935), *Quo Vadis* (1951), *The Robe* (1953), *Demetrius and the Gladiators* (1954), *Sign of the Pagan* (1954), *Ben Hur* (1959), *Cleopatra* (1963), *The Fall of the Roman Empire* (1964), *Gladiator* (2000)

- Shakespeare: *Julius Caesar* (1950; 1953; 1970), *Antony and Cleopatra* (1972), *Titus* (1999)
- Shaw: *Caesar and Cleopatra* (1946), *Androcles and the Lion* (1952)
- Comedy: *Fiddlers Three* (1944), *Carry on Cleo* (1964), *A Funny Thing Happened on the Way to the Forum* (1966), *Up Pompeii* (1971), *Life of Brian* (1979)
- Political commentary: *Roman Scandals* (1933 – also a musical), *Spartacus* (1960 – also an epic), *Sebastiane* (1976 – also art house)
- Sexploitation: *The Arena* (1974), *Caligula* (1979), *Private Gladiator* (2002)
- Musical: *Jupiter's Darling* (1955)
- Detective: *Age of Treason* (1993)
- Mythical: *The Last Legion* (2007)

The cultural context for the making and reception of many of these and other films has been well explored. For example, Maria Wyke (1997) has shown how various film versions of Spartacus have been used in different cultural settings. In the case of the Hollywood version, the diegetic barrier inside the film between Roman and slave mimics the political barriers aimed at by the film's production, self-consciously seeking to break the Hollywood blacklisting of Communists in the 1950s.

What is clear is that many of the American films are based around a duality of Roman and the other. A Roman Imperial court and machine is situated in opposition to internal or external outsiders, be they Christians, slaves, Jews or Egyptians. The link between respect for Roman republican values with the American founding ideal or revolutionary myth has been well explored. The American use of ancient Rome as an exemplar for its own political aspirations during its separation from Britain could easily have led to a filmic presentation of the Roman Republic as an ideal. On the other hand, the need for an other against which to position America necessitates some kind of border. In the 19th century, this involved looking west to the frontier. In the 20th century, this can involve looking east back to Europe across the border of the screen where Imperial Rome can stand in for the evil Empire, the mighty colossus opposed by the plucky freedom fighter or religious sectarian. The Julio-Claudian period, when republic gave way to monarchy, can be used as the ideal metaphor for all that is opposed to American values; sexually licentious, politically vicious and morally corrupt. The borders that exist on screen are between Rome as a civilisation or system and opposing beliefs or social groups. The internal diegetic border is replicated by the structural border of the screen. The American audience is invited to empathise with a point of view antithetical to Rome, positioning itself as an outsider behind the present day border of the screen.

The more recent *Gladiator* has a more nuanced and different relationship with America. A film shot after the ending of the Cold War, it speaks to a dominant yet unsure and troubled America about the nature of Empire and the role of the honest citizen in a world of corrupt politics. Roman values dominate in far-off places as a pale shadow of the corrupt but alluring original. The film was a UK/US co-production, with a British director, Ridley Scott, fully aware of the cinematic past and determined to subvert that past to shape a new mythical Rome for a more modern age.

The British relationship with Rome has always been rather different from that of the USA. Epic is far less in evidence as a genre. Instead, comedy and plays are the dominant genres. Taking the UK films out of the list given above, we have:

- Comedy: *Fiddlers Three* (1944), *Carry on Cleo* (1964), *A Funny Thing Happened on the Way to the Forum* (1966 – UK/US but in a British tradition), *Up Pompeii* (1971), *Life of Brian* (1979)
- Shakespeare: *Julius Caesar* (1970), *Antony and Cleopatra* (1972)
- Shaw: *Caesar and Cleopatra* (1946)
- Political: *Sebastiane* (1976)
- Epic: *Gladiator* (2000 – UK/US but British director)
- Myth: *The Last Legion* (2007)

This lack of epics reflects the dominance of Hollywood over domestic UK film production that has enfeebled the UK film industry, which is able to make fewer and less well-financed products. Where UK filmic expertise does flourish is in television, where Rome has been a strong presence on our screens. Plays and comedy continue to be the dominant genres but are joined now by novels, science fiction and soap-opera.

- Shakespeare: *Julius Caesar* (1938; 1951; 1959; 1960; 1964; 1969; 1979), *Coriolanus* (1984), *Spread of the Eagle* (1963), *Heil Caesar* (1973), *Antony and Cleopatra* (1974; 1981), *Titus Andronicus* (1985)
- Novels: *The Last Days of Pompeii* (1984), *I, Claudius* (1976), *The Eagle of the Ninth* (1977)
- Comedy: *Chelmsford 123* (1989–90), *Up Pompeii* (1969–70), *Further Up Pompeii* (1975; 1991)
- Sci-Fi: *Dr Who – The Romans* (1965), *Dr Who – Fires of Pompeii* (2008)
- Soap opera: *Rome* (2005–07)

The two dominant modes of Roman portrayal in British production are markedly different from the dominant mode of the US, with a literary base (plays and novels) and comedy, as opposed to the epic with its clash of opposite worldviews and social groups. The dualistic vision of Rome as a reflection of the present is absent. What we have instead is either self-conscious celebration of a literary culture in which the Rome on screen stands for the higher civilisation embodied in its literary creation, or deliberately comic deconstruction of the higher/literary representation through farce or satire. An excellent example of this use of comedy to comment on the creation of higher forms of representation is the deconstruction of the epic in *Carry on Cleo*. The film *A Funny Thing Happened on the Way to the Forum* is instructive in being a joint UK/US production. Although the director, Richard Lester, was himself American, he was resident in the UK and had fully absorbed the British performance tradition. While the US play on which the film was based was a purely comedic entertainment, Lester was clear in wanting the film to be a satirical social commentary, a view opposed by the US partners in their production.

Britons are still seemingly caught within the web of Empire, standing on the inside either wishing to join the elite or reliving social tensions by poking fun at it. We are firmly inside the border gazing upon our overlords. Sandra Joshel (Joshel *et al* 2001) has written of the domestication of Empire by bringing it into the domestic arena of the home through television. She was of course referring to *I, Claudius*, a British translation of a literary work into televisual drama, akin to soap opera. The border of the screen is effectively broken down in soap opera with the resulting blurring of fiction and reality. We can indeed become Romans, welcomed inside the border and accepted as citizens of the great world civilisation (is this a comfort for a people whose own Empire has largely gone?). For those who do not quite see the benefits that this brings, there is always the comedy to reassure us that, although we may be native Britons, or of low social status, that really makes us superior to the rather ridiculous Roman elite. It seems that we look on Rome through the screen as an other civilisation, but one we aspire to.

What of possible Romes that have yet to find a screen presence? There are many stories or themes relevant to Britain that could be told on screen but have not been. For example:

- resistance to Roman conquest by Caratacos, Boudicca, Venutios;
- Agricola's campaigns;
- the building of Hadrian's Wall;
- British usurpers of the Empire: Carausius, Maximus;
- Constantine and Christianity beginning in York;
- the events of 410 (Britain in Europe or not in Europe?)

Any of these could make exciting drama or political and social commentary. On the other hand, there are two recent British films which use the mythical loss of the 9th legion in the north of Britain as their theme: *The Eagle*, and *Centurion*. Perhaps creative horizons are at last expanding.

Likewise, there are many periods of Roman history in general that are unexplored. There is a heavy preponderance of films set in the Julio-Claudian period, far outnumbering all other periods or dynasties added together (see Fig 15.1).

FIG 15.1. UK AND US SOUND FILMS PORTRAYING ANCIENT ROME BY PERIOD.

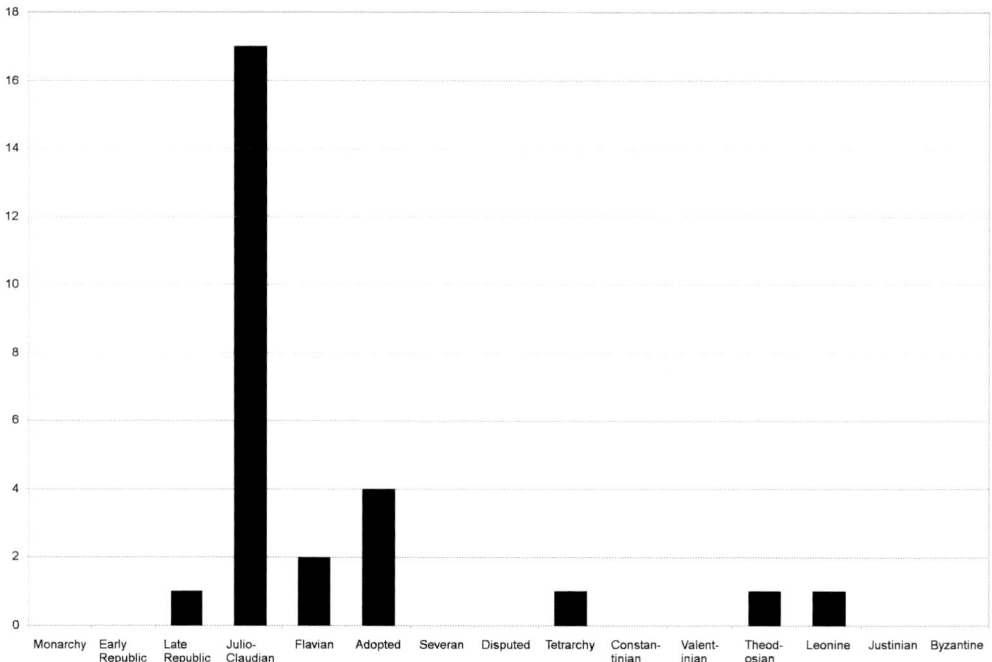

This may be a function of the perceived high status of Rome's golden age as outlined in the Renaissance and 18th century, where Plutarch's *Parallel Lives* became immensely popular. Plutarch was of course the ultimate source for Shakespeare's Roman plays. On the other hand, the obsession with the Julio-Claudian period may also be due to the need for a defined border to cross, so that we can see from within our own civilisation and look upon an other; an other different enough to be useful as a metaphor or an aspiration. The Christianity of the late Empire is too similar to our own world (and the era of the adopted Emperors too lacking in drama). That other eras of Roman history can be fruitful fodder for the cinema industry is clear from the case of Italy (see Fig 15.2).

FIG 15.2. ITALIAN SOUND FILMS PORTRAYING ANCIENT ROME.

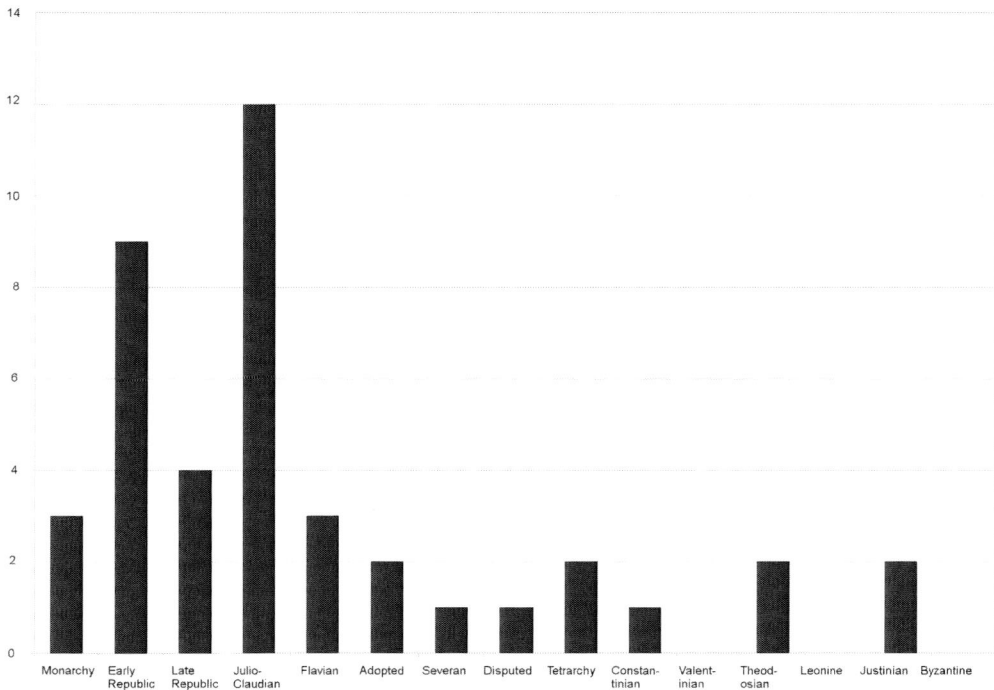

In the UK we do not have an organic inheritance from ancient Rome as part of our histor-ical identity. Instead, we have inherited Shakespeare's use of Julio-Claudian Rome. It has been argued that Shakespeare's Roman plays are inherently different from his history plays that explore English monarchy, yet I think they do share a common concern. *Julius Caesar* and *Antony and Cleopatra* as a pair begin and end with monarchy and have as their narrative the evils of civil war. *Coriolanus* could be seen likewise as an exploration of leadership and defective republican poli-tics. For Shakespeare, Rome stands in for England. It is not an other that we identify ourselves against. Cinema and television versions of Rome in the UK have failed to move very far from

this. It is only an overtly political film-maker like Derek Jarman who manages to find new resonances with Rome, in *Sebastiane* (a film whose dialogue is solely in Latin, that is set in the time
of Diocletian and is an extended exploration of male homosexuality).

It is clear that Rome's place in film and television is a mythical Rome, a Rome created or
explored only for its resonances in today's world. It is not the Rome of history, of the academy,
but of our imagination. In *Life of Brian*, we enjoy the spectacle of a rebellious Jew having
his Latin grammatically corrected for its resonance with countless 20th-century school rooms.
Romane ite domum? No, we need them for the borders they create in our minds.

BIBLIOGRAPHY AND REFERENCES

Cyrino, M S, 2005 *Big screen Rome*, Blackwell Publishing, Oxford

Joshel, S, Malamud, M, and Donald, T, 2001 *Imperial projections: ancient Rome in modern popular culture*,
John Hopkins University Press, Baltimore

MacCallum, M W, 1910 *Shakespeare's Roman plays and their background*, Macmillan, London

Solomon, J, 2001 (1978) *The ancient world in cinema*, Yale University Press, New Haven

Wyke, M, 1997 *Projecting the past: ancient Rome, cinema and history*, Routledge, New York

FILMS [title, year, country, director, (main actors)]

The Sign of the Cross, 1932, USA, Cecil B DeMille (Frederic March, Charles Laughton, Claudette Colbert)

Roman Scandals, 1933, USA, Frank Tuttle (Eddie Cantor)

Cleopatra, 1934, USA, Cecil DeMille (Claudette Colbert)

The Last Days of Pompeii, 1935, USA, Ernest Schoedsack (Preston Foster, Basil Rathbone)

Fiddlers Three, 1944, UK, Harry Watt (Tommie Trinder, Sonnie Hale)

Caesar and Cleopatra, 1946, UK, Gabriel Pascal (Vivien Leigh, Claude Rains)

Julius Caesar, 1950, USA, David Bradley (Harold Tasker, Charlton Heston)

Quo Vadis, 1951, USA, Mervin LeRoy (Robert Taylor, Deborah Kerr, Peter Ustinov)

Androcles and the Lion, 1952, USA, Chester Erskine (Jean Simmons, Victor Mature, Alan Young)

Julius Caesar, 1953, USA, Joseph Mankiewicz (Marlon Brando, James Mason, John Gielgud)

The Robe, 1953, USA, Henry Koster (Richard Burton, Jean Simmons, Victor Mature)

Demetrius and the Gladiators, 1954, USA, Delmer Davies (Victor Mature, Susan Hayward)

Sign of the Pagan, 1954, USA, Douglas Sirk (Jeff Chandler, Jack Palance, Ludmilla Tcherina)

Jupiter's Darling, 1955, USA, George Sidney (Esther Willliams, George Sanders, Howard Keel)

Ben Hur, 1959, USA, William Wyler (Charlton Heston, Stephen Boyd)

Spartacus, 1960, USA, Stanley Kubrick (Kirk Douglas, Laurence Olivier, Charles Laughton)

Cleopatra, 1963, USA, Joseph Mankiewicz (Richard Burton, Elizabeth Taylor, Rex Harrison)

Carry on Cleo, 1964, UK, Gerald Thomas (Amanda Barrie, Sid James, Kenneth Williams)

The Fall of the Roman Empire, 1964, USA, Anthony Mann (Alec Guinness, Stephen Boyd, Christopher Plummer)

A Funny Thing Happened on the Way to the Forum, 1966, UK, Richard Lester (Plautus, Zero Mostel, Phil Silvers)

Julius Caesar, 1970, UK, Stuart Burge (John Gielgud, Charlton Heston)

Up Pompeii, 1971, UK, Bob Kellett (Frankie Howerd)

Antony and Cleopatra, 1972, UK/Sp/Switz, Charlton Heston (Charlton Heston, Hildegaard Neil)

The Arena, 1974, USA, Steve Carver (Pam Grier)

Sebastiane, 1976, UK, Derek Jarman

Caligula, 1979, USA/It, Tinto Brass (Malcolm McDowell, John Gielgud, Helen Mirren, Peter O'Toole)

Life of Brian, 1979, UK, Terry Jones (Monty Python)

Age of Treason, 1993, USA, Kevin Connor (Bryan Brown, Art Malik)

Titus, 1999, USA/Italy, Julie Taymor (Anthony Hopkins)

Gladiator, 2000, UK/USA, Ridley Scott (Richard Harris, Russell Crowe)

Private Gladiator, 2002, USA, Antonio Adamo

Augustus, 2003, UK/It, Roger Young (Peter O'Toole, Charlotte Rampling) (TV Film)

Nero, 2005, UK/It/Sp, Paul Marcus (Hans Matheson, Laura Morante, Rike Schmid) (TV Film)

The Last Legion, 2007, UK/It/Fr/Slovakia, Doug Lefler (Colin Firth, Ben Kingsley)

UK TELEVISION PRODUCTIONS [title, year, director, (main actors)]

Antony & Cleopatra, 1974, Peter Seabourne (Colin Farrell, Susan Jameson)

Antony & Cleopatra, 1981, Jonathan Miller (Colin Blakely, Jane Lapotaire)

Chelmsford 123, 1989–90, John Stroud, Vic Finch (Jimmy Mulville, Rory McGrath)

Coriolanus, 1984, Elijah Moshinsky (Alan Howard, Joss Ackland, Irene Worth)

Dr Who: Fires of Pompeii, 2008, Colin Teague (David Tennant, Catherine Tate)

Dr Who: The Romans, 1965, Christopher Berry (William Hartnell, William Russell, Jacqueline Hill)

Further Up Pompeii, 1975, David Croft (Frankie Howerd)

Further Up Pompeii, 1991, Ian Hamilton (Frankie Howerd)

Heil Caesar, 1973, Ronald Smedley (Peter Howell, John Stride, Anthony Bate)

I, Claudius, 1976, Herbert Wise (Derek Jacobi, Brian Blessed, Sian Phillips)

Julius Caesar, 1938, Dallas Bower (Ernest Milton, Douglas Clarke-Smith, Sebastian Shaw, Anthony Ireland)

Julius Caesar, 1951, Stephen Harrison (Walter Hudd, Richard Bebb, Anthony Hawtrey)

Julius Caesar, 1959, Stuart Burge (Robert Perceval, Eric Porter, Michael Gough, William Sylvester)

Julius Caesar, 1960 (Michael Goodliffe, William Shatner, John Laurie)

Julius Caesar, 1964, John Vernon (National Youth Theatre)

Julius Caesar, 1969, Alan Bridges (Maurice Denham, Robert Stephens, Frank Finlay, Edward Woodward)

Julius Caesar, 1979, Herbert Wise (Charles Gray, Keith Michell, Richard Pasco)

Rome, UK/US co-production, 2005–07, Michael Apted and others (Ciaran Hinds, Kevin McKidd, Ray Stevenson)

Spread of the Eagle, 1963, Peter Dews (Robert Hardy, Roland Culver, Beatrix Lehmann)

The Eagle of the Ninth, 1977, Michael Simpson (Anthony Higgins, Bernard Gallagher, Patrick Malahide)

The Last Days of Pompeii, UK/US/Italy co-production, 1984, Peter Hunt (Laurence Olivier, Franco Nero)

Titus Andronicus, 1985, Jane Howell (Edward Hardwicke, Trevor Peacock, Anna Calder-Marshall)

Up Pompeii, 1969–70, Michael Mills, David Croft, Sydney Lotterby (Frankie Howerd)

16

The Living Frontier:
the Passing of Time on Hadrian's Wall

Richard Hingley

Introduction

This chapter explores the legacies of Hadrian's Wall in the physical and cultural landscape of the north of England. It also addresses how we might develop a rather different appreciation of the archaeological significance of the Wall. Archaeological accounts tend to emphasise the construction of the Wall during the AD 120s and its disuse as a Roman frontier structure in the early fifth century (see for example Symonds and Mason 2009). It is clear, however, that this monument did not suddenly cease to exist when Roman Britain came to an end. An alternative approach suggests that the considerable significance of this monument has, effectively, kept its remains alive throughout its lengthy history. Hadrian's Wall has been uncovered and described by many since the sixth century and these accounts and images have added to the life of the Wall, emphasising its continued presence.

Archaeologists have helped to define their subject by developing ways to determine the sequence of passing time, including the techniques of stratigraphy, artefact analysis and radiocarbon dating. From the late 19th century, a detailed body of knowledge has been accumulated that provides a chronology for the Roman period, emphasising the history and transformation of Hadrian's Wall from the 120s to the fifth century (Maxfield 1982; Symonds and Mason 2009). This body of information provides a foundation for the definition, protection and management of this World Heritage Site (Young 1999). This increased confidence about the chronology of the Wall has also served to separate its remains from the contemporary world, to create and elaborate a clear chronological division between the Roman past and the present day.

From the perspective pursued here, however, the Wall never died – it lives on in the writings, images and physical works of later people, including archaeologists. Taking a lead from artists and popular writers, this chapter explores ways in which archaeological research and fieldwork can help to keep the monument alive.

The Living Wall

Robert Henry Forster was born at Backworth, Earsdon, and helped to direct the excavations at Corbridge from 1907 to 1914 (Bishop 1994, 10–12). By this time Forster had already published a book on Hadrian's Wall in which he titled himself 'the Amateur Antiquary'. In this work he identified the 'two divisions into which antiquaries may be divided' … 'the pedantic and the imaginative' (1899, 5–6). He also defined these two idealised characters. With regard to the pedantic antiquarian, Forster noted:

He is a seething mass of multifarious learning, proficient in many arts and sciences.... As a proof of his mathematical, critical, strategical, topographical, epigraphical, and other capacities ... he can decipher obliterated inscriptions, till they mean whatever he has previously assumed their purport to be. His only faults are in the absence of imagination, and a deficient sense of perspective: but knowing, as he does, everything knowable, and a great deal besides, there is no sphere of imagination left for him ...

This comment reflects the stifling debates over the dating of the various elements of Hadrian's Wall that had dominated recent scholarship (cf Bates 1895, 7).

Forster (1899, 6) had a rather less pedantic approach in mind, observing that:

to the imaginative antiquary the coin, the inscription, the ruin, or the manuscript are but husks of the past: their interest lies in the fact that they contain, as it were, a kind of residual magnetism, upon which his imagination and his knowledge of human nature can work, till he reproduces some picture of bygone times, some chapter of a lost romance, or some echo of long silent poetry: for the true interest of antiquities is, after all, the interest of human life.

Forster's idea of using archaeological items and ancient texts to reflect on life in the ancient past drew upon the earlier Romantic antiquarianism of poets and artists such as Sir Walter Scott (Hingley 2012, 209). Other authors used this imaginative approach to draw political analogies.

Hadrian's Wall had become internationally famous during the middle and later decades of the 19th century, partly because it served to provide a source of imperial reflection. The antiquary John Collingwood Bruce chose the fort of Borcovicum (Housesteads) to present a powerful lecture that compared the Empires of Britain and Rome, stressing the political and religious superiority of the former (Bruce 1851, 40–1; Hingley 2000, 21). Bruce had involved himself in a campaign to promote the regional and national significance of the Wall, a project that included a programme of excavation and antiquarian research (Breeze 2003).

In 1906, the famous novelist and poet Rudyard Kipling constructed imperial folklore for the English in his novel *Puck of Pook's Hill*. Kipling narrated three periods of the history of England, under the Romans, Danes and Normans, and his Roman tales were particularly influential since they drew upon a powerful imperial parallel. Kipling recreated Hadrian's Wall as a metaphor for the British north-western frontiers in India and for concerns about the potential decadence in the British Empire, reflecting, in particular, the problematic recent events in South Africa and India (Roberts 2007, 114). His three Roman chapters formed not so much a contribution to the history of Britain but parables about empire and civilisation that projected contemporary morals for the British (Gilmour 2002, 172). Archaeologists attacked the details of Kipling's imperial rendition of the Wall, pointing out its inaccuracies and anachronisms (see for example Haverfield 1906, 190; Collingwood 1921b, 6). His imperial analogy, however, had a considerable impact on many of the readers of his novel, an influence that has continued to the present day as a result of the writings of W H Auden and Rosemary Sutcliff (Hingley 2011, 46).

After the first decade of the 20th century, authors found it increasingly difficult to romanticise service on the Wall, partly as a result of the difficult international situation and the gradual collapse of the British Empire. In 1937, W H Auden produced the script for a BBC radio programme entitled *Hadrian's Wall from Caesar to the National Trust*, which included his poem *Roman Wall Blues* (Carpenter 1981, 226). Auden wrote in *The Radio Times* that the Wall 'stood as a symbol for certain imperialistic conceptions of life, for military discipline and an international order; in opposition to the Celtic and Germanic tribal loyalties which overwhelmed it' (quoted in Carpenter 1981, 231, 471). He deliberately inverted the sentiments expressed in Kipling's novel to cast a critical gaze on the autocracy and military force that lay behind imperial endeavour (Hingley 2012, 202–3). Kipling and Auden brought the remains of the Wall into a living engagement with the present, despite the rather different political and military circumstances with which they engaged.

These writings, together with the art that has drawn upon the Wall, represent the structure as a living landscape, a tradition that continues to the present day through representation of Hadrian's Wall in the two recent films *The Eagle* and *Centurion*. Many such popular accounts of the Wall draw upon the idea that Forster explored by using archaeological materials to create imaginative pictures of bygone lives.

DISTANCING THE WALL FROM THE PRESENT

While such works aimed to bring the Wall to life, archaeologists were busy constructing a chronological framework that was to serve to separate the monument clearly from the present day. During the final decade of the 19th century, an archaeological focus of attention resulted in the detailed mapping, excavation and interpretation of the chronology and form of the Wall (Haverfield 1899). In his influential article *Hadrian's Wall: A History of the Problem*, R G Collingwood (1921a, 59–66) defined 'The period of scientific excavation', arguing that this commenced in 1891 and lasted until the present day. Collingwood argued that this scientific period of study commenced with the work of a number of researchers, primarily the Oxford ancient historian and archaeologist Francis Haverfield. From 1920, Collingwood built upon Haverfield's work, maintaining his interest until the 1930s. From the 1890s to 1950s, a fairly systematic programme of work created new techniques and questions to explore the physical character of Hadrian's Wall (Maxfield 1982; Browning 1991).

Serious attention was paid to the anatomy of the Wall, exploring the *Vallum* and the structure of the stone curtain Wall. In addition, a new element of the frontier, the Turf Wall, was recognised and examined. The detailed knowledge that arose as a result of this research provides one of the reasons that Hadrian's Wall came to be inscribed as a World Heritage Site (WHS) in 1987 (Young 1999). The preservation of the Wall, together with the detailed knowledge of its location, form and sequence, emphasises its importance as a Roman frontier monument. Hadrian's Wall is probably the best known of the frontier works that formerly defined the Roman Empire.

The point that this chapter seeks to emphasise, however, is that the establishment of the methods and theories of archaeology also focused attention on defining and clearly distinguishing the (dead) past of the Wall from its (living) present landscape (Hingley 2011). The creation of a consciousness that the past is effectively 'a foreign country' was primarily a product of the 19th century (Lowenthal 1985, 233), providing an idea that impacted deeply upon the study of Hadrian's Wall. This tradition has led to a situation in which attempts to bring the Wall to life in art and popular writing have been separated off from the archaeological programmes of work that have aimed to address the 'real' Wall. To explore fully the Roman past of this famous monument required the removal of later accretions that had built up on its site and the display of the uncovered remains of the Roman structures for visitors to inspect. As Mike Pearson and Michael Shanks (2001, 115) have argued in their account of archaeology and performance, 'What is found becomes authentic and valuable because it is set by choice in a new and separate environment with its own order, purpose and its own temporality – the time co-ordinates of the discipline archaeology which give the object its date and context'.

Reviving Hadrian's Wall

Today, various agencies aim to encourage visitors to the Wall from the urban centres of northern England and from overseas and to coordinate visitor experiences (Hadrian's Wall Heritage 2009). A number of art projects and exhibitions manifest this broadening access. One of the most impressive is *Writing on the Wall*, which encouraged artists to write about Hadrian's Wall, resulting in the publication of a volume of collected papers (Chettle 2006). *Writing on the Wall* projects Hadrian's Wall in phenomenological terms as a multinational monument, open to all. It draws upon literary approaches to borderlands as landscapes that provide the context for multiple alternative histories (Hingley 2010, 239).

Writing on the Wall was an international creative writing project, which aimed to link together the local communities and people along the original line of Hadrian's Wall. The project ran from 2001 to 2006 and was part-funded by the Regional Development Agency, One NorthEast, and the Hadrian's Wall Tourist Partnership (Chettle 2006, 2). Steve Chettle has noted that it was inspired by a number of earlier writings on Hadrian's Wall, including Auden's *Roman Wall Blues* and a media report on the Vindolanda tablets. The project included a series of educational and community-based workshops that took place along the route of the Wall. The writers came from Cumbria, Northumberland, Tyne and Wear and Scotland, but also from the countries that had provided auxiliary units to the Wall in Roman times, including poets from Morocco, Romania, Iraq, the Netherlands and Bulgaria (Lewis 2006, 16). It resulted in the creation of art works and artistic texts that were inspired by the archaeological remains and landscapes of the Wall.

The encouragement of tourism over the past decade has led a variety of other events that have drawn upon the impressive archaeological remains. This includes the re-enactment events that regularly occur in order to draw people to particular parts of the monument and also an innovative project that took place on 13 March 2010 in which the entire line of the frontier was marked out after dark by thousands of people through the use of beacons. Such events serve to illustrate the main theme of this chapter – that the disuse of the Wall as a Roman frontier during the early fifth century marked only one form of ending (cf Bender 1998, 9). From early medieval times to the present day, people have recreated the Wall as a vital element of the living landscape. Poets, novelists, antiquaries, archaeologists, clerics and artists have mused on the remains, using the Wall to tell many different stories, creating ideas that have kept its remains alive for all those who take an interest.

Tim Brennan's performance art, based on William Hutton's visit along the Wall in 1801, provides an additional example of the continuing life of the monument (Brennan 2005). Brennan produced this performance as part of a commission, *Performing Northumbria: Empire* at BALTIC, Gateshead, in 2005. This work used the analogy of Roman and contemporary imperialism to interrogate the Roman past and the imperial present. It raised the issue of the relationship of the Roman frontier to attempts to prevent movement between peoples in the world today, an image that serves to re-emphasise the critical comments on oppression that were highlighted by Auden during the 1930s (cf Hingley 2010, 239–40).

The Role of Archaeology in a Revival of the Wall

Animating the Wall draws on the human lives that continue to be tied into its uncovering, maintenance, mapping, marketing and interpretation, whilst also emphasising the evidence for the lives of those who populated the monument in Roman times. In 1974, the travel writer Hunter Davies published a popular account of Hadrian's Wall. Davies had been brought up in Carlisle and educated in Durham, where he had taken a degree that included a course on Romano-British archaeology and Hadrian's Wall. He remarked that he 'always found the subject incredibly boring', but that, 'Slowly, with age, I've come to appreciate that it was a living Wall, then as well as now' (Davies 1974, vii). On the crags in the centre of the Wall's line, Davies came across a group of men clearing and consolidating the impressive remains of the curtain Wall. They were clearing tumbled stones and earth away from the faces of the Wall and rebuilding it with a concrete top. This operation was also revealing the formerly buried remains of the monument and had uncovered, over the previous decades, a number of buried Roman turrets. Davies (1974, 155) noted that 'Hadrian's Wall is a living wall, not just for the local inhabitants, but for tourists and archaeologists, a living, breathing, expanding, growing wall'.

In this regard, one of the main strengths of archaeology lies in the power of excavation to create a link between past and present. The restoration work that Davies observed has ceased, but the archaeological excavations that occur along the line of the Wall draw significant public interest and bring people into an immediate engagement with evidence for past lives. The long-term excavation projects at South Shields and Vindolanda have played a vital part in continuing to animate Hadrian's Wall. Archaeology students and members of the public are fascinated by the idea that the artefact they are handling was once held by an ancient person and the residual magnetism of the past as a source of speculation and knowledge helps to drive archaeological explorations of the Wall today. In a comparable way, the creation of new features for visitors to explore, for example at Vindolanda, South Shields and Wallsend, also add to the living character of the Wall (Fig 16.1).

But the Wall's landscape is not merely Roman in origin. The monument has been pulled apart and rebuilt since Roman times and its landscape contains evidence for human activity of pre-Roman and post-Roman date and also the homes and landscapes of contemporary people (Woodside and Crow 1999; Adkins and Mills 2011). In this context, the archaeological fixation on defining the detailed Roman sequence of the Wall and the military identity of this monumental frontier can sometimes serve to detract from the monument's living significance. It is important to assess the broader range of roles and values of the Wall, issues that relate to the social and cultural character of the monument and the enduring and transforming landscape through which it runs.

Frances Horovitz (1982) composed a poem at the museum at Chesters Roman fort, using the ancient objects to explore the 'balance between masculine and feminine' on the Wall. For Horovitz the Wall was 'great, dominant and striding', but some of the objects in this museum allowed her to imagine the balancing of the feminine and the masculine (Fig 16.2). The development of the archaeological *Research Agenda* (Symonds and Mason 2009) has helped to communicate the importance of some new archaeological directions for research on the Wall, while recent archaeological publications stress the complexity of the communities that occupied the Wall in Roman times and their transformation through time (see for example Bidwell 2008). This represents research that communicates the contemporary significance of the monument and which

FIG 16.1. THE RECONSTRUCTED ROMAN GATEWAY AT SOUTH SHIELDS ROMAN FORT, WHICH WAS OPENED IN 1988 TO PROVIDE VISITORS WITH AN IMPRESSION OF THE APPEARANCE OF A MAJOR ROMAN STRUCTURE ON THE WALL.

has been followed up, at the Great North Museum, Vindolanda and Carlisle, by interpretations for the public that communicate new perceptions of the Wall and its people. These approaches challenge the predominant idea of the Wall as a Roman military monument by exploring more complex issues of identity, an area in which archaeological research is playing a significant role (Hingley 2012, 313).

CONCLUSION

The Roman military archaeology of this frontier is internationally important and the Roman history of the Wall is the reason for the monument's inscription as a World Heritage Site. The point that this chapter has aimed to communicate is that this Roman history is only part of the story of Hadrian's Wall (cf Hingley 2012). This is precisely because the Wall has never ceased to live. Many of the actions that have occurred along the Wall over the past 1600 years have drawn, in physical and conceptual terms, on the imposing remains of this monument. As a result, the social, economic and environmental values of Hadrian's Wall cannot be divided from the physical and conceptual history of the monument as a Roman frontier structure. Neither should these Roman military issues outweigh all other considerations. The preservation and management of the Roman remains of the Wall represents a vital issue for this WHS, but this does not mean that other values and beliefs should be sidelined.

FIG 16.2. A COMMEMORATIVE STONE NAMING THE NYMPH COVENTINA, FOUND AT CARROWBURGH IN THE 19TH CENTURY AND NOW KEPT IN CHESTERS MUSEUM.

It is extremely important in this time of economic crisis that archaeologists seek to contribute to a broad appreciation of the Wall and the landscape that it is situated within. Attempts to read contemporary meaning into the monument have been used here to argue that archaeologists should be fully engaged in developing the living history of the Wall. Archaeology has a major role to play in making the Wall live through the acts of uncovering that help to bring the past to life, but the discovery and interpretation of archaeological deposits should not be entirely the responsibility of the expert who has accumulated a wealth of knowledge and experience of the Wall; it should be the property of all who take an active interest in both the monument and its living landscapes.

ACKNOWLEDGMENTS

These arguments are developed in far greater detail in *Hadrian's Wall: A Life* (Hingley 2012). I am grateful to Paul Bidwell, David Breeze, Stephen Daniels, Nigel Mills, Claire Nesbitt, Michael Shanks, Christina Unwin and Robert Witcher for help with the ideas expressed. I am also very grateful to the Arts and Humanities Research Council for funding the academic research upon which this paper is based, through the Tales of the Frontier project (http://www.dur.ac.uk/roman.centre/hadrianswall/) and through an additional Research Fellowship during 2011.

BIBLIOGRAPHY AND REFERENCES

Adkins, G, and Mills, N, 2011 *Frontiers of the Roman Empire World Heritage Site – Hadrian's Wall Interpretation Framework*, Hadrian's Wall Heritage Ltd, Hexham

Bates, J C, 1895 *The History of Northumberland*, Elliot Stock, London

Bender, B, 1998 *Stonehenge: Making Space*, Berg, Oxford

Bidwell, P (ed), 2008 *Understanding Hadrian's Wall*, Arbeia Society, Titus Wilson, Kendal

Bishop, M C, 1994 *Corstopitum: An Edwardian Excavation*, English Heritage, London

Breeze, D J, 2003 John Collingwood Bruce and the Study of Hadrian's Wall, *Britannia* 34, 1–18

Brennan, T, 2005 *Performing Northumbria: Empire* [online], available from: http://navigatelive.org/timbrennan.html [11 September 2012]

Browning, M, 1991 Archaeology historicized: Romano-British frontier studies and German historiography at the turn of the century, in *Roman Frontier Studies 1989* (eds V A Maxfield and M J Dobson), University of Exeter Press, Exeter, 354–7

Bruce, J C, 1851 *The Roman Wall*, John Russell Smith, London

Carpenter, H, 1981 *W H Auden: A Biography*, George, Allen and Unwin, London

Chettle, S (ed), 2006 *Writing on the Wall: An International writing project for Hadrian's Wall 2001–2006*, ARTS UK, Newcastle upon Tyne

Collingwood, R G, 1921a Hadrian's Wall: A History of the Problem, *Journal of Roman Studies* 11, 37–66

— 1921b The Purpose of the Roman Wall, *The Vasculum* 8 (1), 4–9

Davies, H, 1974 *A Walk Along the Wall*, Weidenfeld and Nicolson, London

Forster, R H, 1899 *The Amateur Antiquary: His Notes, Sketches, and Fancies concerning the ROMAN WALL*, Gay & Bird, London

Gilmour, D, 2002 *The Long Recessional: The Imperial Life of Rudyard Kipling*, John Murray, London

Hadrian's Wall Heritage Ltd, 2009 *Frontiers of the Roman Empire World Heritage Site: Hadrian's Wall Management Plan 2008–2014*, Hadrian's Wall Heritage, Hexham

Haverfield, F, 1899 Five Years excavation on the Roman Wall, *Transactions of the Cumberland and Westmorland Antiquarian and Archaeological Society* 15, 337–44

— 1906 The Romanization of Roman Britain, *Proceedings of the British Academy* 2, 185–217

Hingley, R, 2000 *Roman Officers and English Gentlemen*, Routledge, London

— 2010 Tales of the frontier: diasporas on Hadrian's Wall, in *Roman Diasporas: Archaeological Approaches to Mobility and Diversity in the Roman Empire* (ed H Eckardt), Journal of Roman Archaeology, supplementary series No 78, Portsmouth, Rhode Island, 227–43

— 2011 Living Landscape: Reading Hadrian's Wall, *Landscapes* 12 (2), 41–67

— 2012 *Hadrian's Wall: A Life*, Oxford University Press, Oxford

Horovitz, F, 1982 Audio recording: Poem found at Chesters Museum, Hadrian's Wall, in *Collected Poems* (F Horovitz) [online], available from: http://www.bloodaxebooks.com/titlepage.asp?isbn=1852249250 [June 2011]

Kipling, R, 1906 *Puck of Pook's Hill*, Macmillan, London

Lewis, M, 2006 Who Owns the Stones?, in *Writing on the Wall: An International writing project for Hadrian's Wall 2001–2006* (ed S Chettle), ARTS UK, Newcastle upon Tyne, 16–20

Lowenthal, D, 1985 *The Past is a Foreign Country*, Cambridge University Press, Cambridge

Maxfield, V A, 1982 Mural Controversies, in *Problems and Case Studies in Archaeological Dating* (ed B Orme), Exeter Studies in History 4, Exeter, 57–82

Pearson, M, and Shanks, M, 2001 *Theatre Archaeology*, Routledge, London

Roberts, D H, 2007 Reconstructed pasts: Rome and Britain, child and adult in Kipling's *Puck of Pook's Hill* and Rosemary Sutcliff's historical fiction, in *Remaking the Classics: Literature, Genre and Media in Britain 1800–2000* (ed C Stray), Duckworth, London, 107–24

Symonds, M F A, and Mason, D A, 2009 *Frontiers of Knowledge: A Research Framework for Hadrian's Wall*, Durham County Council, Durham

Woodside, R, and Crow, J G, 1999 *Hadrian's Wall: An Historic Landscape*, National Trust, London

Young, C J, 1999 Hadrian's Wall, in *Managing Historic Sites and Buildings* (eds G Chitty and D Baker), Routledge, London, 35–48

17

The Hadrian's Wall Interpretation Framework: Audience Research

GENEVIEVE ADKINS, NICKY HOLMES AND NIGEL MILLS

INTRODUCTION

In 2009 Hadrian's Wall Heritage (HWHL) commissioned the Centre for Interpretation Studies, Perth College-UHI and Zebra Square to carry out a programme of public engagement research as part of the process of developing the Hadrian's Wall Interpretation Framework. The purpose of the research was to explore and measure the views of a number of different audiences and stakeholders, all of whom were important both to the future sustainability of Hadrian's Wall as an overall attraction and to all of the individual sites and museums. The research was informed by the market data and audience research already in existence. As such, the public engagement research aimed to add to existing knowledge, providing a greater level of detail than previously existed – particularly in terms of visitor and non-visitor perceptions of Hadrian's Wall and the visitor experience. Full details of the research are available as an appendix to the Hadrian's Wall Interpretation Framework (Adkins and Holmes 2011).

The existing audiences for Hadrian's Wall are declining, yet the pool of potential visitors is large. A study by ERA (2004) found that 4.2 million people live within 40 miles or an hour's drive of Hadrian's Wall, 85% of whom are in North East England. A further 1.9 million live within 80 miles. Furthermore, some 5 million tourists, 4.4 million of whom are from the UK, stay within 40 miles of Hadrian's Wall each year. Yet despite being less than an hour's drive away, the majority of these potential visitors choose to visit other places instead. It is this pool of missing visitors – locals and tourists – that needs to be persuaded to explore the outstanding heritage of Hadrian's Wall if its potential as a visitor attraction is to be fully realised.

METHODOLOGY

Review of existing audience research, discussion with site teams (Housesteads, Tullie House, Roman Vindolanda and Roman Army Museum) and wider consultation with organisations along Hadrian's Wall suggested that common key audiences were families and older people visiting with and without children. These audiences might be local, regional or national in origin.

Qualitative and quantitative research into these audiences was undertaken during 2009–10 through focus groups, telephone interviews, site visit interviews and feedback and consultation activities targeted at local, regional and national levels. The purpose of the research was to explore:

- knowledge and perceptions of Hadrian's Wall;
- awareness of key aspects of Hadrian's Wall including World Heritage Status and the number of sites and museums along its length;
- general needs and wants when visiting a heritage site, including interpretation methods and media preferences;
- reactions to the proposed principles and themes of the Interpretation Framework.

Three focus groups of non-visitors (ie participants who had not previously visited Hadrian's Wall sites) were held in identified target catchment areas: Manchester, Edinburgh and Newcastle. A fourth focus group of visitors (ie participants who had previously visited Hadrian's Wall sites) was held in Newcastle. All participants were selected according to the priority audiences identified above, all visited heritage sites in the UK (and selected or jointly selected these) and all were parents or grandparents of children aged nine or over. 'Mood boards' were used to communicate visually the various suggested themes, supported by written and spoken descriptions.

Two community consultation events took place at Hexham and Brampton. These provided local people with the opportunity to find out about the Interpretation Framework, see the mood boards, hear the responses from the focus group and telephone research, and input their own experience and ideas. Telephone and face-to-face consultations were held with representatives of organisations with interests in the management and presentation of the Hadrian's Wall World Heritage Site, as well as two facilitated workshops at which initial research findings were shared and proposed principles and themes discussed. Two site visit interview and feedback activities took place at Housesteads. The first focused on obtaining feedback from existing visitors to the site, including English Heritage and National Trust members. The second focused on obtaining feedback from a sample that had not previously visited the site and were not members of either organisation.

Quantitative data was collected through telephone interviews with 307 people, each interview lasting around 20–25 minutes. Participants lived across the UK and visited heritage sites in the UK at least twice a year. The aim of this research was to measure quantitatively key findings from the qualitative methods, specifically: awareness of key facts about Hadrian's Wall; awareness of the different sites and museums; interest in the principles and proposed themes and narratives of the Interpretation Framework; preferred interpretation methods and media.

KEY FINDINGS FROM THE RESEARCH

Seven key findings emerged from the research and are summarised below.

Finding 1: Hadrian's Wall is not well known and is not perceived as an attractive or easy place to visit

Consultation with those working in organisations along Hadrian's Wall revealed a commonly held assumption: that the general public knows about and/or is familiar with Hadrian's Wall – what it is, where it is and its historical importance. The research findings strongly contradict this. The majority of non-visitor participants in the focus groups and telephone survey demonstrated little knowledge of Hadrian's Wall, best illustrated by responses to question 8 of the telephone survey: 'I am going to say a name of an area in Britain and I would like you to tell me what words or images come to mind when I say it: *Hadrian's Wall*' (see Fig 17.1).

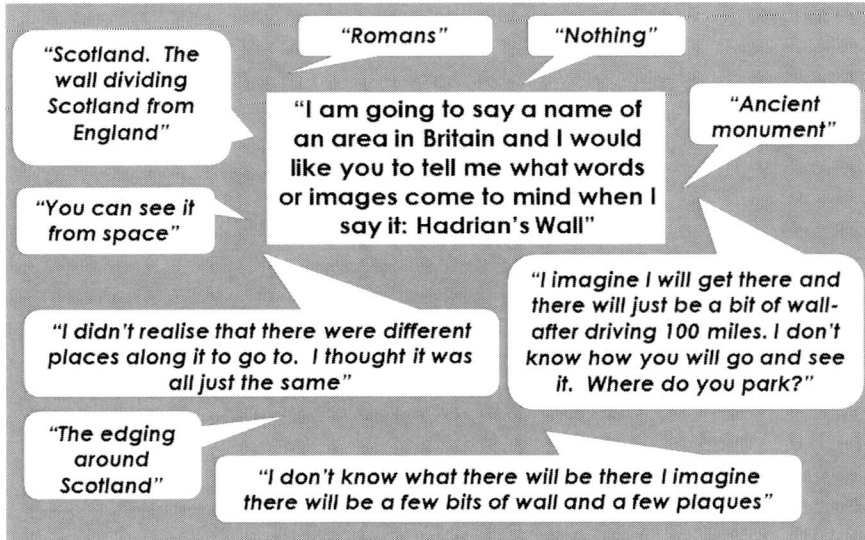

FIG 17.1. ILLUSTRATIVE FOCUS GROUP RESPONSES TO THE MENTION OF 'HADRIAN'S WALL'

Although visitor and non-visitor participants in the Newcastle focus groups were more aware of Hadrian's Wall, the majority of visitor and non-visitor participants in the focus groups and telephone survey were unaware of Hadrian's Wall and especially of the visitor attractions along its length, many describing it simply as *a wall* (see Fig 17.2). However, when informed of the various sites and things to do along Hadrian's Wall, both focus groups and telephone survey participants responded very positively. 57% of telephone survey participants were not aware of the sites and museums along Hadrian's Wall. Once aware, 77% said this was a motivating reason to visit.

> 'I just thought it was a wall and a bit boring. I didn't realise there were different places to go, I thought it was all the same.'
> Response from focus group participant (Adkins and Holmes 2011, 15)

The name of the monument, and the use of this name without any other descriptor or qualifier in marketing and wider communications, appears to play a role in visitor perceptions of the World Heritage Site. Many focus group participants questioned why they would be asked to visit a wall, the name clearly giving the impression that there is little to attract or do once there. This perception, together with a further group of responses to question 8 of the telephone survey that demonstrate visitor perceptions of the landscape and setting of the World Heritage Site (listed below), clearly reveals that a number of barriers need to be overcome if audiences are to be developed and more people are to visit and to appreciate the monument:

> 'remote', 'desolate', 'moorland', 'cold and bleak', 'stones and ruins', 'wild open spaces'.
> Responses from focus group participants (Adkins and Holmes 2011, 6)

A review of marketing literature produced for Hadrian's Wall in North East and North West

FIG 17.2. VISITATION AND AWARENESS OF SITES ALONG HADRIAN'S WALL (BASE 307)

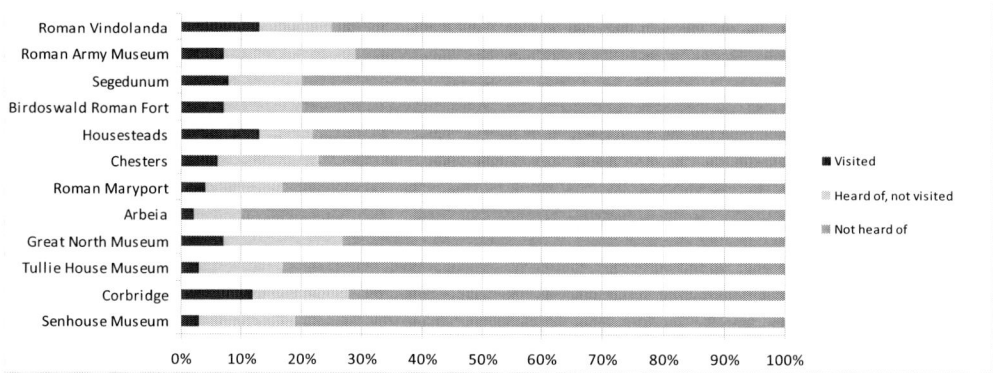

England, including print, advertising and websites, reveals the dominant use of images that reflect these telephone survey responses: open, empty, wild landscapes with no human settlements, activities, things to do, or other people. Such images and landscapes will evidently appeal to some audiences, for example keen walkers along the Hadrian's Wall Path, but for the target audiences of this research and the sites along Hadrian's Wall it is clear that a lack of awareness of Hadrian's Wall and its associated sites, a perceived absence of attractions and of things to do and perceptions of the environment as being harsh and uninviting combine to mean that a visit to Hadrian's Wall is expected to be hard work, with other locations being easier to visit.

In spite of this, the research revealed that improved awareness of the various attractions has a significant impact on motivation to visit. In particular, participants in the focus groups expressed surprise that they were not made more aware of the various attractions and the variety of things to do along Hadrian's Wall. To address these issues, there is a need to:

- broaden the appeal and change perceptions of the World Heritage Site as a place to visit through improved interpretation;
- highlight the breadth and scope of the World Heritage Site and the numerous sites and museums in wider communications and through marketing and advertising;
- target communications at all relevant audiences in the interests of all businesses and communities and in the interests of promoting wider understanding of the significance and interest of the World Heritage Site;
- use a wider and more balanced suite of photographs that include softer and more inviting views and images of people that are more inclusive as regards age, gender and ethnicity.

Finding 2: Widening the interpretive offer to encompass the wider narrative of the Roman Frontier provides a clear opportunity to broaden the visitor offer and start to address issues of perception, appeal and attracting new audiences

In 2005, Hadrian's Wall became part of the Frontiers of the Roman Empire World Heritage Site, currently comprising Hadrian's Wall, the Antonine Wall in Scotland and the German Raetian Limes. The Hadrian's Wall element extends over 118 kilometres and includes the Wall itself with directly associated features, the frontier defences extending down the Cumbrian coast and several outpost forts to the north. In effect, Hadrian's Wall forms the north-west frontier of the Roman Empire.

Consultation with staff in organisations along Hadrian's Wall revealed that some people were unaware of the change and of its implications for the presentation and interpretation of Hadrian's Wall. This lack of knowledge was reflected in focus group participants for whom, on first mention, the phrase 'north-west frontier of the Roman Empire' had little meaning, nor was Hadrian's Wall understood as a frontier or as an edge of the Empire.

'So was it different for people inside the Empire compared to people outside?'

'I just thought you were inside the Roman Empire wherever you lived.'

'So there weren't people or countries outside the Wall? So the countries were different to how they are now?'

> Responses from focus group participants (Adkins and Holmes 2011, 8)

Significantly, when explained, the idea of Hadrian's Wall forming part of a frontier between the Roman Empire and the non-Roman world held immediate fascination for all focus group participants. Unprompted, participants compared Hadrian's Wall to known modern frontiers, walls and barriers built to separate people for political, social and economic purposes; participants were able to relate contemporary issues and troubles to the past and, in doing so, could see the Roman world as complex and many-sided – just as they view 20th-century history and the modern world as studied at school and college.

This immediate and significant change in participants' knowledge and perception of Hadrian's Wall indicates how public knowledge and appreciation of the World Heritage Site could be improved through a broader approach to site interpretation and presentation. By interpreting Hadrian's Wall and its associated sites as part of the north-west frontier of the Roman Empire, instead of providing a narrow focus on the Wall and its archaeology, the scope for visitor understanding and experience is immediately enlarged. Thereafter, as new and refreshed museum displays are developed encompassing a broader range of themes and narratives, the overall offer and visitor understanding of the WHS will be improved. These new experiences will deliver a more appealing, differentiated visitor offer, adding value and motivation to visit Hadrian's Wall. Audiences will have the opportunity to understand the bigger picture, empowering them to make sense of Hadrian's Wall, its many sites and the history and events that left a legacy now celebrated in its World Heritage designation.

It follows that if sites were to be better interpreted to communicate the narrative of the north-west frontier, wider communications, marketing and PR activity would need to adapt to reflect this focus. Thus, whilst retaining the name of Hadrian's Wall and the brand Hadrian's Wall Country, future communications and PR activity needs to promote the wider theme of the north-west frontier and the multiplicity of narratives this encompasses that will appeal to the widest possible audiences – local, national and international. Over time, and with commitment from all those with an interest in the conservation, presentation and interpretation of Hadrian's Wall, a significant change in public understanding, appreciation, visiting and valuing of the World Heritage Site can be achieved, helping to realise the universal values that underpin the inscription of the site and the objectives of the WHS Management Plan.

To address these issues, the Interpretation Framework needs to identify how the interpretive concept of the north-west frontier can provide a structure for interpretation of the World Heritage Site and how this can be embedded in the sites and museums along it.

Finding 3: World Heritage Site status is not widely known, understood or valued

Focus group and telephone survey respondents suggest that World Heritage Status is not fully understood and is generally linked to attractions outside the UK:

> 'If you are on holiday and you see there is a World Heritage Site, you would want to go and see it and you do think it will be something special. But I don't think of sites like that as being in the UK.'
>
> Response from focus group participant (Adkins and Holmes 2011, 9)

55% of respondents in the telephone surveys were aware that Hadrian's Wall is a World Heritage Site; 62% who were unaware thought that this might encourage them to visit; 22% knew that more Roman objects had been excavated along Hadrian's Wall than anywhere else in Britain, including some of the most important finds in Europe. Of those unaware of this, 72% thought this a motivating reason to visit. Whilst these figures demonstrate a general lack of awareness of the heritage assets and their significance, the impact of taking action to increase awareness is clear. These data challenge traditional assumptions that people are aware of Hadrian's Wall and appreciate its historical importance. The issue is one of ensuring that a larger population of current non-visitors is made aware of the significance and interest of the World Heritage Site.

To address these issues, there is a need to communicate more effectively the significance and interest of the World Heritage Site through site presentation and interpretation and through wider information and marketing materials.

Finding 4: People's knowledge of Roman history appears to be shaped by early years education and this has an important limiting impact on their understanding, perception and likelihood of visiting Hadrian's Wall

The public engagement exercise revealed that participants had a limited knowledge of Roman history, including why the Romans came to Britain, why Hadrian's Wall was built and what life was like before and after the Romans.

> 'I know that the Wall was built to keep out the Scots but I have never thought about why the Romans came or what was here before.'

> 'Where does it run from? What does is look like? I am ashamed to say that I don't even know the basics about Hadrian's Wall.'
>
> Responses from focus group participants (Adkins and Holmes 2011, 10)

Although this lack of knowledge was common amongst non-visitor participants, it was echoed to a lesser extent in participants who had visited Hadrian's Wall. Participants in the Newcastle focus groups demonstrated the most knowledge although this did not equate to visiting Hadrian's Wall. In addition, focus group responses suggest that Roman history is understood as facts rather than different viewpoints, ideas or people:

> 'Maybe it's the age you get taught the Romans – in primary school. When you're older and you learn about the Second or First World War you have discussions and you get to know the

different reasons why people did things and all the different viewpoints. In Roman history it is "this happened" and "so-and-so did that".'

Response from focus group participant (Adkins and Holmes 2011, 10)

It appears that having studied Roman history early within their education, participants (now parents and grandparents) remembered very little, viewing Roman history as a very long time ago, and encountered in a distant and largely forgotten part of their schooling. As such, the majority of participants found it difficult to relate to Hadrian's Wall. So distant is their learning and so remote the Roman period that, combined with poor interpretation and limited awareness raising, it appears not to enter their minds to visit.

'It was all so long ago. Battles and armies and not the people. I don't think knowing about the Romans tells you much about life today.'

'It is only now that we have talked about this that I have thought about the Berlin Wall. I never thought about Hadrian's Wall in the same way because it is from so long ago.'

Responses from focus group participants (Adkins and Holmes 2011, 10)

To address these issues, it is important to recognise that people's knowledge of Roman history might be limited and that interpretation should seek to create a framework in which knowledge can be gained, synthesised and developed across the broadest range of audiences.

Finding 5: Participants responded positively to the approaches and themes proposed for the Interpretation Framework

All proposed themes for the Interpretation Framework (see Chapter 18) tested well with focus group and telephone survey respondents as well as with community and organisation consultees. Research participants and consultees tended to understand that all themes were interrelated and that they could most effectively be communicated through narratives of people. Choice of media was also felt to be an important factor in delivering interpretation.

In the telephone survey all themes scored highly, with respondents saying each theme was a good idea and would encourage them to visit or come back to Hadrian's Wall – higher scoring than is generally found in such research. The themes of 'Frontier Lives' and 'Before and After' had the most universal appeal across the sample. In the focus groups, whilst all themes had immediate appeal, some were more immediately appealing, with others becoming more appealing and attracting stronger interest with increased awareness. This seems to reflect the general lack of awareness of Roman history, of Hadrian's Wall and its sites, and the need for sites to provide a range of themes and experiences that reflect the range of audiences and their needs.

Overall, the themes of 'Walls and Barriers' and 'Edge of Empire' appealed most to older respondents who were more likely to have previously visited Hadrian's Wall, echoing focus group participants who thought these themes would appeal best to adults and older children. The 'Edge of Empire' theme, in particular, drew strong responses in the focus groups:

'I think this is a really good idea to make you think of the Wall as part of a bigger picture.'

'I think that is really fascinating.'

'It's a brilliant concept.'

'I like things to be quite thought provoking, to make me think.'

'I like this idea: the Romans around the world.'

Responses from focus group participants (Adkins and Holmes 2011, 11)

Given that participants were also interested in themes of 'Before and After' and 'Walls and Barriers', it appears that the idea of a frontier – of dividing people and of conquest – is of more interest to people than the bare facts about frontiers of the Roman Empire. There is evidence that people do engage emotionally with the idea of a lonely, cold Roman soldier looking out across the empty landscape of the central section of Hadrian's Wall as evidenced by W H Auden's 1937 poem *Roman Wall Blues*. However, the issue is how the idea of a frontier can be interpreted in an engaging way. This is especially important given the positive responses to this theme gathered at Housesteads, where this theme could be picked up in a new interpretation.

The focus groups highlighted that all themes are interrelated and it is not the theme alone which determines the appeal. Participants understood that all themes broadened the potential interest of the site and could be highly appealing if presented well and interactively. This shows that ways of presenting themes that enable people to connect them with their own life experiences are the most effective and accessible – confirming the importance of adopting fundamental principles of good interpretation within the Interpretation Framework and its implementation.

Fig 17.3 shows the percentage of telephone survey respondents who said that each factor was a good idea and would encourage them to visit or come back to Hadrian's Wall. All scored highly, but 'having different experiences and different stories along the Wall' and 'focusing on people, lives and the evidence left behind' scored most highly. These results support the principles of clearly differentiating each site along Hadrian's Wall and presenting themes that connect with visitors, for instance by focusing on narratives of people and life along the frontier as opposed to objects, sites and archaeology.

FIG 17.3. REACTIONS TO THE PROPOSED PRINCIPLES OF THE INTERPRETATION FRAMEWORK

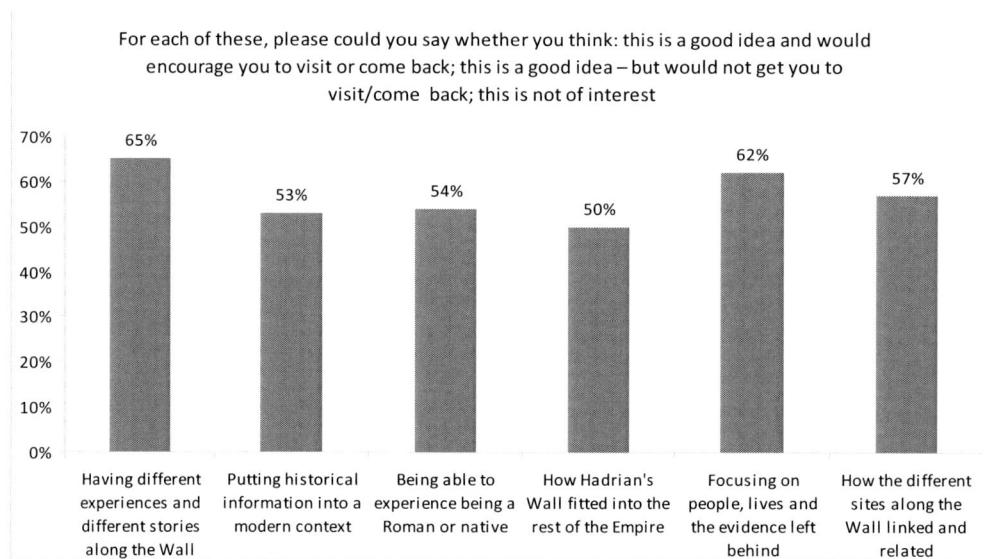

For each of these, please could you say whether you think: this is a good idea and would encourage you to visit or come back; this is a good idea – but would not get you to visit/come back; this is not of interest

Telephone survey responses suggest that a wide range of media was liked. Visitors with children aged under 16 were much more likely to want events, costumed interpreters, hands-on activities and children's trails. The ideal offer would be a combination of different media, providing interest for all the family. An interesting aspect of the data is that responses reflect the media commonly used to interpret historic and archaeological sites and belies the popularity of reconstructions at sites such as Arbeia and Segedunum, and the use of multimedia technology at sites such as Culloden.

Finding 6: Research with non-visitors to Hadrian's Wall produced findings that challenge existing audience research

Two types of research were undertaken at Housesteads: on-site interviews with visitors and first-time visits with non-visitors. Whilst the results of the former mirrored those of English Heritage visitor surveys over past years, the latter reveal clear issues with existing site management, presentation and management arrangements, which efforts are currently being made to address. These issues are worth exploring in more detail as they highlight issues relevant at site level and in the context of the WHS as a whole.

Participants expected the site to inform them of the whole narrative of the Wall in a wider context. Obviously if this was done at each site in the same way, each site would end up presenting similar information and there would be little incentive to visit the other sites. This highlights the need both to differentiate interpretation at each site and to provide visitors with advance information to inform them of what to expect and the options available.

> 'Prior to visiting the site, I had a positive expectation as to what to expect. I knew that the Wall itself was just a wall, but I thought that forts like Housesteads would be a lot more interesting than the Wall. I also knew that Housesteads had a museum which I hoped would not only explain information about the fort itself, but about life in Roman Britain and other things such as the Roman empire, Roman soldiers etc.'

> 'If this is all you see of Hadrian's Wall, I think you will be disappointed. There is no reference to any of the other places along the Wall so I would be worried that visitors would come here and think that all of Hadrian's Wall is like this, whereas in reality you can do different things along the Wall.'
>
> Responses from focus group participants (Adkins and Holmes 2011, 63, 64)

Participants expected a full day out and value for money but struggled to stay for longer than 90 minutes.

> 'It isn't worth the travel time from here (Thirsk). It is a nice drive and all that, but I would like at least 3 or 4 hours for the price of that petrol and the admission ticket. If they gave you money off somewhere nearby, that would help, if they can't add more to Housesteads.'

> 'I liked the countryside setting of the place, it was stunning. That was the best bit of the visit. But how did people who lived here think about the countryside? To me it is beautiful because I live in a city but did they feel isolated or homesick? What about people outside the Wall? I would like that sort of information covered, even though we wouldn't know the facts for sure, we could all have a view.'

'The fort itself was just walls, and I couldn't really imagine what it used to be like. I didn't know what any of the different walls were, even after I looked around.'

'There isn't enough here. You would have to combine it with something else.'

Responses from focus group participants (Adkins and Holmes 2011, 64)

Several respondents highlighted the lack of coordination between the various elements of the site managed by different organisations. English Heritage, the National Trust and the North-umberland National Park are aware of these issues and are addressing them. Of perhaps greater interest are the responses from several participants who felt alienated by the nature and current presentation of the site:

'I did wonder if it was just me who couldn't make sense of it here. I thought that maybe I should know this, and I guess that's why I didn't really want to ask any questions.'

'I like history and I go to a lot of sites, but this one has made me feel inadequate. I don't get a sense of history here because it is so difficult to connect with the information here. I left feeling quite deflated.'

Responses from focus group participants (Adkins and Holmes 2011, 65)

There was also a feeling that there was little of interest for children:

'My daughter got bored really quickly and that made it difficult for me to spend time in there'; 'its just for adults, not young people'.

'The children were underwhelmed. At other sites, it is easy to keep their attention by explaining what they are looking at, and describing events that happened. I found it hard to do that here, as there was a lack of information about the site.'

'We had no idea what this was (the granary), it looked really interesting, but we just couldn't work it out.'

Responses from focus group participants (Adkins and Holmes 2011, 66)

All of the participants mentioned the need to bring the site to life to make it more appealing for them to visit. The most frequently made suggestion was for re-enactments and costumed interpreters. Most participants also suggested guided tours by volunteers or paid staff. Activity back-packs for children were also suggested:

'It would be good to have a funny, exciting guided tour.'

'Housesteads would be better if they had things like historic re-enactments, character actors, guided tours, an interactive museum etc.'

Response from focus group participants (Adkins and Holmes 2011, 68)

Participants suggested improvements to the museum including interactives, children's informa-tion, a larger model of how Housesteads looked and a short film recreating the site. They also suggested more information at the site, making it clear and easy to read, and including some 'fun' or unusual facts:

'More information definitely, but not the way it is written now. It needs to make you want to read it. All of the panels looked the same to me, and were all a bit boring.'

Response from focus group participant (Adkins and Holmes 2011, 68)

Participants like the idea of Housesteads connecting with the wider Wall, and to other sites as part of the World Heritage Site. They felt this would equip them with information to help them decide where else to visit on their trip:

'It would be good to get ideas of where to go from Housesteads. Something which tells you to come here to get X about the Wall, or go there for information about a different subject. I like that, because I would plan to go to two sites in one day.'

'The bus service AD 122 had a commentary from the driver about the points of the Wall that the bus was passing. I found this very informative, and helped me get a sense of the whole Wall.'

'It (the suggested theme of walls and barriers) is a different reason to come. You can see the Wall and understand a completely different subject. I would then go to another attraction on the Wall for a different story.'

Responses from focus group participants (Adkins and Holmes 2011, 68, 69)

These responses highlight the need for organisations looking to develop audiences for the historic environment and Hadrian's Wall to undertake more research with non-visitors to identify their knowledge, perceptions and needs. Only if these are better recognised and understood can an audience-development agenda be pursued along Hadrian's Wall. The focus group and telephone surveys give clear insights into the needs and opportunities to attract current non-visitors. Given the decline in existing visitor numbers, it is vital that all organisations along Hadrian's Wall better recognise and respond to the needs of all audiences if new and future audiences upon whom the long-term sustainability of the World Heritage Site depends are to be encouraged to visit.

Finding 7: Respondents identified common elements that make a good visitor experience at a heritage site

In addition to exploring audience perceptions of Hadrian's Wall, the public engagement exercise sought to establish what makes a good visitor experience, from the perspective of the identified target audiences. Over half of respondents in the telephone research (56%) identified the following as characteristics of a favourite site that they visited regularly:

- lots to see and do that appeals to the visitor group, such as activities for children;
- some familiar elements than can be relied upon;
- some changing elements, such as temporary displays or events;
- located within easy travelling distance;
- sites that visitors can feel connected to, usually through good interpretation;
- sites that provide clear information about what is available, and that enable people to plan and manage their visit and travel;
- good facilities and amenities;
- availability of a saver ticket or season ticket that provides good value for money.

CONCLUSIONS

Visitor numbers to Hadrian's Wall have been declining in the context of increased competition for audiences' leisure time and discretionary spending. The audience engagement research identified that a number of factors are contributing to this decline, including: low awareness of Hadrian's Wall and its various sites; lack of awareness of its historical and cultural importance; a perception of narrow focus with little of wider interest; duplication and questionable quality of existing interpretation; difficulties in accessing sites and information. These issues must be addressed if new audiences are to be persuaded to visit Hadrian's Wall. New approaches to interpretation need to be adopted based on sound audience development and interpretation principles, improved facilities and appropriate and accessible information provided on a coordinated, Wall-wide basis.

The public engagement exercise confirms other tourism and interpretation research in telling us that people are interested in people and in narratives and information that they can relate to their own life experience and the world around them. Interpretation is most effective when visitors are able to relate to its messages, so it is important to deliver interpretation that encourages such relationships. One way of doing this is by focusing interpretation on the narratives of people and life on the frontier, and by communicating these narratives in ways that are diverse and personally engaging.

A second way is to seek contemporary resonances. By making connections between modern life and the past, people are able to relate it to their existing knowledge and experiences, providing an environment in which they can be stimulated to compare, question, reflect and construct new understandings and knowledge about the past and the present. Hadrian's Wall, part of the north-west frontier of the Roman Empire, offers an unparalleled opportunity to explore many issues that affect contemporary society. In this way it can offer people new insights into both the Roman and modern World including colonialism, multiculturalism, identity, government, conflict, war, walls and barriers. As such, it provides an unrivalled learning resource for all ages and interests to engage with issues that reflect UNESCO's WHS values, providing a profound and affecting experience.

Hadrian's Wall is but a single element of the defensive and administrative infrastructure that made up the north-west frontier of the Roman Empire. The frontier was not static and its location, nature and organisation changed over the 350 years of Roman occupation in response to political, social and economic pressures and issues at the heart of the Empire. The frontier also represented and symbolised many different aspects of Roman civilisation and cannot be understood without reference to the reasons why the Romans occupied Britain. Most archaeological museums naturally focus on the particular sites and collections with which they are associated, providing only a small amount of contextual information. No museum or site anywhere in the UK explores the bigger picture of the Roman Empire. The wealth of museums along Hadrian's Wall and the underlying similarity of their collections provides both a need to differentiate interpretation so that each provides a complementary visitor experience, and an opportunity to explore wider issues. There is a unique opportunity to do this in a way that will accrue wider social, economic and conservation benefits to a large and important geographical area.

By broadening the interpretive focus of Hadrian's Wall to encompass the wider frontier narrative, focusing on themes and issues that people can connect with, Hadrian's Wall has the potential to become more than just a Wall, taking on a richer and more significant place in the UK's historic environment that better reflects and communicates its WHS designation.

BIBLIOGRAPHY AND REFERENCES

Adkins, G, and Holmes, N, 2011 *Frontiers of the Roman Empire World Heritage Site – Hadrian's Wall Interpretation Framework Public Engagement Appendix*, Hadrian's Wall Heritage Ltd, Hexham

Adkins, G, and Mills, N, 2011 *Frontiers of the Roman Empire World Heritage Site – Hadrian's Wall Interpretation Framework*, Hadrian's Wall Heritage Ltd, Hexham

Economics Research Associates, 2004 *The Hadrian's Wall Major Study Report*, available from: http://www.newcastle.gov.uk/wwwfileroot/legacy/regen/ldf/06_06_hadrianswallmajorstudy_2007.pdf [12 September 2012]

18

The Hadrian's Wall Interpretation Framework

Nigel Mills and Genevieve Adkins

Arguably Hadrian's Wall is more relevant today than it was in the past: it stands as a symbol of our identity as well as our heritage and serves as a cultural link across continents, not simply as a tourist attraction but a means which connects our understanding of the world today.

Roz Elliott, Deputy Head, Burnside College, Wallsend

Introduction

All Year 7 pupils who attend Burnside Business and Enterprise College in Wallsend explore aspects of Hadrian's Wall, including its history. The college is located near Segedunum Roman fort and was designed with a ground plan based on the shape of a flattened Roman legionary helmet. Roz Elliott is Deputy Head and, for her and her students, perhaps the most important aspect of the Wall and all that it represents is how it helps to promote community cohesion by providing a context through which to explore contemporary issues of identity and multiculturalism. The soldiers stationed at Segedunum and at other forts along Hadrian's Wall came from many different parts of the Empire. The students can explore what it might have been like to have been stationed in a foreign land, to marry locally, to adapt to local ways of life yet maintain links with home, and relate this to their modern world.

This resonance with contemporary society is as fundamental to engaging visitors through interpretation as it is in providing a resource for formal teaching and learning. Put another way, what is perhaps most important for public understanding of, and engagement with, the World Heritage Site is not what happened in the past, what the Romans *did* for us, but their relevance to the modern world: what the Romans mean to us today.

There are 11 principal managed sites and museums along Hadrian's Wall. There are also extensive parts of the World Heritage Site that are not managed but are visited and which have potential to add significantly to the visitor's enjoyment and understanding of the site. Audience research (see Chapter 17) suggested that existing interpretation was perceived to be poor, not very interesting and essentially the same at each site.

In response to these perceptions, and working with partners along Hadrian's Wall, a flexible framework has been developed to guide interpretation development (Adkins and Mills 2011a). The objective is to enable the creation of a network of differentiated yet connected sites that engage and excite visitors, encouraging multi-site visiting, longer stays and repeat visits. Central to the development of the Framework were the six principles of interpretation developed by Tilden and especially his first principle, that 'any interpretation that does not somehow relate what is being displayed or described to something within the personality or experience of the visitor will be sterile' (1977, 9).

In the context of Hadrian's Wall, there seemed to be two main conceptual areas through which to link the Wall to the experience of the visitor, as detailed below.

The first is by relating the daily experiences of those people who lived and died along the Wall 2000 years ago to those of modern visitors – military and family life, food, transport, fashion, craft skills etc. People are interested in people. By focusing interpretation on people and daily life, and by communicating in ways that are diverse, personally engaging and which challenge assumptions, a more varied, inspiring, affective and effective visitor experience can be created. This has the ability to generate stronger feelings and attitudes, enhance understanding and engage new and more varied audiences.

The second is by exploring the bigger picture of the Roman frontier narrative and relating it to the wider social, political and economic forces that people see every day on their television screens and in newspapers. Viewed in this way, the sites and museums along Hadrian's Wall have an unparalleled opportunity to explore many issues that affect contemporary society as illustrated by the approach taken at Burnside College. This approach to interpretation responds to Tilden's fourth and fifth principles: 'the chief aim of interpretation is not instruction, but provocation' and 'interpretation should aim to present a whole rather than a part, and must address itself to the whole man rather than any phase' (1977, 9).

The process of developing the Framework was organic and iterative. Starting from an understanding of visitor perceptions of current interpretation provision, of interpretation concepts and approaches and of the wider frontier narrative, initial principles were set out, tested with partners and then used to inform interpretation planning at most of the major sites currently proposed for development: Vindolanda, the Roman Army Museum, Tullie House, Housesteads and Roman Maryport.

Consultant design and interpretation planning teams were appointed by the site teams to work with them to develop interpretation plans for each site as part of their project design and planning. The briefs used in the appointments of the consultant teams identified the key principles at the heart of the Framework: that new interpretation should be audience focused, based on sound principles of good interpretation, and encompass the wider narrative of the frontier and the Empire and modern resonances. Working to the principles set out in the Interpretation Framework, the role of staff at Hadrian's Wall Heritage was to work with the site teams to help formulate interpretation plans designed to draw on the particular strengths and opportunities represented by each site and their potential to contribute a distinctive, differentiated offer within the overall concept. The consultant teams included Event at Roman Maryport, Redman Design at Tullie House, The Centre for Interpretation Studies (Perth) and Studio MB at Vindolanda and the Roman Army Museum, and CMC Associates and Studio SP at Housesteads.

THE NEED AND OPPORTUNITY FOR THE INTERPRETATION FRAMEWORK

From an academic perspective, each site along Hadrian's Wall once played a unique role within the north-west frontier, and differences and similarities in the evidence from each site are fundamental to academic understanding of the monument. However, the audience research suggests that audiences do not currently perceive there to be many differences between the sites; even different types of site are viewed simply as 'Roman'. This seems to be the result of three main factors. First, a lack of background knowledge that would help audiences make distinctions between, say, a fort and a temple. Second, the perception that existing interpretation focuses primarily on describing and presenting archaeology and objects – information rather than inter-pretation. Third, the perception that sites are presented in a very similar way and offer little variation in visitor experience.

If audiences, particularly local people, believe there to be little difference in the sites along Hadrian's Wall, and the visitor focus group participants associate it with being old-fashioned and not worth a visit, then the perceived lack of variety is a core issue that must be addressed if audiences to Hadrian's Wall are to be developed.

A review of existing interpretation at sites along Hadrian's Wall revealed that audience percep-tion largely reflects the evidence on the ground. Many staffed sites feature displays that, while clean and well maintained, appear out of date when compared to more recent exhibitions that audiences had visited. Many sites feature object-rich displays supported by descriptive graphic labels that provide few opportunities for interaction and engagement.

Whilst it is true to say that all sites have their own unique evidence, similar types of site served essentially similar functions. Put simply (and with tongue a little in cheek), in AD 122 Hadrian decreed that a Wall should be built. It took three legions six years to build and there were so many forts and so many milecastles and turrets. Each fort was occupied by a detachment of troops who went about their daily life in the fort and in the garrison settlement beside it, had religious beliefs, wrote letters to each other, and died, sometimes violently. End of story. It does not need 11 sites and museums to say that.

For the visitor it is not sufficient to present the sites according to their relative similarities and differences; this is more the realm of typology and in some ways describes the current way the sites are presented with the emphasis on providing the visitor with information about the site. To quote Tilden again: 'Information as such is not interpretation. Interpretation is revela-tion based upon information. But they are entirely different things. However, all interpretation includes information' (1977, 9).

Interpretation provides a means of looking at the sites afresh and moving beyond their tangible remains to explore the intangible past they represent, which can provide great meaning for audiences. Put simply, sites themselves are not the entire story, or even most of it. More overt differentiation is needed and interpretation can provide this. At the heart of the Interpretation Framework is recognition of the opportunity to communicate the narrative of the north-west frontier of the Roman Empire.

Hadrian's Wall is but a single element of the defences, structures and strategies that make up this north-west frontier. Hadrian's Wall is also only part of a story that begins with the Roman occupation of southern Britain and encompasses the gradual movement of the frontier north-wards into Scotland, the construction of Hadrian's Wall and the Antonine Wall, subsequent campaigns and the aftermath of the decline of centralised Roman administration.

By broadening the interpretive focus of Hadrian's Wall to encompass the north-west frontier and the wider sites, resources and narratives, Hadrian's Wall has the potential to become so much more than just a Wall, taking on a richer and more significant role in the UK's historic environ-ment that better reflects its World Heritage Site designation. No museum or site anywhere in the UK deals with this story at an appropriate scale.

The WHS designation provides further scope to extend interpretation to encompass UNESCO's aspiration of creating the concept of World Heritage: to promote understanding, respect, toleration and cooperation between the peoples of the world through appreciation of their distinctive contributions to World Heritage. The narrative of Rome's north-west frontier can offer new insights into both the modern and the Roman world, acting as a metaphor through which to explore issues affecting contemporary society including colonialism, multiculturalism, identity, conflict, war, walls and barriers, trade and commerce. As such, it provides an unrivalled learning resource for all ages and interests to engage with issues that reflect UNESCO's WHS values, providing a profound and affecting experience.

A FRAMEWORK, NOT A STRATEGY

The purpose of the Framework is to create a structure within which more detailed strategic planning and coordination can take place and through which each site and museum can build on its own particular strengths and opportunities to create distinctive, differentiated and complementary experiences for visitors. Realisation of these opportunities will in turn deliver wider benefits:

- enhance the visitor experience and visitor enjoyment for the widest possible audiences;
- increase visitor numbers and, more importantly, encourage visitors to stay longer and to visit more sites;
- improve awareness and understanding of the WHS, its significance and the need to conserve and protect it, thus supporting the objectives of the WHS Management Plan;
- promote UNESCO's WHS values which seek to share the heritage and experience of people around the world.

The term *Framework* was used very deliberately to describe a flexible approach which sets out guidelines to inform audience development and interpretation along Hadrian's Wall. The guidelines presented in the Framework are not prescriptive; instead they are intended to help the many different organisations with an interest in Hadrian's Wall – from local authorities and national agencies to community groups and private landowners – to develop approaches to interpreting the World Heritage Site in a coherent, complementary and differentiated way that will deliver long-term benefit for all.

GUIDING PRINCIPLES

The Framework is an advocacy and guidance document. It recognises that developments and improvements will take place at different rates and timescales according to the resources and the opportunities that become available. A more prescriptive approach would have required significantly more time to develop and would have been redundant within a few years. Instead, the Framework focuses on understanding and encouraging adoption of the highest quality interpretation designed to meet audience needs across the WHS. Using best practice audience development and interpretation principles and applying these within a thematic framework that broadens the scope of interpretation beyond the archaeology of the Wall, sites and museums have the opportunity to develop differentiated but complementary visitor experiences, adapting and responding to opportunities over time.

The first recommendation is to put audiences first; a commitment to audience development and to improving the visitor experience through good interpretation as a means of doing this. This recognises the need to broaden the appeal of Hadrian's Wall to the widest possible audiences for whom it may have meaning, resonance and value. The Interpretation Framework advocates that audience needs and the visitor experience should be at the heart of decision-making and recognises that a dynamic and responsive approach is required to engage all audiences and encourage repeat visitors. To achieve this, the Framework advocates the following audience development principles:

- a belief that our cultural heritage should be accessible and inviting and that interpretation is key to achieving this;
- an understanding of the barriers to participation for different audiences and an understanding of the factors that drive participation;
- an understanding of the needs of different audiences and a commitment to meeting these needs;
- an awareness that the narrative of the north-west frontier of the Roman Empire and of the people connected to it can be motivating for audiences and can encourage participation if presented in appropriate ways;
- the desire to make people feel welcome and build relationships with visitors.

(Adkins and Mills 2011b, 8)

The need for these principles is reflected in responses obtained through the focus group research:

'I think sometimes, if you have someone there talking about the place who knows all about it, if they have a personal interest and they're telling you lots of things you've never heard before, that just makes it really interesting.'

'There's nothing worse than displays in glass cases.'

'Keeping the children occupied is key. There needs to be things to do to stop them getting bored.'

'I think it helps put things in context.'

Responses from focus group participants (Adkins and Holmes 2011)

The second recommendation is to apply good interpretation using a set of principles informed by consultation, good practice guidelines, interpretation research and audience research:

- commit to interpretation that is dynamic and people oriented, relevant (though potentially challenging) to their views, understanding of and interest in the world around them – providing interpretation that is exciting, challenging, engaging, fascinating, participative, enjoyable and fun;
- recognise opportunities to identify contemporary resonances as a key means to engage visitor interest, foster understanding and promote UNESCO's broader values in relation to the WHS – enabling Hadrian's Wall to act as a metaphor through which to explore contemporary issues, contributing relevance, meaning and value to the visitor experience;
- appreciate that Hadrian's Wall is itself an object that illustrates the overarching theme of the Roman Empire's north-west frontier, and is not, on its own, the whole story;
- enable visitors to grasp 'the bigger picture' and to understand that each site tells a different part of the story or presents the story in a different way appropriate to different audiences;

- differentiate each site along Hadrian's Wall so that each one is an attraction in its own right and makes a unique contribution to the overall visitor offer and experience;
- understand that in order to engage more effectively with existing and new audiences, interpretation needs to be underpinned by sound academic research and that objects and sites should focus on communicating themes within an overall narrative structure for the north-west frontier of the Roman Empire.   (Adkins and Mills 2011b, 9)

Responses from the focus group research again illustrate the need for these guiding principles:

'I like things to be quite thought provoking and make me think.' (p 11)

'My children are more interested if there's a story behind it, people's experiences; it really captures their imagination, something to relate to. The story of someone's life would be great.' (p 24)

'To me the size of the empire is really interesting and the idea of different walls around the world now is brilliant.' (p 27)

'I think this is a really good idea to make you think of the wall as part of a bigger picture.' (p 11)

'The idea that things are still ongoing is really interesting; it goes against the idea that the wall is a wall. It's a process still ongoing.' (p 20)

'This idea really works, it's really good to hear about people and how they lived.' (p 15)
                    Comments from the focus group research (Adkins and Holmes 2011)

A THEMATIC STRUCTURE

Building on these principles, on the audience research and on two workshops undertaken with stakeholders, an overarching interpretive concept was developed through which to structure interpretation of the Hadrian's Wall World Heritage Site:

Hadrian's Wall is at the centre of the dynamic story of the north-west Frontier of the Roman Empire. This frontier evolved from the first to the fifth centuries AD in response to changing political, social, economic and demographic forces within the Roman Empire, and the changing status and role of Britain as an Imperial Province. The heavily militarised frontier zone has left a rich physical and cultural legacy through which we can explore its story and understand its resonance with the modern world.   (Adkins and Mills 2011a, 30; 2011b, 10)

This concept was then mapped into nine themes proposed as the focus for interpretation at sites and museums along Hadrian's Wall. It is not suggested that each site should necessarily focus on a particular theme. Rather, the themes provide a menu which can be mixed and matched, building on the particular opportunities and strengths of individual sites, their collections, their settings, history, locations and accessibility, to enable each site to develop its own distinctive, audience-facing offer.

1. *People of the Empire* – the Roman Empire was multicultural and as concerned with issues of citizenship, identity and belonging as we are today. Modern parallels can be drawn with

the archaeological and historical record to inspire reflection and a new understanding of this aspect of Rome's legacy.

2. *Frontier Lives* – we can become personally involved in the daily lives, emotions and cares of individual Roman citizens through the compelling personal stories revealed in the writing tablets from Vindolanda and Carlisle and through the wealth of inscriptions found across Hadrian's Wall.

3. *Edge of Empire* – Hadrian's Wall was the centre of the north-west Frontier of the Roman Empire, a key element in the frontier ring created by the Emperor Hadrian. As such it symbolises the military power of the Empire and the imposition of military occupation on Rome's territories.

4. *Britain – a Roman Province* – Britain was part of a vast Empire with long-range social and commercial links. The area around Hadrian's Wall reflects this story and reveals many aspects of life in the provinces, including exploitation of mineral resources, commerce, citizenship, politics and relations between Romans and local people.

5. *The Roman Army* – the Roman Army was the key instrument in establishing and maintaining the Roman Empire. It operated as an effective and mighty military machine and its multicultural soldiers were also administrators, engineers, a police force and loyal citizens in retirement.

6. *Before and After* – before, during and after the Roman occupation of the north-west frontier, local people occupied the area. Through archaeological research we are learning more about these people, about the long-lasting effect of Rome on people, culture and environment, and on ties to our European neighbours. The frontiers of the Roman Empire form both tangible and intangible links between the many countries once within the Empire, and those outside the Empire.

7. *Power and control* – empires are often synonymous with conflict, struggle and barriers. Once a great divide, the frontiers of the Roman Empire provide a unifying element in the modern world and offer opportunities to explore and understand contemporary struggles and barriers, and share universal values that resonate with the purposes of World Heritage designation.

8. *The Frontier and its Environment* – the landscape, its geology and its flora helped shape the frontier and the nature of Hadrian's Wall. The Romans exploited, adapted to and left their mark on the environment of Hadrian's Wall.

9. *Exploration, Discovery and Values* – the archaeological and historical evidence that enables us to explore the story of the north-west frontier is revealed through antiquarians, archaeologists, workmen and volunteers. This is a dynamic process with which we can actively engage and contribute our own interpretations. It is also a process through which we come to understand and value the legacy of the past.

(Adkins and Mills 2011a, 30; 2011b, 10)

Delivering Change on the Ground: Sites

Those responsible for the various sites and museums along Hadrian's Wall will undertake the detailed interpretive planning for the sites in their care, a process that will evidently be informed by organisational practices and procedures. They have the opportunity to use the Framework to guide development of interpretation to deliver the benefits that it is believed all those with an interest in the WHS wish to see. The Framework provides guidance on how the principles and themes might be used to implement change on the ground:

Identifying Audiences
Existing audience data and research needs to be reviewed to highlight visitor and non-visitor groups, both of whom should be a target for enhanced interpretation. The interests and needs of different audiences should be identified and tested. Audience research is different to market research and the two should not be confused although they may overlap.

Identifying Assets
Interpretation is based on sound information. The archaeological information from a site, including history of research, collections and visible remains, should be reviewed to identify opportunities for interpretation and presentation with a view to broadening audiences for Hadrian's Wall. This review needs to include mundane objects as well as those that are distinctive or special in some way.

Identifying Themes and Narratives
These assets can then be mapped to the themes of the Interpretation Framework to identify potential themes and narratives that the assets can be used to illustrate. This is not to suggest that every object needs to be displayed as part of a narrative. Some objects are outstanding in their own right and may not need further explanation nor to be used to contribute to a narrative.

This process should include development of a central concept or theme statement that draws together all key themes to provide a clear identity and message that can be communicated and promoted simply. The process is iterative in that as potential narratives and themes emerge, other objects and assets that contribute to or illustrate the narrative may be identified. The process is also comparative in that it needs to be undertaken in the light of the approaches taken at other sites, to help define a different and distinctive offer.

Identifying Access Opportunities
Access to sites along Hadrian's Wall is extremely variable and is therefore a primary consideration within any strategy that seeks to develop audiences through enhanced interpretation. An access review should be undertaken, identifying opportunities for on- and off-site interpretation.

Identifying Opportunities for Differentiated Interpretation and Presentation
The focus group research highlighted that responses to themes are inextricably linked to how themes are delivered. Ways need to be identified in which emerging themes and narratives can be delivered that are different from, yet complementary to, those at adjacent and more distant sites.

This requires an assessment of the widest possible interpretive methods and media. Special consideration should be given to approaches that enable the greatest levels of active participation and engagement and response to audience questions, as well as the conservation and management needs of sites.

The process should be iterative, allowing for dialogue around audiences, assets, themes and opportunities for differentiation to enable the most effective solution for each site within the overarching interpretive concept. Two illustrations of the application of this process are provided in Chapter 19; the Roman Frontier Gallery at Tullie House and interpretation planning for the proposed new visitor facilities at Roman Maryport.

Delivering Change on the Ground: Strategic Context

The audience research (Chapter 17) has shown that it is not simply interpretation on the sites themselves that needs to change if the full interpretive and audience development potential of the World Heritage Site is to be realised. A series of related activities and provision also need to change and improve.

The clearest finding is the need for a single public face and coordinating voice to provide visitors with easily accessible and inspiring information that enables them to be aware of the full range of experiences and opportunities available and to make informed choices about where, what and how to visit. The existing arrangement, whereby each organisation provides information about and promotes its own site or sites, results in confusion, perceived duplication, perceived lack of value for money and decisions not to visit Hadrian's Wall.

Visitors find the multitude of different organisations confusing. While the different sites need to maintain their own identity, they also need to be seen to be part of a coherent whole. The most important requirement is for there to be a central website portal that must be visitor-facing, with content based on serving visitor needs and inspiring people to visit. Website development needs to start from consideration of the reasons why people will choose to visit the website in the first place, such as to seek inspiration for or to plan a visit, or to access educational resources. These points are illustrated by responses from focus group participants:

> 'A website with all the information about the area as a whole would be great, with all the info about pubs and restaurants.'

> 'You could market it like the Yorkshire dales, as a whole area to go to with lots going on.'
>
> Responses from focus group participants (Adkins and Holmes 2011)

The website needs to be supported by a limited suite of printed publications that present the World Heritage Site as an integrated destination with a range of complementary and differentiated offers. This suite would include a simple map and interpretive guides (for adults and children, and for national and international audiences) that bring the overarching narrative to life and show how the different sites complement each other.

Research has also shown the need for a new signage scheme that helps visitors orientate and navigate their way along Hadrian's Wall and to its different sites, and for all sites to be perceived as part of a single destination and to clearly relate to one another. This requires sites to provide more effective cross-site referral and to contribute positively to the vision of Hadrian's Wall as an integrated destination.

Local people and businesses throughout the WHS have a major role to play in the effective orientation of visitors and in encouraging multi-site visits. This involves an in-depth understanding of the WHS and its landscapes, places of interest, the opportunities available at different sites and enthusiasm and interest in communicating this knowledge to visitors. There is an opportunity for local people and businesses to be actively involved in the process of bringing the site and its stories to life for visitors.

Alongside interpretation, presentation and promotion, the research indicated the importance that value for money plays in influencing decisions to visit. All focus group participants identified having to purchase separate tickets for each site and car park (rather having a single, joint, discounted ticket allowing access to all or a selection of venues) as a barrier to visiting, when factored on top of distance/time and travel costs and additional expenses such as drinks, food and souvenirs.

> 'I wonder about the cost of it … do you have to pay to go to each different site individually, or can you get a special ticket that you can use in all the sites? Because otherwise it would end up being quite expensive.'

> 'I think if you've got a year pass to somewhere, you're much more inclined to go and visit. Paying individually works out very expensive.'

> 'The best way of getting us to go is to give us more information about what is there, and some special offers with money off.'
>
> Responses from focus group participants (Adkins and Holmes 2011)

Ultimately, effective delivery of the Interpretation Framework depends on the acceptance and buy-in of partners and stakeholders to best practice principles of interpretation and audience engagement. It also depends on the same acceptance and buy-in from funders and strategic agencies.

BIBLIOGRAPHY AND REFERENCES

Adkins, G, and Holmes, N, 2011 *Frontiers of the Roman Empire World Heritage Site – Hadrian's Wall Interpretation Framework Public Engagement Appendix*, Hadrian's Wall Heritage Ltd, Hexham

Adkins, G, and Mills, N, 2011a *Frontiers of the Roman Empire World Heritage Site – Hadrian's Wall Interpretation Framework – Primary Theme: The north-west frontier of the Roman Empire*, Hadrian's Wall Heritage Ltd, Perth

— 2011b *Frontiers of the Roman Empire World Heritage Site – Hadrian's Wall Interpretation Framework – Overview and Summary*, Hadrian's Wall Heritage Ltd, Perth

Tilden, F, 1977 *Interpreting our Heritage*, 3 edn, University of North Carolina Press, Chapel Hill

19

Applying the Hadrian's Wall Interpretation Framework

Nigel Mills, Tim Padley, John Scott, Lucie Branczik and Genevieve Adkins

Museological provocation is a tricky art form. It is easy to excite folk sensually with artefacts, much harder to make them think. I visited a week after the [Roman Frontier] gallery had opened and there were already many handwritten visitor comment labels. One states what I was struggling to articulate: 'I have visited Hadrian's Wall numerous times … this is the first time I have seriously considered the social and personal consequences of the wall'.   (Lewis 2011)

Introduction

Hadrian's Wall is one of the greatest monuments of the ancient world. It tells us as much about ourselves as about the past. We should take pride in it and help unlock its potential to teach, inform and stimulate our own and future generations. The purpose of the Interpretation Framework (Adkins and Mills 2011) is to enable us to do just that; to create a structure within which more detailed strategic planning and coordination can take place and through which each site and museum can build on its own particular strengths and opportunities to create distinctive, differentiated and complementary experiences for visitors. Realisation of these opportunities will in turn deliver wider benefits:

- enhance the visitor experience and visitor enjoyment for the widest possible audiences;
- increase visitor numbers and, more importantly, encourage visitors to stay longer and to visit more sites;
- improve awareness and understanding of the WHS, its significance and the need to conserve and protect it, thus supporting the objectives of the WHS Management Plan;
- promote UNESCO's WHS values which seek to share the heritage and experience of people around the world.

In Chapter 18 we explored the development and structure of the Framework. In this chapter we look at implementation on the ground of the approaches advocated in the Framework through two case studies: the Roman Frontier Gallery at Tullie House Museum in Carlisle which opened in June 2011, and proposals for new galleries intended to form part of a new visitor attraction at Roman Maryport.

THE ROMAN FRONTIER GALLERY – TULLIE HOUSE

The Great North Museum and Tullie House Museum, with their large museum collections representing many different parts of the frontier zone, can be seen as eastern and western gateways and orientation points to Hadrian's Wall and to Hadrian's Wall Country. From the perspective of the Interpretation Framework, their role is to provide both a physical and conceptual overview of Hadrian's Wall, introducing and exploring the overarching concept of the north-west frontier of the Roman Empire, in contrast to the site-based museums which have the opportunity to focus on more specific themes and narratives.

The Hadrian's Wall Gallery at the Great North Museum was designed prior to the creation of the Interpretation Framework. The new Roman Frontier Gallery at Tullie House responds to the Hadrian's Wall gallery in providing a markedly different visitor experience, endeavouring to apply fully the principles and approaches advocated in the Interpretation Framework. It takes a much wider view of Hadrian's Wall, placing it in the context of the narrative of the north-west Frontier of Imperial Rome and the position of Britain as a military province within the Empire. Several key factors inspired development of the overarching interpretive concept for the Gallery.

First and foremost were the particular strengths of the Roman collections at Tullie House and the nature of the Roman settlement at Carlisle which they reflect. Roman Carlisle was the major urban centre on Hadrian's Wall and in the north of England. It was the only urban centre in the north to be granted *civitas* status. The collections reflect the cosmopolitan and commercial nature of urban life and the juxtaposition of Roman and native traditions. More clearly than anywhere else along the Wall, they allow us to explore civilian as well as military life. The collections also cover the whole period of the Roman occupation of the north of England, from the first arrival of the Emperor Vespasian's troops in the winter of AD 72/73 and the construction of the first fort at Carlisle, to the rebellion and temporary creation of the Gallic Empire under Carausius, formerly Governor of Britannia, in the fourth century and whose name survives on an upturned milestone. Finally the collections include many well-preserved wooden and leather objects including writing tablets, shoes and fragments of textiles.

Second was the desire and opportunity for Carlisle to be a western counterpoint to the Hadrian's Wall Gallery in the Great North Museum in Newcastle. The Hadrian's Wall Gallery displays the collections of the former Museum of Antiquities at Newcastle University which include an extraordinary group of inscriptions and sculpture from across the Wall. Hadrian's Wall itself was therefore the natural focus for interpretation in the new gallery. The centrepiece of the new displays is a scale model of the full length of the Wall, surrounded by the inscriptions and sculpture and placed in context by landscape images.

The different strengths of the collections at Tullie House and the absence of any really strong sculptural objects helped to create the opportunity for a very different approach to interpretation. At both the Great North Museum and Tullie House, a third factor was the absence of any clearly visible Roman archaeology in the form of a fort, bathhouse or other remains. Interpretation was therefore free to focus on the collections rather than on visible archaeology, using the collections to introduce the archaeology of the Wall and the wider frontier.

Fourth was David Mattingly's book *An Imperial Possession – Britain in the Roman Empire 54BC – 409AD*, first published in 2006. In the book Mattingly explores the narrative of the occupation of Britain by the Romans. 'Its fundamental theme is the fate of Britain as an imperial possession during nearly four centuries of foreign domination' (Mattingly 2007, 3). In his Introduction, Mattingly states that:

> In attempting to write a new history for the globalised twenty-first century, I have been much influenced by recent dramatic changes of emphasis and interpretation. Studies of the pre-Roman Iron Age have been revolutionized by new theoretical approaches and Roman history is also starting to be affected by post-colonial perspectives. This book is very much concerned with the experience of people in Britain under Roman rule and as such it is far more social history than political history … This is a post-colonial history, in the sense that it questions aspects of the consensus model and attempts to widen debate about the nature and impact of Roman rule in Britain.   (Mattingly 2007, 3)

Nowhere in Britain is there a museum that explores the whole narrative of the Roman occupation. Museums naturally focus on particular sites and collections, referring to the wider narrative as context rather than the primary theme. Given the nature of the collections at Tullie House and of the Roman settlement in Carlisle, the opportunity and the need to provide a different experience from that at the Great North Museum and at other sites along Hadrian's Wall, David Mattingly's book provided the academic rationale, the raw material and the inspiration for a radically new way of looking at Hadrian's Wall in the context of the Roman occupation of Britain and of the evolution of Rome's north-west frontier. More importantly, the Frontier Gallery provided the opportunity to move this approach from the academic to the public domain. The narrative of the frontier was inextricably linked to that of the occupation, in many ways defining the occupation and its nature. What better place therefore to introduce the public to the wider narrative than on the frontier itself?

The overarching concept for the Frontier Gallery was to invite visitors to explore the narrative of the Roman occupation of Britain from the perspective of the north-west frontier of the Empire and of Carlisle, its most northern urban centre, in particular. The audience development and interpretation principles advocated in the Interpretation Framework were used in developing and applying this concept, in particular the belief that our cultural heritage should be accessible and inviting, dynamic and people oriented, and relevant (though potentially challenging) to their views, understanding of and interest in the world. A primary objective was to stimulate visitors to think and to ask questions about the Roman occupation and its resonances with the modern world.

Articulation of this concept into a structure for the Gallery was developed through dialogue between interpreters (Nigel Mills and John Scott from The Hadrian's Wall Trust, Genevieve Adkins from the Centre for Interpretation Studies, Perth College) and the museum curator, Tim Padley, Curator of Prehistoric and Roman Antiquities, Tullie House Museum. The structure was developed around four key themes.

The first theme focuses on the idea that Britain was at the edge of the Empire but very much part of it. Rome was the largest and most influential empire ever to have existed in Europe and Britain was its most northerly territory or province. This empire was created by Rome's army, which occupied conquered lands and heralded new ways of living, trading, communicating and worshipping. This empire without borders saw Britain become home to Romans from across the Empire – from modern France to Germany, Syria, Egypt and Morocco. Key sub-themes included the idea of a common identity across the Empire expressed through imperial power and identity, language, ritual and beliefs, monumental architecture and the introduction of coinage and a monetary economy primarily through a paid, professional army.

The second theme recognises that the frontiers of the Roman Empire ebbed and flowed according to the success of the army, imperial ambition, politics and external pressures. The north-west frontier was no exception. Before Trajan there was no concept of frontiers – the objective was to conquer the whole known world. Areas adjacent to territory directly controlled by Rome were often linked through alliances and trade. A key sub-theme was that Hadrian's Wall represents only part of the frontier narrative that began with the advance of Vespasian's troops into the north of England on their way into Scotland, included the construction of both Hadrian's Wall and the Antonine Wall, and continued with the major third-century campaign under Severus and onwards to the end of Roman rule. To emphasise the point that Hadrian was not the only Emperor involved in this narrative, the Emperors Vespasian, Hadrian and Severus were chosen as key figures around which to construct the displays.

Theme three explores the idea of Britain as a Roman province. Rome began its conquest of Britain in AD 43. This was partly for political reasons, but was also to increase the Empire's wealth, growth and power. The colony was expected to produce a return, to help pay for the army, the administration and to become a part of the Empire. It was, in the modern sense of the word, a colony. The Empire achieved these aims through control of the colony and its people and the exploitation of its natural resources. Key sub-themes included the need for the colony to produce an economic return (and the administration of the province for this purpose), the promotion of the Roman way of life amongst the elite and amongst the multicultural commercial class, the impact of Rome and interrelationship with native peoples and the eventual decline and collapse of centralised Roman rule.

The fourth theme further explores the idea of Britain as a Roman province by looking in greater detail at Roman Carlisle – a frontier town. Carlisle was the largest town in the north of Roman Britain. An urban way of life was a key element of Romanisation; towns were where trade and commerce was carried out, where the elite could show off and buy into the Roman lifestyle and where the influence and dominance of Rome could be expressed through public buildings. Carlisle was the military and administrative hub for Hadrian's Wall and the centre for trade and commerce in the region; it was the only town in the north to be given the status of *civitas* – to have its own civilian government. Urban areas would have been very strange to most native Britons. Key sub-themes included trade and commerce, citizenship and Roman town life, and civilian government.

A fifth theme, the Living Wall, was developed around the concept of resonances with the modern world and in particular the perspectives of people today, for whom the experience of frontiers is part of their daily life and worldview (see Fig 19.1). The decision to include this theme was inspired by two main considerations. The first was the application of sound interpretation principles; that good interpretation should stimulate and challenge visitors to think, and that one way of doing this is to relate what is being presented to the wider life experience of the visitor – not just the practicalities and emotions of daily life, but moral and ethical issues that affect us all. The second was the status of Hadrian's Wall as part of the Frontiers of the Roman Empire World Heritage Site and in particular UNESCO's wider agenda and objective in promoting the concept of World Heritage, that of promoting peaceful co-existence and partnership between the nations of the world through respect, understanding, toleration and cooperation. What better place to encourage people to think about that agenda than a place which owes its status as World

FIG 19.1. THE ROMAN FRONTIER GALLERY – THE LIVING WALL.

Heritage Site to conflict and military occupation? The narrative of the Roman frontier could act as a metaphor through which to explore significant contemporary issues.

This fifth theme was also innovative in that interpretation and presentation at other World Heritage Sites of which we are aware focuses on the Outstanding Universal Value of the site (the reason for being granted World Heritage Status), with little attention paid to the wider objectives of UNESCO in creating the designation. This presented another opportunity to widen the scope of interpretation to real purpose and to create the foundations for a unique learning resource of national and international significance.

It was this conceptual and big picture approach and especially the Living Wall theme that inspired Redman Design to tender for the design contract, and it was their understanding of and enthusiasm for the approach which helped them win it. Interpreters, curator, educationalists and the design team then worked together to turn the concept into reality including some key decisions about the approach to design and display that were made as the process unfolded.

An early decision was to respond to the very contemporary and slightly odd, elongated shape of the space available by playing to its strengths and working with it rather than forcing a new shape into it (see Fig 19.2). This was allied to a decision that there should be changes of mood and atmosphere through the Gallery, from an initial impactful and immersive experience with strong imagery and low ambient lighting through the dynamic frontier theme to a wider, lighter, more free-flowing space beyond. The glass eastern wall of the Gallery, separating it from an underpass, provided the opportunity to keep the central space light and open, with a strong contemporary feel, contrasting with the dark atmosphere and focused lighting of the first section.

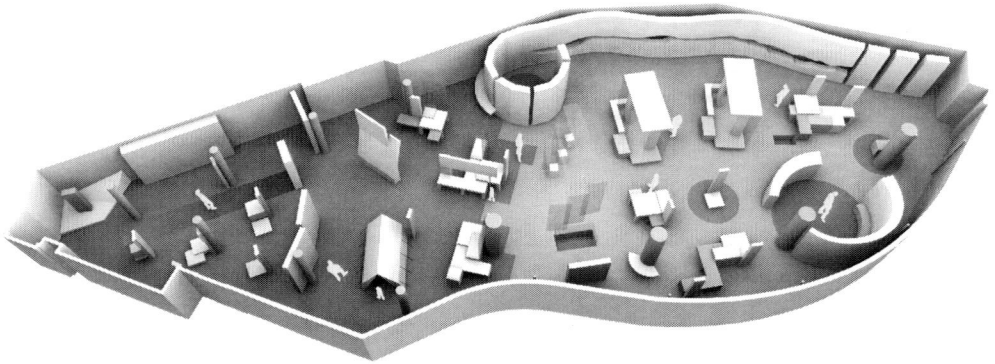

FIG 19.2. THE ROMAN FRONTIER GALLERY – LAYOUT.

A second decision was that objects would be carefully selected to illustrate the storylines, seeking to limit the number of objects on display to those required to bring the narrative to life. Allied to this was the decision that interpretation should be layered and should follow through from header and text panels into the display cases themselves, with further in-depth information being provided through a series of handheld resources entitled The Curator's Cut.

A fourth decision was to borrow objects from other museums if it was felt that they could add impact and strengthen the narrative. The British Museum kindly agreed to loan a number of key objects or replicas of objects from their main and reserve collections. High quality sculptural items from different parts of the Empire were especially useful in illustrating the connections between Britain and the Empire as a whole, and the nuances resulting from Britain's position as one of the most remote provinces. High quality replica busts of Vespasian, Hadrian and Severus were central to communicating the simple message that the narrative is not all about Hadrian! The decision to use a replica, supplied by the Great North Museum, of the famous tombstone from Hexham Abbey depicting a Roman cavalryman riding down a barbarian was initially controversial, but seen as essential in making a bold and dramatic statement at the start of the exhibition, encapsulating the underlying concept of the whole Gallery.

Further key decisions were that whilst there should be a general direction of flow to enable visitors to orient themselves and to engage with the overall concept of the Gallery, there should also be scope for them to return to and revisit sections easily to obtain more information. There should be differentiated spaces for contemplation and activity within the Gallery as a whole, but interactive elements for children and family visitors should be integrated throughout the Gallery, rather than concentrated in a particular area. The Gallery opened in June 2011 and received a highly complimentary review in the December 2011 edition of the *Museums Journal* (Lewis 2011).

ROMAN MARYPORT

The site of the Roman fort at Maryport was purchased by Hadrian's Wall Heritage Ltd in 2008, through a grant provided by the North West Regional Development Agency, as the first step in creating a new museum and visitor attraction that would firmly place the World Heritage Site on the west coast of Cumbria and contribute to the regeneration of local communities. The project is being developed in partnership with the Senhouse Museum Trust, who own and run the existing small museum adjacent to the site. The purchase included a complex of traditional farm buildings, intended to be the setting for the new development.

The Senhouse Collection is internationally famous for the unique collection of 22 altars dedicated to Jupiter that have been found at the site, of which 17 were from a group of pits excavated in 1870 at a distance of 300m north-east of the fort. Recent excavations (Haynes and Wilmott 2011) have demonstrated that the pits containing the altars were in fact part of the foundations for a large timber building constructed in the late Roman period, with the altars used for setting and packing large posts. Simply as museum objects the altars are impressive but have limited interest for visitors. For the average visitor one altar is much the same as the next and the Latin inscriptions seem obscure and irrelevant to modern experience.

The altars' extraordinary interpretive opportunity lies in the narratives revealed and illustrated by their inscriptions about the people who dedicated them, and in the power of these narratives to reach out and to resonate with the modern world. All of the altars were dedicated by commanders of the regiment garrisoned at Maryport in the second century AD. The earliest regiment attested at the fort is the First Cohort of Spaniards, and no fewer than six commanders of this regiment are recorded on the altars. From the inscriptions, and from evidence elsewhere in the Empire, it is possible to reconstruct the career paths of several of these officers.

These career paths indicate the integrated and cosmopolitan nature of the officer class of the Roman army. The officers at Maryport came from Italy, Provence (southern France), Noricum (modern Austria), North Africa and possibly Spain. They moved between posts in Britain and the provinces of Upper Pannonia (modern Austria), Lower Pannonia (Hungary), Lower Moesia (Bulgaria and Romania) and Judaea (Israel), travelling on occasion from one end of the Empire to the other to take up their next appointment (Breeze 2006, 399).

One officer, Marcus Maenius Agrippa, left his *curriculum vitae* on a monument in his home town of Camerinum in Italy. He came from a rich family that moved in the social circles of the Emperor Hadrian. His first command was a regiment of Britons on the Lower Danube (modern Bulgaria). He moved to Britain with Hadrian to take command of the regiment at Maryport from AD 122 to 124. He returned to the Lower Danube to take command of a regiment of Gauls, later coming back to Britain as Prefect of the British fleet, ending his career as Procurator of Britain, the most senior appointment in Britain after the Governorship.

Lucius Antistius Lupus Vernianus came from Sicca in North Africa where he served as a town councillor before furthering his career by joining the army. Cammius Maximus came from Solva in Noricum. T Attius Tutor also came from Solva and rose through the ranks to take charge of one of the largest and most prestigious auxiliary regiments in the Roman army. These narratives are potentially inspirational for the visitor, conjuring up images and questions of career advancement, of training and opportunity, of journeys, transport, supply and communications, of ethnic origins, language and diverse cultural experiences far beyond simple inscriptions on pieces of stone.

As with Carlisle, the location and role of the Roman settlement at Maryport adds power to the narrative. The Roman settlement here was most probably the western supply port for the frontier garrison, playing a similar role to that of Arbeia on the east coast, hence perhaps also its importance in the career path of an officer like Maenius Agrippa. Viewed from the perspective of Rome, Maryport was one of the most remote places in the whole of the Empire, yet was seen

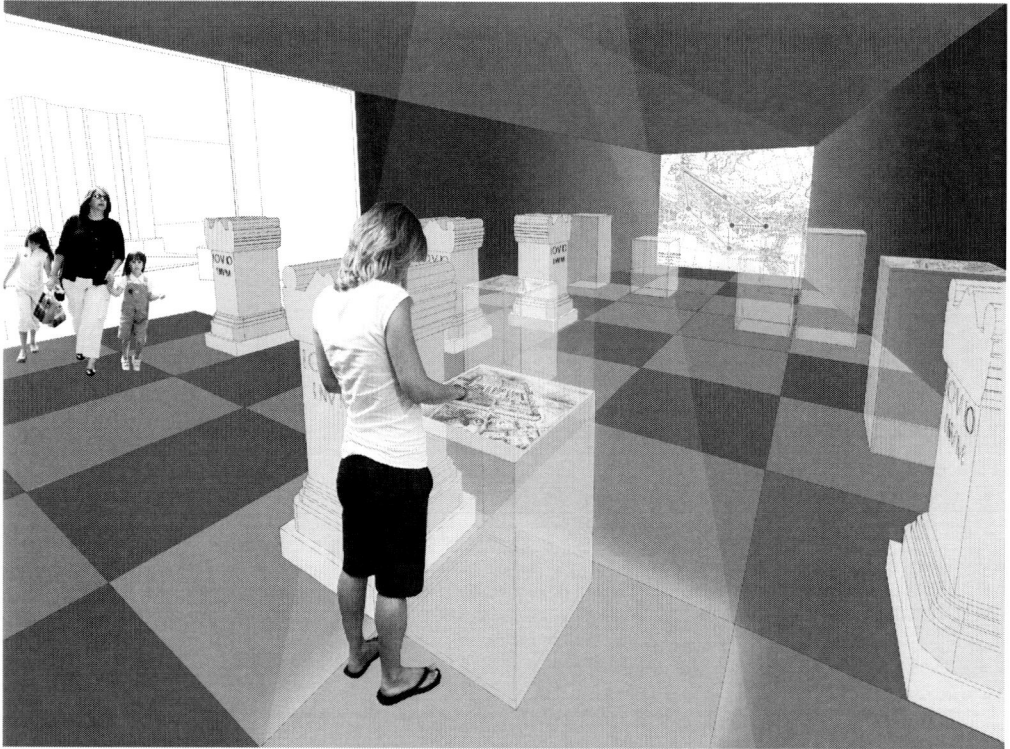

FIG 19.3. JOURNEYS ACROSS THE EMPIRE.

as an important career posting by ambitious officers. Its location and narrative also invite the visitor to explore seaborne supply and communications, the most important means of connecting and supplying the Empire yet largely ignored by and unknown to the public, whose knowledge naturally focuses on roads and buildings.

A further element in the approach to interpretation planning for Roman Maryport was recognition of the opportunity to contribute to the regeneration of the town and of other west coast communities, not only through the creation of an exciting and engaging museum and visitor attraction but also through the creation of inspiring learning opportunities. The west coast communities such as Maryport, Whitehaven and Workington have owed their prosperity to the sea and to looking outwards to the world, since their creation in the 18th century as planned trading towns up until the 19th century and their roles as industrial, trading and commercial centres. What better inspiration for young people today than the example of the commanders of the regiment at Maryport in Roman times?

A further key element was the aspiration to link the new galleries to an ongoing programme of excavation focused primarily on the garrison settlement, the *vicus*, located adjacent to the fort. Understanding these settlements is identified as a key research priority in the Archaeological Research Framework for Hadrian's Wall (Symonds and Mason 2009). Aerial photographs and resistivity surveys have revealed what is currently the largest and most complete *vicus* along

Hadrian's Wall, located on the top of the ridge to the north of the fort. An ongoing programme of excavation would enable this key research objective to be met at the same time as enabling visitors to engage with the live research process.

The thematic structure for the Roman Maryport Interpretation Plan was developed around these key elements by the interpreters Nigel Mills and John Scott from The Hadrian's Wall Trust and Lucie Branczik from Event Communications. The overarching concept is that of little Maryport, big Empire. It explores the relationship between the Empire and one of its most far-flung outposts, revealed through the career paths of the officers commanding the regiment. It is a journey through time and place using people-focused narratives based on the characters revealed through the inscriptions and realising the opportunities to explore the multiple identities of people and places.

This concept is explored through seven key themes, linked through the concept of a journey from different parts of the Empire to Maryport, experienced by the visitor through the career paths of the officers (see Fig 19.3). As with the Roman Frontier Gallery, objects would be carefully selected to illustrate the themes and narratives, allowing space for key objects to speak for themselves, and using loaned and replica objects where the local collections were deficient.

Theme one: Rome and the Empire

As with the Roman Frontier Gallery the first objective is to immerse the visitor in the sights and sounds of the Empire. The focus here though is the Empire's vast geographic expanse and its cultural diversity, as reflected in the diverse places that were the original home towns of some of the commanding officers, introducing some of them who will feature recurrently as the narrative unfolds. This section also explores how these different places came to be part of the Empire, setting the scene for the occupation of Britannia.

Theme two: Sea crossing

The officers travelled by sea across the Channel on their way to their posting at Maryport. Although sea transport held the Empire together and underpinned trade in bulk goods, sea journeys seem to have been feared by soldiers and there were many superstitions involving sea monsters. Roman Maryport most likely owed its significance to its role as an important supply port for the frontier garrison.

Theme three: Occupying the Province

This section explores the earlier stages of the occupation of the Province of Britannia, leading up to the establishment of the fort at Maryport and complementing the later part of the narrative of the northern frontier revealed at Tullie House.

Theme four: Managing the Province

A key role of the regiments and of their commanding officers was to assist in managing the Province. This role is exemplified by the career of Marcus Maenius Agrippa. The Empire relied on a vast supply network which facilitated the movement of people, and of huge quantities of bulk goods, but which had to be organised, maintained, managed and protected. The Empire also relied on a complementary communications network which ensured that officers such as those in command of the regiment at Maryport could travel to different postings as required. Underpinning the role of managing the Province is that of military occupation and the role of

Maryport and the west coast of Cumbria in the strategic management of the frontier. This section also provides an opportunity for a wide range of interactive learning activity.

Theme five: New Postings and Fort Life

This theme explores in detail the career postings of the officers at Maryport, the evidence on which our knowledge of these career postings is based, and how Maryport appears to have fitted into the career ladder. This section highlights the altars themselves and the officers who dedicated them, alongside military life in the fort.

Theme six: Settling in Maryport

Explores life in the *vicus* and relates this to the unfolding evidence revealed by the proposed ongoing programme of excavations on the *vicus* site. Initially the displays would be based on objects (either on loan or through replicas and images) from other *vici* across Hadrian's Wall, as well as those currently in the Senhouse collections. As the excavations progress, these loaned objects would be replaced or complemented by objects from Maryport itself.

Theme seven: Dig Detective

Explores the process of archaeological research through interactive displays linked to the ongoing programme of excavation on the *vicus*. Key elements in this process include the identification of research priorities, different research techniques and how to use them, decisions on where to survey or excavate, the process of excavation, the process of conservation and finds study, data analysis, interpretation and reporting, and storage.

CONCLUSION

The two examples discussed in this chapter – the Roman Frontier Gallery at Tullie House and the Interpretation Plan for Roman Maryport – illustrate the application of fundamental interpretation and curatorial principles to the display of archaeological information. First, the approach to interpretation is founded in the nature and strengths of the particular museum collections and of the archaeological sites and their contexts from which the collections derive. However, in the interests of good interpretation, the approach does not allow itself to be restricted to these collections where objects that are needed to illustrate important parts of the narrative are either missing or simply not available. At the Roman Frontier Gallery the use of objects from the British Museum enables key aspects of the wider Empire to be brought to life, while the replica sculpture of the cavalryman riding down the barbarian provides a powerful initial reference point for the whole gallery. At Roman Maryport, the narrative of the *vicus* is crucial to understanding the significance of the site, but pending the results of excavation can still be illustrated by reference to other similar sites across Hadrian's Wall.

Second, these examples illustrate the way that archaeological information can be brought to life through the use of sound interpretation principles. Tilden's first principle of good interpretation is that 'any interpretation that does not somehow relate what is being displayed or described to something within the personality or experience of the visitor will be sterile' (Tilden 1977, 9).

People are interested in people. By focusing interpretation on people and daily life, and by communicating in ways that are diverse, personally engaging and which challenge assumptions, a more varied, inspiring, affective and effective visitor experience can be created. This has the ability to generate stronger feelings and attitudes, enhance understanding and engage new and more varied audiences. Underpinning this approach is the use of objects to illustrate narratives or themes that people can engage with. This is precisely the approach used by the Director of the British Museum, Neil MacGregor, in his brilliant Radio 4 series and publication *A History of the World in 100 Objects* (MacGregor 2010). At Maryport, this is powerfully illustrated by the potential of the narratives of the commanding officers to be brought to life from a group of stone altars that, for many visitors, would elicit a purely passing interest.

Tilden's fourth and fifth principles are that: 'the chief aim of interpretation is not instruction, but provocation' and 'interpretation should aim to present a whole rather than a part, and must address itself to the whole man rather than any phase' (Tilden 1977, 9). These principles have been clearly applied in developing the Roman Frontier Gallery at Tullie House through the Living Wall and in the interpretation planning for both sites by looking outwards from the sites themselves to the bigger picture beyond. Judging by the review in the *Museums Journal*, from the comments of visitors and from the positive reactions from schools and educationalists, the approach has been highly successful at Tullie House although effective marketing is needed to ensure that potential visitors are aware of the gallery's existence.

Three final points should be made. The first is an observation that a particular strength of archaeological training is that one is taught to understand that individual objects have many different meanings, and can contribute in many different ways to understanding the past: functional, processual, symbolic, economic, social etc. It is a paradox that when it comes to presenting these same objects to the general public, the reaction of many archaeologists and curators is to retreat into an academic cul-de-sac which reduces the object to its simplest functional form, rather than being used to illustrate diverse themes and narratives.

A corollary to this observation is that the role of interpreters in the design of museum galleries is currently undervalued. Key to the design of the Roman Frontier Gallery was the initial collaboration between curatorial and interpretation professionals to develop the underlying concept for the gallery, inspiring the exhibition designers and giving them confidence to create an imaginative and unique space. Too often it is the exhibition designers who lead development of the concept, with interpreters reduced to a secondary role of simply writing interpretive text within an essentially architectural design.

The final observation is that good interpretation and good display recognise that objects can also speak for themselves – it is all a question of balance. The new display of the remarkable series of milestones from the Antonine Wall at the Hunterian Museum in Glasgow illustrates eloquently how effective such an approach can be. Similarly, and although a replica, the sculpture of the cavalryman riding down a barbarian is a bold and striking image that sets the tone for the whole Frontier Gallery and needs no further explanation.

Bibliography and References

Adkins, G, and Mills, N, 2011 *Frontiers of the Roman Empire World Heritage Site – Hadrian's Wall Interpretation Framework*, Hadrian's Wall Heritage Ltd, Hexham

Breeze, D J, 2006 *J Collingwood Bruce's Handbook to the Roman Wall*, 14th edn, Society of Antiquaries of Newcastle upon Tyne, Newcastle upon Tyne

Haynes, I, and Wilmott, T, 2011 Jupiter: best and greatest, *Current Archaeology* 259, 20–5

Lewis, P, 2011 Review of The Roman Frontier Gallery, Tullie House Museum and Art Gallery, Carlisle, Cumbria, *Museums Journal*, December, 46–9

MacGregor, N, 2010 *A History of the World in 100 Objects*, Allen Lane, London

Mattingly, D, 2007 *An imperial possession. Britain in the Roman Empire*, Penguin, London

Symonds, M F A, and Mason, D J P (eds), 2009 *Frontiers of Knowledge – a research framework for Hadrian's Wall, part of the Frontiers of the Roman Empire World Heritage Site*, Durham County Council and Durham University, Durham

Tilden, F, 1977 *Interpreting our Heritage*, 3 edn, University of North Carolina Press, Chapel Hill

Contributors

Genevieve Adkins is Director of the Centre for Interpretation Studies, University of Highlands and Islands, Scotland. Following an early career in heritage tourism, she was appointed Head of Interpretation and Education at Historic Royal Palaces in 2000, playing a role in its transformation into a financially independent charitable trust. She was subsequently appointed by the Scottish Government to lead the development of the visitor experience at over 345 historic monuments in the care of Historic Scotland. Recently appointed Vice-President of the ICOMOS ICIP working group, she is a champion of the professional development of interpretation and interpretation professionals.

M C Bishop is a freelance writer, publisher and archaeologist who has excavated within the Roman forts at Chester-le-Street, Newton-on-Trent and Osmanthorpe, and in the civil settlements outside the forts at Brough-on-Noe, Inveresk and Roecliffe. He co-authored the publication reports on the Roman sites at Corbridge and Housesteads and has catalogued collections of material in the museums at Aldborough, Corbridge, Chesters and Housesteads. Having initiated the Roman Military Equipment Conferences, he was founding editor of the *Journal of Roman Military Equipment Studies*, and is also co-author of a diachronic study of Roman arms and armour.

Lucie Branczik graduated from the Courtauld Institute with honours in History of Art. Since 2006, she has worked as an interpreter at Event Communications, Europe's leading exhibition design group, recognised as a pacesetter for pushing the boundaries of existing practice and constantly exploring new ways to interpret, present and connect with audiences. Her project portfolio includes the Dutch Maritime Museum, Amsterdam; the Royal Institution of Great Britain; and Chichester District Museum. In 2010 she led the interpretive team for The Crystal, an urban sustainability centre in London commissioned by Siemens. For M Shed in Bristol she managed audience research sessions and developed the masterplan, content and displays for the museum as a whole.

David Breeze is Chairman of the International Congress of Roman Frontier Studies and is an honorary professor at the Universities of Durham, Edinburgh and Newcastle. He was formerly Chief Inspector of Ancient Monuments for Scotland. He is a past President of the Society of Antiquaries of Newcastle upon Tyne and is currently President of the Cumberland and Westmorland Antiquarian and Archaeological Society. He has excavated on Hadrian's Wall and the Antonine Wall and has written about both frontiers. His latest book is *The Frontiers of Imperial Rome*, the first account of all Roman frontiers from an archaeological perspective.

Mike Corbishley has been teaching heritage education at the Institute of Archaeology, University College London since 2003. Throughout his career he has specialised in introducing archaeology to teachers. In 1972 he helped found and run the Young Archaeologists' Club. He has variously worked as a school teacher, an adult education lecturer and an archaeologist. He was appointed the first Education Officer for the Council for British Archaeology in 1977. In 1984 he joined English Heritage, later becoming their Head of Education. He has written a number of books for children and teachers about archaeology, heritage and the ancient world.

Jim Devine is the Director of Interpretive Media Limited, a multimedia development and consultancy company specialising in innovative technical solutions for the cultural heritage sector and commercial clients. He has over 20 years' experience in the cultural heritage sector and in academia, publishing on key issues in heritage interpretation and education. He co-authored the IT Strategy for Glasgow Science Centre, and produced the major 'What Clicks?' report for the Scottish Museums Council. He served two elected three-year terms on the Board of Directors of the Museum Computer Network, and served on the Advisory Board of the 'Horizon Report', produced by the US-based New Media Consortium, which examines emerging technologies for their potential impact on, and use in, education and interpretation within the museum environment.

Erik Dobat worked for a television company in Germany after leaving school and in 1998 founded Boundary Productions to produce high quality documentaries about archaeology. He studied Archaeology of the Roman Provinces at the Ludwig Maximilian University in Munich and graduated (M.Phil.) from the University of Glasgow in 2004. In 2005 he started to experiment with video content for mobile phones. Recent advances in smartphone technology have made the presentation of reasonable quality video content possible and in 2009 he developed a concept for location-based smartphone services for the Frontiers of the Roman Empire World Heritage Site. The first application was released in 2011 and he is currently working on new smartphone projects and DVDs for use in schools.

Matthias Flück studied Prehistory, Roman Archaeology and Ethnology at the Universities of Basel and Bern (Switzerland). His 2007 Masters thesis on Roman Archaeology was published in *Jahresbericht der Gesellschaft Pro Vindonissa 2007*. He has participated in excavations in Southern Germany, France and Switzerland and from 2008 to 2011 he was responsible for the analysis of the archaeological structures and the synthesis in the interdisciplinary report and publication project '*via et porta praetoria*' which will be published as Vol 22 of the *Veröffentlichungen der Gesellschaft Pro Vindonissa*. In 2008–2009 he was in charge of the development of a new digital and physical model of Vindonissa for the Vindonissa-Museum in Brugg and in 2011–2012 he directed a large-scale excavation in the southern civil settlement of Vindonissa.

Christof Flügel is chief consultant for the archaeological museums in Bavaria at the Bavarian Museums Service (Munich, Germany). His main interests focus on Roman military small finds as well as the archaeometric analysis of Roman ceramics. He has also conducted excavations with the German Archaeological Institute, Rome, at Carthage (Tunisia). He is a member of the Scientific Board of the Austrian Archaeological Institute in Vienna and of the Archaeological Institute at the University of Padova (Italy).

Snežana Golubović has worked at the Archaeological Institute in Belgrade since 1999 as a Research Associate on various projects, most recently on a Ministry of Science project entitled: 'IRS – Viminacium, roman city and military legion camp – research of material and non-material culture of inhabitants using remote detection, geophysics, GIS, digitalization and 3D visualization'. She has participated in excavations at Mediana and Viminacium since 1981 and regularly collaborates with the Archaeological Institute. She has also participated in numerous international congresses and symposia and published many articles and papers in a variety of periodicals.

Susan Greaney is a Senior Properties Historian working in the Curatorial Department at English Heritage. During her first four years at English Heritage, working on interpretation at unstaffed properties through the Free Sites Project, she oversaw the production of over 30 reconstruction paintings of historic sites. She has a strong research interest in prehistory, particularly the monuments and landscapes of Neolithic and Bronze Age Britain, and is currently developing the content of the new visitor centre at Stonehenge.

Tom Hazenberg (Hazenberg Archeologie) is an archaeologist and entrepreneur. Following his studies in Leiden he worked as a researcher and project manager for the Agency of Cultural Heritage and ADC ArcheoProjecten. In 2001 he founded his own company, Hazenberg Archeologie, with offices in Leiden and Arnhem, currently one of the largest archaeological consultancies in the Netherlands. He and his colleagues specialise in archaeological research, consultancy and in presenting archaeological information to the public in interesting and entertaining ways. He is particularly interested in the Lower German Limes and North Sea Basin in Roman times.

Don Henson is a consultant in public archaeology and heritage education, and Honorary Director of the Centre for Audio-Visual Study and Practice in Archaeology at the Institute of Archaeology, University College London. His interest in public heritage covers both theoretical issues of public engagement with the past and practical issues of narrative creation and communication within heritage. He has a keen interest in the portrayal of the past and of archaeology on television and in feature films, and in the use of audio-visual media in communicating archaeology to diverse audiences.

Richard Hingley is Professor of Roman Archaeology at Durham University (UK). He researches and publishes widely on such topics as the archaeology of the societies of the Western Roman Empire, the nature of Roman imperialism and the historiography of Roman studies. He has been working for the past five years on a project assessing the afterlife of Hadrian's Wall and he is the author of a number of books, including: *Roman Officers and English Gentlemen* (2000), *Globalizing Roman Culture* (2005), *Boudica: Iron Age Warrior Queen* (2005), *The Recovery of Roman Britain* (2008) and *Hadrian's Wall: a life* (2012).

Nicky Holmes graduated in sociology and social policy before beginning her research career at National Museums Liverpool. During her time there she carried out numerous visitor and non-visitor research projects which culminated in a successful Heritage Lottery Fund bid. Following this, she worked in various commercial research agencies but always maintained an interest in widening access to culture and heritage. She established the market research agency Zebra Square in 2005 and has continued to conduct research into heritage and tourism for a wide range of clients including English Heritage and Historic Scotland, as well as for individual museums.

Martin Kemkes studied Provincial-Roman Archaeology, Classical Archaeology and Ancient History at the Universities of Cologne and Freiburg. Between 1993 and 2003 he worked at the Kurpfälzisches Museum in Heidelberg as well as at the Württembergischen Landesmuseum in Stuttgart. Since 2003 he has led the branch museums at the Archäologischen Landesmuseum Baden-Württemberg and is responsible for the Limesmuseum Aalen and the Römermuseum of Osterburken, the most important museums at the UNESCO World Heritage Site Upper

German-Raetian Limes in Baden-Württemberg. He is spokesperson for the 'Roman Museums along the Limes' working group and also a member of the German Limes Commission.

Miomir Korać has worked at the Archaeological Institute in Belgrade since 1981, where he is currently Principal Research Fellow, engaged in studies of Roman provincial archaeology, especially of the Roman province of Moesia Superior. In 1997 he took over as director of Project Viminacium. From 2000 to 2005 he was manager of the project 'Expert Systems and Use of Artificial Intelligence in Archaeology and Internet Data Base/Dynamic Presentation of the Most Important Archaeological Sites', funded and supported by the Ministry of Science and Technological Development of the Republic of Serbia. Since 2005 he has led another project, funded by the same Ministry, on 'The Use of Geophysical Methods GIS, GPR, GPS and New Methodologies in Research of the Roman City and Legionary Camp of Viminacium'. He has been involved in numerous innovative projects in integrated and interdisciplinary research.

Michaela Kronberger studied Archaeology and Art History in Salzburg and Vienna. From 1991 onwards she undertook several years of scientific work at the Austrian Archaeological Institute and the Department of Urban Archaeology of Vienna, focusing particularly on Roman material culture, Roman urbanism, 3D visualisation and ancient landscape reconstruction. Since 2005 she has been Curator of the Department of Archaeology and History until 1500 at the Wien Museum, the former Historical Museum of Vienna, in charge of the archaeological collection and several outposts of the Wien Museum. She has curated several exhibitions and was responsible for the development of the concept and realisation of the new Roman Museum in Vienna.

Nigel Mills (the editor of this volume) has a long-standing interest in, and experience of, the application of interpretation principles to public presentation of the historic and natural environment. Following academic research in landscape history and archaeology, he developed a career in countryside and heritage management, through which he became familiar with the work of Freeman Tilden in interpretation and of Steve van Matre in earth education. At the IFA conference in 1987 he co-organised a keynote session entitled 'Presenting the Past'. He has endeavoured to apply these principles in his various roles since, as a Countryside Manager for Derbyshire County Council; as Project Manager for Groundwork West Durham; as Director of Creswell Heritage Trust; and as Director of World Heritage and Access for the Hadrian's Wall Trust.

Jürgen Obmann studied Prehistory and Mediaeval History at the Ludwig Maximilian University in Munich, and Roman Archaeology at the Universities of Exeter and Cologne, where he received his doctorat and where he also worked on archaeological archives and as an assistant lecturer. He has been involved in work on the Upper German-Raetian Limes in Baden-Württemberg and Bavaria since 2005 and has been the Management Plan coordinator for the Limes in Bavaria since 2011. He is the author of several monographs and has written or co-authored over 30 articles.

Tim Padley studied Archaeology and Geography at the University of Exeter, before going on to obtain a Masters Degree in Scientific Methods in Archaeology at the University of Bradford. He moved to Carlisle in 1980 as the finds researcher for the Carlisle Archaeological Unit, and has witnessed first-hand much of the recent archaeological development of the city. In 1997 he became Curator of Archaeology at Tullie House. He provided all of the artefacts and much of the background information for the Roman Frontier Gallery, as well as writing the text.

John Scott has over 20 years' experience in the management of cultural sector projects and attractions, primarily in the East Midlands area. Working in the environmental, arts, economic development and heritage sectors, his aim has been to bring these disciplines together and share cross-sector best practice. His experience of interpretation, education, community engagement and visitor management is complemented by qualifications in Business and Performance Management and Heritage Management. At Creswell Heritage Trust as Projects Manager (and latterly Assistant Director), he played a pivotal role in the development and delivery of a £6.5m museum capital project and currently, as Hadrian's Wall Management Plan coordinator, he has to balance the many facets of this particularly complicated World Heritage Site.

R Michael Spearman has worked with exhibitions and computer applications for cultural projects since 1982. Having trained as an archaeologist, he was Curator of the National Museums of Scotland's Celtic and Viking collections for ten years. He then became founding CEO of the £15m lottery-funded digital image library, SCRAN, before returning to the Museum to establish its Multimedia Team. The Team was responsible for developing the Museum of Scotland's strategic approach to the use of new technologies to improve public access to collections. In 2003 Dr Spearman and the Team formed CMC Associates Ltd, concentrating on 3D image research and creative media for the cultural and heritage sector.

Jürgen Trumm studied Roman Archaeology, Prehistory and Ancient History at the Universities of Freiburg im Breisgau (Germany) and Lausanne (Switzerland). He has participated in numerous excavations in Germany, France, Switzerland and Hungary. Between 2003 and 2006 he directed an important rescue excavation of the southern area of the legionary camp of *Vindonissa* (Windisch, Switzerland), where he created the on-site presentation *Archäologiestätte via et porta praetoria* in 2007. Since 2008, he has been responsible for *Vindonissa* field research at the Kanton Aargau archaeological service (Brugg, Switzerland).

Sandra Walkshofer is an historian, author and documentary film producer from Carinthia (Austria). She is CEO of Boundary Media KG, a company that produces film and multimedia content for different platforms such as DVDs, mobile devices and the internet, including the recent smartphone application 'Mainlimes Mobil', the content for which was developed in 2009–2010.

Christopher Young is an archaeologist who originally specialised in Romano-British pottery. He has worked for English Heritage for many years and has been involved in the management of Hadrian's Wall in different capacities for around 30 years, and more recently with the Frontiers of the Roman Empire World Heritage Site. He developed English Heritage's first guidance on the reconstruction of archaeological sites, published in 2002. As Head of International Advice, he covers international heritage issues, including the World Heritage Convention. He advises on management plans and nominations for new World Heritage Sites in England and on policies for protecting and enhancing those sites.

Index

HERITAGE MATTERS